STEPMOTHERING
Another Kind of Love

STEPMOTHERING
Another Kind of Love

THE WAY TO

HAPPINESS AND SUCCESS

AS A STEPMOTHER

by
Pearl Ketover Prilik

FORMAN PUBLISHING

Published by Forman Publishing Inc.,
Los Angeles, California 90049

Distributed by Publishers Marketing Services
11661 San Vicente Blvd.,
Los Angeles, California 90049

Library of Congress Catalogue Card Number 88-082265

ISBN 0-936614-06-4

Printed in the United States of America

Designed by Irving Perkins Associates

10   9   8   7   6   5   4   3   2   1

To my husband, D.J.
Applause maker, underwriter,
soulmate, and very best friend

ACKNOWLEDGMENTS

The writing of this book has been a journey of personal and professional discovery. The ending of this adventure is both joyous and inexplicably painful. Although I'd like to think I could have done it all alone, I know that this book would not have come into being as a unilateral endeavor. And so I'd like to acknowledge some of the people without whom this idea would not have become a reality . . .

My publishers, the Formans, Claudia and Len, for seeing a book in a concept, for their commitment and practical assistance throughout the process from query letter to completion.

My editor, Ann LaFarge who mid-wifed this book—her steady and determined perseverance, the changing colors of her demeanor alternatingly encouraging, cajoling, prodding, questioning, clarifying, demanding—helped shape the jumble of impressions and research into a form that is eminently more accessible and readable than it would have been outside her capable hands.

Dr. Emily Visher for her thorough reading of this manuscript and for sharing her time, personal thoughts and professional expertise on this subject.

My parents—my father who taught me to dream and my mother who taught me to act; the contribution of their individual personas coalesced and directed within me.

My own stepfamily—the basic inspiration for the writing of this book:

Cori, my stepdaughter: my love for her is refreshing, clear, and uncomplicated. Guiding her passage across the threshold into womanhood provided the magic of a trip backward into my own girlhood—a young woman who continues to soften each day with her commitment and trust, and sparkles my life with courage and laughter.

Brett, my stepson: my deep feeling for him taught me much about what I now know about love, trust, and commitment; about building dreams and realizing them—a young man who enriched my understanding of the limitless horizons of life itself, all in his own incomparable way.

Josh, my son: all the wonder and magic of bearing him into this world has brightened with each day that followed; loving him continues to be one of life's greatest joys—a young man, my sunshine child, who has taken the warmth and depth of the tropical sea and colored the very definition of family and of my life with a shimmering vitality that is all his own.

And of course, my husband, D.J.: a proper acknowledgment would fill another volume. His confidence, forbearance, enthusiasm, and support were continuous and without complaint. Without his love and his very practical assistance in keeping us all afloat, this book would not and could not have been written.

Most of all I would like to acknowledge my tremendous gratitude for all the stepmothers who participated in this study. Wonderful women who freely shared the personal pain, joy, frustration, and satisfaction that defined their experience as stepmothers. The intensity of their experiences spilled from their pages and helped to create these; giving flesh, vitality, and life itself to this subject. It is their voice that resonates throughout these pages. Thanks to all the women who opened their lives to me, entrusting me to speak about them. I thank them all for this honor and hope I have done them justice.

CONTENTS

PART III
*Changes,
Challenges,
Crises*
209

They Call Me "Steppie"

The subject of stepmothering continues to change with each new stepmother, with every new experience, with each individual life. That constantly changing relationship provides the collective lore of stepmothering. Shimmering and lovely, dark and light, magical and illusive. Another kind of love.

In this spirit I throw my experience into the pool of shared moments. Like most stepmothers, I began by feeling confident about my mothering abilities, expecting that my own very positive experience as a mother would translate into sufficient preparation for stepmotherhood. I quickly discovered that this new kind of mothering, mothering without the touching, the giggling, the luscious intimacy of biological motherhood was not as natural and easy as I had imagined it would be. My confidence thinned—but my resolve quickened.

Constant talking, family conferences, letter-writing to my husband, my stepchildren, and my son, and the keeping of a personal journal helped me over the rough spots. By far the greatest help in my uncharted course as a stepmother was my husband, the father of my two stepchildren and a father, in all ways but biologically, to my son. His support was absolute and continuous.

I also did research in an attempt to better understand my new role. As part of that research, I asked stepmothers to relate their most rewarding experience with their stepchildren. Many responded by describing the first time their stepchildren said "I love you." My own most rewarding experience was a little note written on a sheet of loose-leaf paper and left for me on the kitchen counter by my stepdaughter. I've long since forgotten what the note said, but it was signed "Love and Chicken Soup." Somehow, I just knew that the "chicken soup" was a recognition of my caring and love for her, and a reciprocation as well as an acknowledgment of that love. "Love and Chicken Soup" became, for us, a special secret message, signifying caring.

Many stepmothers have struggled to express exactly what it was that they gained from their relationship with their stepchildren; so it's only fitting that I attempt to meet that challenge in this book. What have I gained? I have gained a definite sense of my own personal limitations—limitations that include the realization that I cannot accomplish everything according to my specifications and within my time parameters. More important, my relationship with my stepchildren has lessened the desire to do this. I have learned that my personal limitations are not the end of the world.

I have learned, too, that feelings sometimes supersede thought and logical expressions, and that when one is dealing with intimate relationships this is okay. I have ultimately learned that a family is not *created* out of desire but rather *evolves* through time and shared experience.

From my relationship with my stepchildren, I have learned that parenting is never to be taken lightly or for granted. I have learned that true relationships stand free from biological, legal, or other external bonds. True relationships develop from shared commitment, loyalty, respect, and common history. They may, if one is very fortunate, come to rest under the banner of love.

Like so many other stepmothers, I sometimes miss those elements that will always be missing from my relationship with my stepchildren, in particular the unconditional love that I feel, at all times, for my son—a love that stretches back in time to predate his very existence. I miss having felt my stepchildren kick inside my womb, having held them as infants and rocked them to sleep. I miss the confidence, the validation, the sweet smiles and conspiratorial womanliness of motherhood, present in my relationship with my son and absent from my relationship with my stepchildren.

I expected the same kind of love. I found a different kind. I find that I am often a "better" parent toward my stepchildren than I am toward my own son—a more logical, compassionate, calmer parent. There is something noninflammatory in my relationship with my stepchildren; the heat that often fires the bond with my son burns more sedately with my stepchildren.

Like any other stepmother, I, too, would appreciate some recognition of our role from the general public. I would enjoy getting a friendlier welcome from teachers, other children's parents, doctors, and others who are at present more than a little uncomfortable with my role as a stepmother. *I* am proud of my role and I know that I am an integral and important figure in my stepchildren's lives, and *they* know it, and my husband, my family, and friends know it. I have grown strong and resilient during my years as a stepmother, and my confidence is high. I must, however, acknowledge that it would have been *so nice* to have gotten a few "strokes" along the way.

We who are stepmothers nurture our stepchildren on a daily basis. We build a family out of the experience and memories that ultimately shape our relationships. We guide, advise, care, and share, and we know when and how to encourage our stepchildren to grow up and away, as they all ultimately must. Perhaps we really are magical creatures, entrusted with the opportunity—and the challenge—of giving our stepchildren another chance, another "ride on the merry-go-round."

Like that last fairy in "Sleeping Beauty," stepmothers cannot hope to change the past; but like that well-intentioned, high-spirited fairy, we can and do shape the future.

P.K.P.
Lido Beach, N.Y.
1988

PART I

Stepmothering: What It Means

CHAPTER 1

A Book Just for Stepmothers

Remember what it felt like to be a child—the brightness of the snow, the sense of high expectation as you held a gift wrapped in bright paper? Remember how long the summers used to be—steamy days that stretched endlessly into sweet velvet nights? The coldness of ice cream sticking sweetly to the tip of your tongue? And remember the scary parts of being a child: lying in bed, moments after the bedtime story ended, thinking of princes and princesses, castles and wicked stepmothers? Jumping, as the door clicked shut too quickly, leaving you alone in a darkness livened with liquid squishy things? Do you remember your fear?

What did you do? Did you pile your Raggedy Anns and Andys, your teddy bears, and plush puppies into a fortress? Did you whisper promises and pacts with a God you were still sure could hear? Or did you just plop a finger into your mouth and suck away the chill? If you were lucky, the door opened and brought light and help and comfort. If you weren't so lucky, no one came, and with the covers pulled up over your head, and your chilled feet tucked under your body, you'd burrow as far into your pillow as possible and somehow get through the night. Alone.

Many stepmothers don't have to return to their childhood to bring back these memories: They feel this way right now. Women who have married men with children are often ill-prepared for the job of being a parent. Deprived of literature, support, or even a clear understanding of the role they are expected to play in their new families, such women often find stepmothering a frightfully overwhelming endeavor.

Stepmothers have been isolated from one another, stigmatized by society, and virtually shunned from professional and lay research. The full-time or custodial stepmother has been ignored, overlooked, forgotten, or treated with a chillingly polite distaste. This cold-shoulder treatment has exacerbated the normal stresses experienced by anyone trying to raise a family. Stepmothers have been left to confront the challenges of their new families in a vacuum. Expected to assume primary leadership of a family that is of someone else's origin, bolstered by little or no support, too many stepmothers fail.

Nobody Taught Us How

Let's face it: Most little girls do not spend their childhoods dreaming of becoming stepmothers. Stepmothers belong to the make-believe part of childhood. In the brightness of daylight, even the most imaginative of us didn't expect to grow up and become a stepmother, yet millions of little girls do just that. I was one such child. Chances are, if you are holding this book, you, or someone close to you, is a stepmother, too. For too many of us, the reality of stepmothering is as strange as stepping into the pages of a childhood fairy tale.

A Need for Role Models

Stepmothering doesn't have to be strange or mysterious. In order for women to begin to feel less disenfranchised, less like oddballs, they need role models. Such models cannot be found in fiction. Although the existence of wicked-stepmother mythologies is interesting from a psychological perspective, such tales cannot guide a stepmother in the practical challenges she faces on a daily basis. Nor are the stepmothers on television helpful when applied to real-life concerns. "The Brady Bunch" and "Eight Is Enough" are simply modern fairy tales. Their saccharine stepmother "saints" are as unhelpful to real stepmothers as the story of Cinderella. These fantasy role models seem to tell stepmothers "Take your choice—Crone? Or Saint?" Neither choice is a viable alternative when attempting to manage a real-life family. Stepmothers must begin to look to one another for the guidance and support they seek.

There's Comfort in Numbers—and in Each Other

Stepmothers are a very real presence in today's world. Millions of women are currently living their lives as full-time or custodial step-mothers. Fifty million individuals are involved in stepfamilies in our country. Four million individuals become available for remarriage, and a possible stepfamily, each year. With such huge numbers, there is no good reason for stepmothers ever to feel alone. Certainly stepmothering has its problems—the following pages will address these concerns—but problems are not insurmountable. Step-mothering can be, and often is, one of the most rewarding and important roles a woman can have.

In order to boost the chances for happiness and success, step-mothers need to confront the realities of modern-day stepmother-ing, beginning with the statistics. Although they are startling, they need to be explored without fear.

Scary Statistics

The outlook for second marriages is dismal: Nearly half of second marriages fail. The reason most often cited for this high failure rate is "problems with the husband's children." This figure includes both residential and nonresidential stepchildren, but these problems are obviously intensified for custodial stepmothers. Given the fact that stepmothers are often expected to assume primary parenting immediately after the wedding ceremony and in virtual isolation, this high figure is not surprising. This pattern can only be broken by building confidence and dealing with issues directly.

First, facts must be faced: Many women are not happy as stepmothers. They feel isolated, alienated, and betrayed; they feel as though "someone changed the rules"; they feel tricked and trapped. Too often these feelings of resentment can be directly traced to the unrealistic expectations these women held going into their relationships with their stepchildren.

Ruth was one such stepmother. Even after thirteen years of caring for one stepdaughter and two stepsons, Ruth still bears a load of unattainable goals. She traces her current unhappiness to the very beginning of her stepmothering. "Naïvely, I did not think there would be problems in becoming a stepmother. I was confident in my mothering capabilities, my ability to nurture. I expected to be able to handle any emotional turmoil with maturity, love, and rational behavior. I also expected that the children would love me immediately, especially when they saw how wonderfully different I was from their own mother.

When the wedding was over, the problems began—with a vengeance. It was a shock to me, and a shock to Tom, and a shock to our marriage. I'd never seen Tom red-faced with anger before. Neither of us knew how to cope. Things have gotten better over the years, but we still have flare-ups, and I still feel alone. I wish I had some sort of support group, like alcoholics and battered women have."

Like most stepmothers, Ruth began her "career" with a host of unrealistic expectations. Because she was separated from the experiences of others like herself, Ruth never did realize that her disappointment was commonplace. The failure of a stepmother's initial expectations for her relationship begins a cycle of negative emotions that often destroys her sense of well-being. The failure of these unrealistic expectations causes too many stepmothers to enter a cycle of confusion—frustration—depression—anger. If left unbroken, this cycle leads directly to the divorce court.

Breaking the Pattern

In reality, stepmothers are less alone than ever before. Changing patterns of child custody and the phenomenon of late-marrying women mean that there are more stepmother marriages each year.

But despite the numbers, stepmothers continue to be threatened by feelings of disappointment and personal inadequacy. These problems can be faced and solved by sharing the information gleaned from experts in the field: stepmothers themselves.

In studying almost one hundred responses to an extensive questionnaire sent to stepmothers around the country, I found that certain common concerns emerged. Although every stepmother thought she was unique, the issues related to being a stepmother began to sound increasingly familiar. I'll discuss each of these concerns in depth so that stepmothers can begin to realize that they are *not* alone: The experiences they encounter, and the challenges they face, are common to most stepmothers.

Take a look at this list, and ask yourself how many of these problems *you* have had to deal with:

- Lack of a clearly defined role:
  "Who am I?"

- Lack of a common title:
  "What do they call me?"

- Negative stigma of stepmothering:
  "Just the word itself is creepy."

- Unrealistic and/or poorly defined expectations:
  "What did I *think* it would be like?"

- Unfamiliarity with stages of child development:
  "When does he stop whining?"

- Confusion about nurturing responsibilities:
  "Am I supposed to do it *all*?"

- Issues relating to stepchild's biological mother:
  "Who has the final say?"

- Difficulty forming a family from different lifestyles:
  "You do it *this* way?"

- Raising two sets of children in the same household:
  "What do you mean, you can't share a room with him?"

- Legal blurriness regarding stepmother's rights:
  "What happens to my relationship with the kids if we divorce or you die?"

- Loss of personal freedom:
  "I never have any *time*."
- Lack of support, feedback:
  "Am I all alone—or are there others like me?"

Who Are We?

These common concerns suggest common strategies. In order to begin to feel happy and fulfilled, stepmothers must first feel clear and confident about their role. Before you can begin to form realistic expectations and attainable goals, it is important to untangle the knot of stepmothering first by answering this question: WHO IS A STEPMOTHER?

It is little wonder that stepmothers are confused about their role. There is no general agreement today about exactly who is to be called "stepmother." It is difficult for stepmothers to get information, to link up with others like themselves, or even to begin to articulate common concerns when the very term "stepmother" is up for debate. This ambiguity is more than semantically troubling; the vagueness of the title "stepmother" is indicative of the problems faced by stepmothers today. It is hard to feel fulfilled in a role, or happy to be a member of a group, that has no accepted definition.

Stepmothers—in the Past and Now

It wasn't always this way. Once upon a time, the stepmother's role was fairly straightforward: The term "stepmother" referred to a woman functioning as a mother substitute for her husband's (motherless) children. In fact, the "step-" prefix comes from the Middle and Old English prefix "stoep-" meaning "bereaved" or "orphaned." This term implied—as was usually the case—that the biological mother had died. In the rare case that parents had been divorced, the children typically continued to live with their father. The remarriages of these custodial fathers made stepmothers relatively commonplace.

As the nineteenth century ended, the courts began to exhibit a change in custodial preference: Mothers, rather than fathers, began to be routinely awarded custody of very young minor children— children the court deemed to be of "tender years." At first the children were returned to their fathers when this period of tender years ended, but over the course of time the notion of tender years expanded and grew in popularity. By the 1960s, the courts were more likely to award sole and continuous custody of children to their biological mothers.

The preference for maternal care, coupled with an ever-increasing rate of divorce, created a high number of noncustodial fathers and resulted in the blurring of the role of stepmother. Society, accustomed to referring to women married to *custodial* fathers as "stepmothers," continued to use the term when referring to women married to *noncustodial* fathers. "Stepmother," which for many years had consistently referred to a woman assuming a primary parenting role, began to assume a very different connotation: A stepmother was seen simply as the consort of a father whose children lived somewhere else.

Full-time stepmothers now find themselves in an untenable position as a result of these blurred roles. Recognizing that the custodial nature of their relationship separates them from the wives of noncustodial fathers, they often seek to identify themselves as "mothers" to their stepchildren, only to find that such attempts at replacing "mother" bring disastrous results. And bring them back, full circle, to the original question: "Who *am* I?"

The custodial stepmother straddles two worlds. Often, as my grandmother was fond of saying, "She can't find a place for herself." She lives in limbo, poised between the poles of the "weekend stepmother" and the biological mother.

The Bottom Line

The noncustodial stepmother may find it possible to back off from parenting roles with her stepchildren—a posture suggested by many experts in the field—but the intimacy of day-to-day living with full-time stepchildren precludes such detachment. The full-time stepmother, unlike her part-time counterpart, cannot simply grit her teeth and wait for her stepchildren to go home. The custodial stepmother's children *are* home. It is this unalterable fact that erases all but the most cursory similarity between her role and the role of the weekend stepmother.

The full-time stepmother's confusion grows as she seeks to separate herself from the all-inclusive usage of the term "stepmother." There are no roles that can be compared to her own. Most women who care for children on a full-time, live-in basis are either "mommies" or "nannies" (now often called "caregivers"; the parameters of these caretaking roles are clear and familiar. Stepmothers also live with children and care for them on a full-time basis, and yet their role does not fit any such familiar parameters.

Stepmothers in a state of confusion seem to select a role based on what they are *not*. Full-time stepmothers know that they are not nannies and therefore erroneously assume that there is only one full-time choice left: "Mommy." The problem with opting for "Mommy" is that it just doesn't work. The stepmother who tries to be "Mommy" will confront two clear and often immediate problems: (1) There are distinct differences between stepmothers and biological mothers, and (2) the role of "Mommy" is already filled.

Where does this leave the full-time stepmother? Nowhere. Too many stepmothers discover only who they are *not*. Unlike weekend stepmothers, they assume immediate leadership of a family. Unlike biological mothers, they are denied the luxury of bonding and developing a relationship with children based on a process of nurturing and shared experience. Many feel terribly isolated—alienated both from those stepmothers who do not share the same day-to-day concerns and from biological mothers who possess a blood relationship and a shared history they cannot hope to replicate. This alienation, coupled with the very real demands of ongoing child-care, often makes stepmothers resentful and angry. When stepmothers feel rejected as "mommies" they often become angry about the implication that they are "nothing" to their stepchildren. Many begin to speak disparagingly of themselves. Deprived of the "Mommy" label, they seem to feel that their caretaking responsibilities make them nothing more than "maids" to their stepchildren.

In order to take the sting out of the mother/stepmother debacle it is important to understand the ways that stepmothers and mothers are different. When these differences are clear, stepmothers may begin to define themselves as STEPMOTHERS: neither mothers nor nannies but with a real role—and a name for it—that is all their own. The fact that they are STEPMOTHERS—and not something else—is the bottom line.

A Matter of Perspective

The dilemma facing many stepmothers today is reminiscent of an episode aired on Rod Serling's classic show of the 1960s, "Twilight Zone."

The story involves a young girl whom we meet in a hospital, where she is recuperating from surgery; her face is swathed in bandages. The girl is awaiting the removal of the bandages with obvious and extreme trepidation. Solicitous nurses and doctors surround her and offer their support. We quickly come to understand that this surgery has been the last in a series of corrective operations taken to reverse the girl's horrible disfigurement. The major part of the story is given over to the girl's fears of nonacceptance, her revulsion at the possibility of the surgery's failure, and her consideration of the alternatives for the future course of her life.

At the end of the episode, the bandages are slowly and ceremoniously cut away; the musical score builds as the final bandages fall. Everyone gasps. The girl turns to the camera. She is beautiful, but she, too, gasps in horror as she views her reflection in a hand-held mirror. The operation is pronounced a failure; she will be ostracized, sent away. The viewers' confusion is lifted as the camera pans, for the first time, to the faces of the doctors and nurses: It is they who, by our standards, are horribly disfigured.

Too often, stepmothers are caught in a similar predicament. They mirror their successes and failures upon a standard that has little to do with their lives. Millions of stepmothers are doing wonderful jobs and should be filled with pride. However, because they are using an incorrect measure for their success, and because they are often unaware that others share their concerns, they feel incompetent and unrespected. Isolated, alienated from other women in child-rearing capacities, too many stepmothers begin to doubt their abilities, their marriages, and themselves.

Such haunting doubts, if left unattended, can lead a stepmother to one of two unhappy and unnecessary conclusions: that her unhappiness springs from her own lack of personal worth and competence, or that her marriage itself was a mistake.

The Third Alternative: Becoming Confident and Happy as a Stepmother

There is a third alternative. Instead of admitting defeat and throwing in the towel, a stepmother can choose to become successful and confident in her role. Helping her to do so is the object of this book.

Stepmothers are *not* alone. The problems, challenges, daily crises, and joys of being a stepmother are common terrain to millions of women. Stepmothers are *not* biological mothers. They are *not* merely the wives of their stepchildren's fathers. Stepmothers are— STEPMOTHERS.

Connie's Message

Connie's experience is typical of the happiness a stepmother can and should attain. Connie has been a stepmother for the past seventeen years; her two stepdaughters are now grown women and out on their own. Connie's life has not always been easy, but she never permitted outside influences to affect her feelings for her stepchildren.

Connie realized early in her marriage that she was going to be mostly on her own: Because of different religious beliefs, both Connie's family and her husband's were strongly opposed to the marriage and to her raising of her stepdaughters. Perhaps it was this very isolation, although hurtful at first, that helped Connie to accept the fact that she alone was responsible for her happiness. By meeting all her problems head-on and insisting that her husband do so, too—and by maintaining open communication with both families—she has weathered the prejudices of a small town and the particularly tumultuous adolescence of one stepdaughter.

Connie has recently become a (step)grandmother. Her long years as a stepmother place her in the position of being able to reflect back. She feels that she has gained a great deal from her relationship with her stepchildren. "What have you got to tell us?" I asked her when we met.

"Mostly, that nothing is forever," Connie replied. "Children grow up and away. My stepdaughters gave me years of their childhoods and their lives. I have a past full of everything I experienced with these children and a future of that past locked in love forever. They gave that to me and I earned it. There seems to be a place for being a stepmother that was born into me—a place in me, where these children just fit, perfectly. And when you want that to happen, you just don't let anything get in the way."

Connie has been able to shape a happy life for herself despite family resistance, religious differences, small-town narrowness, and her stepchildren's stormy adolescent years. Connie would like others to understand that *all* stepmothers would welcome support and respect. "Millions of children have stepmothers. Anything that can be done to give stepmothers a personhood, an identity that will build the future for these millions of children, is going to help. Stepmothers are not babysitters or substitutes or part-time help. "Stepmothers," Connie said with a smile, "step in where others have stepped out and we should be proud of the name stepmother! I am."

For the purposes of this book, the term "stepmother" has been returned to those women for whom it was originally invented— women who have chosen to marry men with children and to assume full-time responsibility for the care and upbringing of these children—their own stepchildren.

It is time for stepmothers to wear the name with pride—to shatter the myths, throw off the covers, and find their own real place in the world. Millions of women continue to be trusted to raise their husband's children. It is critical that we begin to accept the fact that we can do this successfully and happily!

CHAPTER 2

Forming Achievable Goals

Stepmothers tell me that they are often cautioned against unrealistic expectations. "Don't expect instant love." "Don't expect quick acceptance." "Don't expect a big happy 'Brady Bunch' family." Although all of these don'ts, and a host of others, are apt, they aren't very helpful.

I asked stepmothers to reflect on their "beginnings"—beginnings that were often turbulent. They stated with almost a single voice, "We didn't know what to expect." Stepmotherhood is probably the one personal endeavor that women enter without support, familiarity, or what the psychologists like to call "rehearsals." Girls and women generally do not discuss stepmothering; when a woman becomes a stepmother, it is often without the vaguest notion of what to expect. Fear of the unknown is perhaps the greatest fear of all. It is time to alleviate some of that fear by examining what we can expect, learning to build confidence about the stepmother role, and then forming truly realistic, achievable goals.

14

What to Expect

EXPECT CONFUSION

It will take a little while for everyone to settle in. Even under the most ideal circumstances, children have to be moved: Places must be found for possessions. Mealtimes, bedtimes, school adjustments, and homework schedules must be established. The business of daily living in new circumstances will create more or less chaos, depending on the individuals and situations involved.

EXPECT UNEASINESS

Because the situation is new and everyone has not lived together before, there will be a period of awkwardness. This is normal. Try to remember that you and your new husband will be more familiar, comfortable, and connected to each other than the children are with you.

EXPECT WARINESS

Most stepchildren will be reluctant to trust anyone new. Stepchildren have already suffered the loss and dissolution of one family. They often bring a skepticism born of fear, or cynicism born of hurt, to their father's new marriage. Families are built from commitment and shared experience. Stepmothers, like other good parents, will be involved in the business of "making memories." As more experiences are shared and remembered, even the most reluctant children will begin to feel and act like members of a family, and the wariness will disappear.

EXPECT NEEDINESS

The notion of family wasn't just the result of some caveman's whim. The family unit evolved to ensure that biological needs, including the very perpetuation of the species, could occur safely. The timeless function of the family as a safe zone, a buffer or haven from the pressures of the outside world, continues today. People, especially children, expect and need—and demand—a lot of nurturing within the family. Stepmothers will find that their stepchildren need a lot of parenting—a lot of attention. Stepmothers who attempt to assume cooler roles find that emotional distancing is both counterproductive and impractical when *living* with children.

EXPECT TO WORK HARD

The overwhelming majority of stepmothers feel that responsibility for the family rests squarely on their shoulders. Almost to a woman, they report either accepting or being given primary responsibility for the smooth functioning of the family, whether or not they work outside the home. Stepmothers are expected to create and maintain family routines including housekeeping, child-care, and the diplomatic duties of negotiating with the children's biological mother.

EXPECT TO BE TESTED

Stepmothers often feel as though they are sitting in a twenty-four-hour exam. Everything they do or say is scrutinized, criticized, and "graded" by their stepchildren. Such testing is a normal, rational way for children to measure the stepmother's commitment to them and the reliability of the new family.

This period of testing can be very trying. During the stepmother's initiation period, rules, expectations, and opinions will be countered, questioned, or ignored.

Dora, frazzled by responsibility for her young stepchildren, warns stepmothers to "expect to be hated, used, lonely, confused, cursed at, belittled, compared to others, in the middle, and exhausted." This period *does end* and, as Dora tells us, "When it's over, a stepmother can expect to be a stronger, wiser person."

EXPECT TO FEEL LEFT OUT

Stepmothers often feel left out. When the old photo albums appear at Grandma's, when everyone is talking about holidays, trips, or times that preceded the stepmother, she feels a pang. Such pangs are understandable, but allowing them to blossom into intolerable pain is unconstructive. Stepmothers may be excluded from the children's past, but they are *not* left out of the present—a present that may at times include reminiscing. Sharing family memories can inspire the stepmother to share *her* past life, too.

EXPECT TO MAKE BIG EFFORTS

Many stepmothers operate on the mistaken notion that good families and good relationships "just happen." This is as counterproductive as the attitude of the sexually dissatisfied woman who just lies there, waiting passively for her husband to figure out how to make sex glorious for her. Many women seem to operate under the mistaken notion that if you have to ask for something, it is somehow not as valuable as something that is intuited by another. Whether it's good sex or a good family, such passivity is just not practical. Refusing to get to work on making things better is going to make things worse. Building a new family takes work, patience, and perseverance.

EXPECT TO HAVE NEGATIVE FEELINGS

Some stepmothers are shocked to discover that they feel resentment, anxiety, jealousy, indifference, or even downright dislike for their stepchildren. These negative feelings are perfectly normal, but they are difficult to admit and still more difficult to face. For example:

Resentment. Stepchildren alter the course of the couple's relationship. They interrupt the "honeymoon phase" of the marriage and introduce problems that have nothing to do with the couple's interaction with each other. Too often, stepmothers begin to feel that the marriage would be "perfect if not for the children." This feeling of lost perfection will cause resentment to grow.

Anxiety. Children often do not respond to a stepmother's overtures, and this reticence can cause her to feel incompetent. Stepchildren do not come with instruction manuals. Their lack of affection, openness, or receptiveness may shake a stepmother's confidence in her ability to nurture and may cause her self-confidence to plummet. Lowered self-confidence will make the stepmother more susceptible to vulnerability and increased anxiety.

Jealousy. Stepmothers are often embarrassed by their jealous feelings toward their stepchildren. The sight of a twelve-year-old girl curled up on Daddy's lap may make a stepmother's stomach unpleasantly queasy. Often these feelings of jealousy have little or nothing to do with the stepchildren themselves but rather refer to the stepmother's ambivalence about her husband's former relationships and the claims of others for his attention and affection. Stepchildren also provide a constant reminder of their father's relationship with another woman—their mother.

Envy. It's normal for a stepmother to feel some envy for the biological mother, whether she is living or dead. Envy springs from a feeling that someone has (or had) something that you don't have and would like: Biological mothers have, or had, a relationship with their children that may threaten an insecure stepmother, and the more insecure a stepmother feels, the more intense her feelings of jealousy and envy will be. Such feelings are best countered by meeting them head-on: "I wish I'd known you when you were a baby" or "I wish the kids were really *ours*" are healthier responses than sulking or seething.

Dislike. Stepmothers often suffer from guilt stemming from unpleasant feelings about their stepchildren. They dislike their stepchildren for different reasons. Some children behave badly. Some may have very different value systems from their stepmother. Children may remind their stepmother of faults she chooses to overlook in her husband. They may also remind her of their biological mother—whom she chooses to ignore.

Annie was having a great deal of trouble relating to her sixteen-year-old stepdaughter. Although Annie had raised the child since age two, she found that she could "hardly look at the girl" as she began to mature. Annie finally was stunned to realize that a great part of this problem was that her stepdaughter had developed a striking resemblance to her biological mother. Annie stated woefully, "I don't know what to do! I knew her mother in high school and I didn't like her at all!"

Sometimes a stepchild is just not somebody a stepmother feels good about. Sometimes personalities clash. Stepmotherhood may be defined as "motherhood without the illusions." A stepmother, unlike a biological mother, is often able to acknowledge to herself that she would not, if given the choice, have chosen these particular children. Many stepmothers are plagued with guilt as a result of this acknowledgment and are reluctant to admit the glaring differences between themselves and their stepchildren. The world will not collapse from such an admission, and although stepchildren are not exchangeable, a mutual admiration society is *not* necessary to raise a child successfully.

BUT . . .

A warning on negative emotions. Although there may be no such thing as an unacceptable feeling, feelings inappropriately shared may cause unnecessary pain. Raising kids is difficult, often frustrating work. Raising kids is an emotional business. It's okay to feel whatever you feel, but it is never okay to put down, hurt, or alienate your stepchildren, or your husband. It *is* okay to hate your stepchildren's behavior and to share your discomfort and disapproval of that behavior with your husband—tactfully, please. Real negative feelings about stepchildren—jealousies, dislikes, anxieties—are better dealt with by yourself, with a professional, or with an understanding friend who can be trusted.

If negative feelings begin to dominate your life, or if they get in the way of the care and raising of your stepchildren, it is time to get help. Sometimes, simply ventilating these feelings by writing in a journal or letting off steam with a trusted friend will help. If such measures don't alleviate your concerns, and you are still troubled, seek professional help in a self-help group for stepmothers, a mental health clinic, or with a private therapist.

EXPECT YOUR LIFE TO BECOME CHILD-CENTERED

Much of your time and energy will center on child-related concerns: Little League, Brownies, school conferences, homework, table manners, household chores, college choices, after-school or summer jobs, dating, colds, inoculations, braces, cavities, making a bow that stays tied, finding a date for the prom, scanning the shelves for just the right reference book. The list goes on and on and on. Expect compromises on your personal privacy as well.

EXPECT LOVE TO TAKE TIME . . . AND PATIENCE

Warm feelings may take a long time to materialize. We allow that time to our stepchildren, but we can't afford to take a long time before making a commitment to *them*. The needs of children and the demands of child-care are immediate and pressing. Stepmothers may find that their relationships with their stepchildren are initially lopsided: Our commitment has been made to them without reciprocity. This demands patience in large doses.

EXPECT TO DEAL WITH THE CHILDREN'S MOTHER, WHETHER SHE'S ON OR OFF THE SCENE

Issues relating to the biological mother are positively volatile! (An entire chapter of this book has been devoted to this issue.) Suffice it to say, at this point, that stepmothers always have difficulty coming to grips with their stepchildren's biological mother. Different issues evolve depending on the circumstances and starting with whether she is alive or dead. If the biological mother is living, the stepmother will have to deal with the logistics of visitation, telephone communication, and the mother's absence or involvement in her children's lives. If the mother is dead, the stepmother will expect to confront the issue of death both in the abstract and the specific. The stepmother may expect the grieving of her stepchildren and their divided loyalties between the memory of their mother and the actuality of their stepmother.

EXPECT CHILDREN TO RESIST ANY EFFORT TO BE "MADE OVER"

No one enjoys being made over. The very attempt at making over a stepchild presumes that there is something unacceptable about the individual. Making over stepchildren, whether it is by such direct overtures as buying a new wardrobe or as indirect as subtle suggestions about hairstyles, friends, or hobbies, is bound to meet with resistance. Suggesting or facilitating a makeover says that the stepmother is not pleased with the stepchildren as they are. HOLD OFF.

THE BOTTOM LINE (AGAIN): EXPECT STEPMOTHERING TO BE DIFFERENT FROM ANY OTHER TYPE OF CHILD-REARING

Although stepmothering shares certain similarities with other types of child-rearing roles—mother, wife of noncustodial father, adoptive mother, or foster mother—the stepmother is different from all of these in the following ways:

Biological Mother: There is a period of bonding and nurturance that is socially approved and supported.

Part-Time Stepmother: There is a finiteness to the relationship, a time limit to the physical interaction proscribed by legal agreements between the biological parents.

Adoptive Mother: The adoptive mother has *chosen* to accept full parenting responsibility for a child whose biological mother has relinquished all rights and responsibilities through legal surrender or death. In either case, great pains are taken to protect the adoptive mother from the intrusion of the biological mother.

Foster Mother: The foster mother recognizes that her relationship with her foster children is temporary and that the long-term goal of the foster relationship is to return the child to the parent(s).

Stepmothering shares characteristics of all other types of mothering, but remember: Stepmothering is a way of life all its own.

Building Confidence

Once stepmothers have a general idea of what to expect, they need to begin to learn about their own families. In order to avoid feeling overwhelmed and out of control, they need to understand as much as they possibly can about their individual situations. No family is exactly like another. Each stepfamily is different from every other one. In order to begin building confidence and enhancing the possibility for success and happiness, stepmothers need to assess their own set of circumstances—the particular characteristics of the situation in which they live and the actual children with whom they share their lives.

Stepmothers who understand the unique dynamics of their own families will minimize surprises and will find that they are more confident and comfortable with their stepfamilies. Ideally, stepmothers will find out the facts about their new situations before they marry and/or begin to live with their stepchildren, but stepmothers who are already past this point, and already living with stepchildren, can benefit from reflection about the particular characteristics that make up their families.

CONFIDENCE BUILDER NUMBER 1: ASSESS YOUR SITUATION

In order to begin formulating concrete goals that can be achieved and that will lead to a feeling of accomplishment, stepmothers might use the following questions as a guide to putting their individual situations into a workable perspective. Understanding a situation, one's own reactions to it, and opinions about it is invaluable in building personal confidence.

1. Where Will You Live?

Husband's house? Stepmother's house? New house? If you're moving into or living in your husband's house, how do you feel about the furnishings? Will there be opportunities for you to redecorate or personalize the house to your taste? If you are planning to live in your own house or apartment, will your husband expect you to make changes? How do you feel about any such proposed changes?

Fran is a middle-aged stepmother of two teenaged girls. A state of "decorative warfare" developed between Fran and the girls and nearly drove her mad. Fran had married a widower and moved into her husband's house after their marriage. The house was decorated in a taste that was generally pleasing to Fran. Indeed, in an odd twist of fate, Fran had been a friend of the girls' mother and had actually helped her shop for some of the furnishings! Sensitive to her stepdaughters' loving memories of their mother, Fran planned no major redecorating; she was happy with the house the way it was. However, Fran was unprepared for her stepdaughters' *absolute* insistence that everything in the home remain *exactly* as it had always been. Fran found that she was not "permitted" by her stepdaughters to make even the slightest change.

If she moved a coffee table or rearranged a lamp, the moved articles reverted mysteriously to their former place. Finally, Fran confronted her stepdaughters, only to be told sweetly but adamantly that they had "just put things back where they belonged."

2. Will You Be Expected to Work Outside the Home?

If you will be continuing your present job, how will your new responsibilities fit into your daily life? If you will be leaving your job, have you planned your transition from the work world to work at home? Will it be a sacrifice—or a relief—to give up your life in the workplace?

3. Will There Be Time and Money for Fun?

Will money be available for the family, for you, for your husband, and for you and your husband as a couple to have fun? Are there activities that can be enjoyed as a family? As a couple? Individually? Will your own financial picture change, and is that change accept-able to you?

4. How Will You and Your Husband Share Responsibilities?

Most stepmothers report that they assume the overwhelming pro-portion of child and domestic duties after their marriages, whether or not they work outside the home. How much responsibility do you *really* want to assume? Do you need to feel in control of the family? Do you want your husband to share the chores? Do you expect your stepchildren to help? Does your husband concur?

5. How Do You Feel About Marriage and Stepmotherhood?

If you've been married before, have you worked through any resid-ual feelings from that former relationship? If divorced, have you resolved what went wrong with your previous marriage? If wid-owed, have you completed the grieving process for your former husband? What do you want from this marriage? How are you prepared to get it? How will your personal life change as a result of marriage and stepmotherhood? How will you choose to handle any problems that you can foresee? Do you know any other step-mothers?

Stepmothering calls many emotional issues into play. Step-mothers need to be more self-confident and self-assured than typi-cal "brides." In order to strengthen self-esteem, stepmothers need to think carefully about personal issues; stepmothers need to "get their act together." It is very important that stepmothers know them-selves well enough to understand how their own personal issues affect their feelings about marriage and the role of stepmother.

6. What Will "They" Call You?

Stepmothers are often unhappy about what their stepchildren choose to call them. If you expect to be called "Mom" or "Mother" by your stepchildren, you may be severely disappointed when the children insist upon calling you by your given name. On the other hand, you may find yourself uncomfortable being called "Mom" by a child you don't even know. What would you like to be called? *You* decide. The unique relationship between you and your stepchild calls for a unique name as well—a derivative of stepmother such as "Steppie," or a nickname that is used only by your stepchildren, highlights the special and exclusive quality of your relationship to these children—one that is different from all the other relationships in your life.

7. Will You Have Support? How Do Family and Friends Feel About Your Becoming a Stepmother?

Stepmothers need support outside the family. Will you have a strong support system? Do you have friends or family who feel positive about your becoming a stepmother? Too many stepmothers, during times of stress, hear only "You knew what you were getting into." Stepmothers need others who will be there for them. Do you have someone who will help you through the rough spots? Do you have people who are eager to share in your family's joys?

8. How Does Your Husband Feel About Living with His Children?

Did your husband actively choose to have his children live with him? Did the children begin to live with your husband by default? Would your husband really prefer another living situation for the children if circumstances were different? What are your feelings about the suitability of fathers raising children? How suitable do you feel your husband is to raise his children, either without assistance or with you beside him? Will you make a good parenting team?

CONFIDENCE BUILDER NUMBER 2: FOCUS ON YOUR STEPCHILDREN

Another important step in the building of confidence is getting to know your stepchildren. It is nothing short of amazing that many women attempt to begin relationships with children based on little or no personal contact, to marry without thinking in depth about the individual personalities of their stepchildren. Some brides, swept away in the "honeymoon phase" of their marriage, tend to dismiss their stepchildren as minor characters in a romantic play or items in a "package deal." If they think about their stepchildren at all (and many do not), they consider them merely as extensions of their husbands.

Some stepmothers go to the opposite extreme: Infatuated and excited by the prospect of a new family, they romanticize their stepchildren. Little children are gushed over as if they were cuddly cherubs. Older children are giggled with as friends or helpmates. Dismissing children either as extensions of their fathers or as willing characters in some vague soap opera of instant family bliss is a dangerous mistake. Stepchildren of any age will have tremendous impact upon a marriage. The unique personalities, personal histories, and individual perspectives that children bring to a stepfamily will affect the daily life of the marriage. The existence of stepchildren propels a couple into a family. Stepchildren's contributions as individuals can enrich or damage a family. Relationships are not forged with strangers. The wise stepmother will get to know her stepchildren as well and as quickly as she possibly can.

Getting to Know Them

Any relationship is based on an exchange of personal information. Women certainly realize this in other areas of their lives. However, in the rush of infatuation for their husbands, or in the case of later-arriving stepchildren, many stepmothers don't take the time to find out *who* their stepchildren are. This is an "occupational hazard" for biological parents as well. Many adults are simply not in the habit of thinking about children as individuals; they refer to "their" children, implying both ownership and a sense of children as extensions of themselves. Many parents have just not gotten around to thinking about their children as separate individuals.

Learn about your stepchild's view of the world. Ask questions. Listen carefully to responses. Watch reactions to various situations. Aim for sensitivity. Stepchildren do not, it is true, come with instruction manuals; however, their daily behavior will be your guide.

What are these children like when they are relaxed and "themselves"? Is the child who acts out during initial meetings with the stepmother really a shy child under less pressured circumstances? Is the little child sulking in the depths of that movie seat a chatterbox at Grandma's house? The more aware you are of your stepchildren's personalities, the more comfortable and confident you will feel with them.

Stepmothers usually aren't given any choice about how they will view their stepchildren. When the initial expectations of "instant love" and "instant family" dissipate, as they usually do with startling speed, stepmothers often panic: They realize that they don't "know" their stepchildren at all.

Stepmothers do not possess that maternal selective blindness that familiarity and love bring with the passage of time. However, the stepmother's ability to "see" the individuality of her stepchildren can actually become an advantage rather than a liability. Her objectivity permits her to understand her stepchildren in a way that others, who are too close to the situation, may overlook. One of the stepmother's most important contributions to the family is her new and fresh perspective. This objectivity permits her to be aware of children's feelings when they are unhappy, frustrated, or distressed. It also allows stepmothers to tune into talents, strengths, and interests that the children's father or other family members might have missed.

WHAT ARE YOUR STEPCHILDREN REALLY LIKE?

The following questions may be helpful in focusing on the actual children in your new family.

1. How Old Are They?

Children of different ages will have different needs that must be addressed. Various stages of child development will call for different parenting skills. For many women with limited, or rusty, child-rearing experience, a good child-care guide is essential. You'll find a shelf filled with child-care books at your library or bookstore. Children develop physically, emotionally, and intellectually at different stages of their lives. Familiarity with a child's typical stages of development will help stepmothers frame expectations that are age-appropriate. An understanding of the physical, emotional, and intellectual capabilities of children at various ages will prepare stepmothers for typical behavior, attitudes, problems, and needs.

(Chapter 5 has been devoted to a more detailed examination of stages of child development.)

2. Boys or Girls or a Combination?

Boys and girls today are privileged to live in a world where all options are open to them regardless of their sex. However, gender-related differences, be they emotional, physical, or cultural, have certainly not been eliminated. It is very important for stepmothers to explore their own personal feelings as they relate to the differences between boys and girls. What are *your* feelings about any innate differences? Do you expect or accept different types of behavior from boys and girls? Do you anticipate that boys and girls will have different interests and/or abilities? Do your feelings mesh with your husband's?

3. How Do the Children Get Along with Their Father?

It is important to understand the type of relationship the children had with their father prior to your arrival on the scene. Did the children live in a single-parent situation with their father? Did the father have assistance raising the children? From a housekeeper? A grandparent? Has the father just recently assumed physical and/or legal custody? Will the children need time to adjust to their *father*, as well as to their stepmother, as a primary caregiver?

4. What Circumstances Resulted in Father-Custody?

The circumstances that lead to children living apart from their biological mother will affect the stepmother's relationship with them. The facts surrounding the children's separation from their mother will have contributed to their receptivity to new relationships and the speed with which they can be expected to develop trust in you. Are you prepared to handle the special problems these children may bring? (Problems may include fear about death, fear about critical illness or disability, and familiarity with drug or other substance abuse.) Are you prepared to cope with the effects of abandonment (real or perceived)? Neglect? Abuse? Many children, living apart from their biological mother, have suffered through a variety of traumatic experiences. The more you know about the history of these experiences, the better prepared you will be to cope with future problems.

5. How Do the Children Feel About Their Mother?

Children's feelings about their biological mother may run the gamut of emotional possibility. Do they feel abandoned? Resentful? Defensive? Confused? The children's relationship with their mother will affect their ability to trust their feelings about themselves and will have an impact upon their relationship with you.

6. Are There Any Special Problems You Should Know About?

Special problems that might confront a stepmother can range from a physical, emotional, or learning disability to unacceptable social behavior. Stepmothers may have to cope with social, school, mental, or physical problems. Any identifiable problems should be explained clearly to you. You may have to push your husband for this information.

7. What Are the Children's Interests?

Taking the time to learn about children's interests is a lovely way to begin a relationship. Many children are uncomfortable with their father's marriage; they are not quite sure what this relationship really involves. Stepchildren are often pleased by evidence of their stepmother's interest in their lives. A note of warning: As with all other beginning relationships, stepmothers should exercise caution and not push. Stepchildren may have mixed feelings about their fathers and stepmothers "talking about them"; they may feel flattered by the attention but at the same time may feel threatened by their loss of exclusivity with their father.

8. What Have the Children Been Told About You?

In order to begin thinking about your stepchildren, it is important to understand what, if anything, the children already know about you. What do they know about your relationship with their father? Do they know that you plan to marry? Do they know that they will be living with you? Have you been "bad-mouthed" by anyone? Do the children fear the title "stepmother"? Have they accepted the fact that *you* will be *their* stepmother?

9. How Will the Children React To Surprises?

Keep surprises to a minimum. Children do not enjoy major life changes posed as surprises. "Surprise! We just got married, and we're all moving tomorrow!" is unlikely to prompt a happy reception. Ask as many questions of your fiancé/husband as possible. Ideally, most of these questions will be posed and answered before you meet or begin living with your stepchildren. However, learning about each other is a lifetime process!

Stepmothers who have a clear sense about general expectations, and who have taken the time to learn about and think about their individual situations, will have a far easier time creating a role for themselves in their new lives.

Up until now, the stepmother has concentrated on learning about others. Now it's time for her to turn her attention to herself and begin to answer the question "Where do I fit in?" In the next chapter, we will examine the various aspects of the stepmother's role and offer practical guidelines for stepmothers who are struggling to find their new family identity.

CHAPTER 3

A Role of Your Own

Stepmothers are often treated as so many Alices at some huge "mad tea party." Although people are usually polite, and some sort of decorum prevails, the expectations applied to stepmotherhood are sometimes difficult to understand. The mixed-messages relayed to a stepmother by those around her are always confusing and sometimes just short of maddening.

Stepmothers who try to fulfill the expectations of others find that such expectations often clash and nobody is satisfied. As I spoke with stepmothers about what they felt others expected from them, the following three consistent and clashing expectations emerged:

1. Stepmothers should care for their stepchildren as their "own," BUT stepmothers should never attempt to replace the biological mother.

2. Stepmothers should never identify themselves as stepmothers, BUT stepmothers should never identify themselves as "Mother" either.

3. Stepmothers should forget about fairy-tale non-sense, BUT stepmothers should laugh (cheerfully) at allusions to wicked stepmothers.

Failure is built in for a stepmother who attempts to meet any of these expectations because they contradict each other. The resulting confusion makes us feel off-balance and unsure of ourselves.

What can a stepmother hope to "be" for her stepchildren? Can she be a "mother"? Should she just forget about being a parent and define herself as "Dad's wife" or "friend" to her stepchildren? How can she create a role for herself that reflects her responsibilities and expresses her commitment to her stepchildren?

Why "Mommy" Won't Work

The majority of stepmothers at some point attempt to define themselves as "Mother" to their stepchildren. Most, when questioned, are uncomfortable about being referred to as "stepmother"; they prefer to be referred to, acknowledged, and treated as their stepchildren's "mothers." And why not?

Certainly stepmothers perform the duties of "Mom"! When asked to define their role as stepmothers they offered a litany of child-care responsibilities:

> "I'm the same as Mother," states a young stepmother of an eight-year-old. "He is treated exactly the same as my two sons."

> "I'm the MOM!" proudly claims a particularly bubbly stepmom. "I perform the same duties for my stepsons as for my biological boys: cooking, cleaning, laundry, attendance at school conferences and functions, Scout leader, etc., etc., etc. . . ."

> "I do everything the 'lady of the house' (sometimes known as Mother) would do, and I'm in the Football Mother Club for my stepson. A school volunteer. I make homemade goodies and send care packages to my stepdaughter at college. I carry out all the responsibilities a real mother would do."

And so it went: Stepmother after stepmother defined herself as "Mother" and validated the definition by a recital of her responsibilities—lists which were at times often daunting in their scope. But despite this litany of commitment, stepmothers are *not* replacements for their stepchildren's biological mothers. This misdefinition is at the root of much of the dissatisfaction plaguing stepmothers today.

What is all this fuss about anyway? A woman raising a child is a mother. Right? Stepmothers are on the scene every day. Stepmothers sit in those uncomfortable little chairs on conference night; they pace the floor when a child is late. Stepmothers stuff their pockets with soggy tissues. Stepmothers clean up after a sick child. Stepmothers swallow their meals while trying to ignore table manners that drive them up a wall. Stepmothers advise little children about bullies and bigger ones about pregnancy. They worry about scraped knees, monsters under beds, coughs that linger, and kids that are too noisy or too quiet. If a stepmother isn't a mother, who is? After all, as one stepmother quipped, why should the term be reserved for some woman who "just happened to be there at the moment of birth"? *Why isn't a stepmother a mother?*

THE ROLE IS FILLED

The primary answer to this question is that the role is already filled. Stepmothers who try to be Mother open themselves up to unnecessary disappointment and pain. Stepmothers are a vital part of their stepchildren's lives, but engaging in a "motherhood" competition diminishes the importance of their role.

A DIFFERENT (NOT LESS IMPORTANT) ROLE

The stepmother can and most often does function in a nurturing capacity, offering emotional support as well as care for her stepchildren. Her responsibilities may replicate or even surpass the responsibilities of custodial biological mothers. However, the stepmother's role is a *different* role. Because it is so important to stepmothers that their role be defined with dignity, it is essential to spend some time examining those specific features that differentiate biological mothers from stepmothers.

Dedication and time cannot erase these differences. The inability to accept them is often the cause of the dissatisfaction many step-mothers feel. Failing to be recognized as their stepchildren's "mothers," they feel disappointed and hurt. Such feelings are absolutely avoidable if stepmothers will stop pretending or striving to be something they are not. Stepmothers who claim or strive to be mothers indicate their own ambivalence about their role. Only by refusing to compete for someone else's role will you begin to form a place in your life that belongs to you and you alone.

WHAT'S THE DIFFERENCE?

Remember "Sleeping Beauty"? In this tale a wicked fairy places a curse upon a baby princess, condemning the infant to an early death. A protective fairy is powerless to lift the curse, but she *can* modify the spell: She does so, softening the sentence of death into a lengthy and peaceful slumber. So it is with stepmothers. Stepmothers cannot erase the past, but they can and often do determine the course of their stepchildren's future.

A biological mother and her infant begin their relationship free from any personal history. The infant has neither the ability and experience nor the language to pass judgment. The infant learns about the world from the daily interaction with the mother. The biological mother and child have the luxury of a period of bonding. During this time the baby comes to expect certain reactions to the signals that he sends and begins to form a set of expectations that will be enlarged into a broader set of expectations about the world. The stepmother, however, meets a child who is usually able to talk and whose personal history has already helped to formulate expectations about the world. The child's personal history excludes the stepmother.

The biological mother creates expectations, whereas the step-mother must modify, or coexist with, the child's previously set expectations *before* she can even begin to create a relationship of her own with that child.

THE "IDEAL" MOTHER

"Mother" is perhaps the most basic of all human roles. Mother may be the figure who sets the emotional tone for the rest of our lives, either supplying us with a nurturance we seek to replicate or depriving us of the nurturance which we seek to find. The search for recovery, or discovery, of that early nurturing period may last a lifetime. Mothers are fascinating subjects of study; they've been examined at length by sociologists, psychologists, and poets. Motherhood is perhaps one of the *only* roles that is clear in its idealized state.

The ideal mother is the consummate nurturer. She is perceived as "all-giving," offering a sort of extended coverage plan of sustenance and support. Hers is a socially acceptable role. Greeting cards, comic strips, plays, novels, art, social sciences, humor, all reflect the common acknowledgment of the primacy of the "mother" role. Mothers are always available, uncomplaining, loving, nonjudgmental, supportive, unselfish. So ingrained is our familiarity with this idealized role that stating that a woman is, or is not, "acting like a mother" is culturally defined and needs no further explanation.

BAD PRESS FOR STEPMOTHERS

On the other hand, the expected behavior of a stepmother springs from the fear of abandonment and rejection by the mother. Fairy tales and myths popularized the role of the "bad mother" in the character of the evil stepmother. The stepmother has been conceptualized as an "antimother" figure, perceived as life-threatening and malevolent. Stepmothers are portrayed as the antithesis of ideal mothers: unavailable, complaining, unloving, judgmental, critical, and selfish. A witch.

Although stepmothers may in fact supply stepchildren with the bulk of nurturance and support, their very presence testifies to the reality of another deep-seated fear: the disappearance of Mother. The daily *presence* of a stepmother suggests the *absence* of the birth mother.

MORE DIFFERENCES

The birth of a planned child creates or intensifies a deep emotional bond between a man and a woman. A woman who marries a previously married man has to make certain adjustments in her romantic vision; she has to come to terms with her predecessor. She must "rewrite history," employing a form of selective amnesia. In this way, the new couple chooses to forget certain specifics of a past marriage or relationship. They "forget" that the husband has loved another woman and was loved in return. The new couple chooses not to linger in the past; they do not often discuss former relationships and, in the course of time, the past is allowed to recede naturally. As time progresses, the couple's shared experiences assume a primacy and validity that erase the power of the previous relationship. So complete is this rewriting of history that many such couples come to think about their present marriages as their only "true marriage."

No such illusions for stepmothers! It is difficult to forget about the past when its products are sitting at the breakfast table each morning! It's difficult to rewrite history in the presence of firsthand witnesses. The stepmother, unlike the biological mother, must create a relationship with children that includes another woman, a woman who is, unlike an adoptive mother, known to the children as their "birth" mother and who is often actively involved in their lives. In addition to this competition for the primary nurturing role, the stepmother must acknowledge the ongoing existence of the woman who once shared her husband's life.

It is not often that you hear "I hope this baby loves me" from a biological mother. The expectation of biological mothers is that their children will love them simply because they *are* mothers. There is something almost mystical in the expectation and acceptance of the love between child and mother. The taboo against voicing negative thoughts against one's mother is primal and generally universal. Biological mothers may typically demand and be accorded "love" despite apparent contradictions in their behavior toward and concern for their offspring; nowhere else do we find a nine-month investment expected to pay such long-range and continuous dividends as in the case of motherhood.

Stepmothers long for this unconditional love and fear they will never receive it; they probably won't. Stepmothers continually describe situations where biological mothers are granted love and loyalty despite the quality or quantity of their involvement with their children. Stepmothers often feel that no matter how much they labor they must continue to earn each and every "I love you"—if they earn any at all.

Given the differences between biological motherhood and step motherhood, it is easy to understand why many women simply opt to "become" mothers to their stepchildren. Given the choice, who would choose to be a "witchy, wicked, evil" stepmother? But choosing to try to be a mother to her stepchildren is probably the greatest error a stepmother can make. Women may choose to nurture, to love, and to commit to their stepchildren in varying capacities, but stepmothers who attempt to crown themselves "Mother" and wait for a shower of unconditional love and acceptance will subject themselves to a long wait—ending, most likely, in painful disappointment.

WHAT IS "UNCONDITIONAL LOVE"?

Unconditional Love. Everyone seems to want it, everyone mourns its absence; yet what *is* it? The very notion of love given without any conditions suggests a relationship plagued by irrationality. The notion of one person giving without hope of reciprocity suggests the possibility for huge abuse and disappointment. Who needs it? Stepmothers may be confused when they stumble upon a troubling discovery; Unconditional "love" is not really very loving, nor is it desirable at all! In fact, the unconditional love that is so coveted by stepmothers and so easily awarded to biological mothers is often a catchall label for a host of otherwise unacceptable emotions. Unconditional love is often little more than another way of saying, "You have to." Unconditional love is an acceptable repository for unfulfilled needs, guilt, unexpressed rage, and fears of abandonment.

Real love has little or nothing in common with unconditional love. Love that is granted despite mistreatment, despite abandonment or reciprocity, is something the stepmother will not receive. Looked at in this light, it's hardly worth having. The love that a stepmother will ultimately find will be firmly rooted in shared commitment and respect.

DEVELOPING INNER STRENGTH

The stepmother's search for "mother-love," although painful, causes a surge of personal growth and understanding. The search for unconditional love causes the stepmother to explode unwittingly some dearly held myths about the state of motherhood. She may discover that her relationship with her stepchildren causes them to review and adjust their views of their relationships with their own mother. Such analysis causes many stepmothers to begin thinking about themselves in ways that they may never have gotten around to. Over and over again, stepmothers reported that their relationships with their stepchildren ultimately resulted in their becoming stronger. One of the ways they built that inner strength was by examining and adjusting dearly held personal myths about mothers in general and in particular. How many individuals truly have the nurturing, mutually satisfying supportive relationships of the idealized biological mother? Most people have difficulty with their mothers. In exploding the myth of the ideal mother, stepmothers begin to realize that they are capable of building a healthy and workable relationship with their stepchildren—on their own terms. As stepmothers.

Almost every stepmother I interviewed distanced herself from the role of stepmother and protested that she acted as mother to her stepchildren. An overwhelming percentage were quick to point out that their stepchildren called them "Mom." Many other stepmothers added that people didn't even know that their family was a stepfamily. The vehemence with which stepmothers identified and justified their identification as mothers was loud and clear.

BUT IS IT REAL?

Although stepmothers seemed clear about their need to be acknowledged as mothers, a truer sense of their self-image emerged when they were asked, "Where would the children go in the case of your husband's death?" Almost every stepmother assumed that her stepchildren would return to their biological mother (if she was living). This assumption held despite the past or current relationship with the mother. More revealing of the stepmother's acknowledgment of the tenuousness of her role was the fact that in cases where the biological mother was no longer living, most stepmothers assumed that the children would go to live with another blood-related family member. Obviously, the majority of stepmothers considered that their "motherhood" relationship with their stepchildren was dependent upon an intact marriage. Scratching the surface, one finds that many stepmothers seemed to regard their relationships as subject to control by forces outside the family: courts, the wishes of biological mothers, grandparents. This is not real motherhood!

Given these differences and the likelihood that stepmothers accept them, at least surreptitiously, why do stepmothers continue to insist upon motherhood as the definition of their role?

DOES IT SEEM THE OBVIOUS CHOICE?

Stepmothers may opt for motherhood simply because it's more familiar. When my son was about three years old, he was particularly fascinated by pregnant women. He asked lots of questions, which I tried to answer as simply and factually as possible. One day in the park he stared with rapt attention as an obviously pregnant young woman strolled past. "Mommy," he said, "I can't wait to grow up and have a baby inside me." I explained that only women grew babies inside them and hastened to add that he would play a very important part in the creation of a baby some day. I watched his little face darken as he took in this disappointing news. After a quiet moment he brightened and announced, "Mommy, when I grow up, I'm going to change and be a woman!" He had worked through a solution to his problem; because he couldn't understand the nature of his future role, he opted for a choice that was familiar and comprehensible. It made sense to him and it seemed to settle the problem; *but the choice wasn't his to make.* Changing into a woman was not possible.

Changing and becoming a biological mother is not possible for stepmothers, either.

DANGER SIGNS: THE OPPOSITE EXTREME

A small percentage of stepmothers do not attempt to function as mothers to their stepchildren: They go to the opposite extreme. These stepmothers described their relationships with their stepchildren as non-nurturing. They attempted to distance themselves from their stepchildren as a result of suffering perceived rejection or due to an inability to compromise with their husbands about different child-rearing styles. This small number of stepmothers tried to assume the various roles of "housekeeper," "Dad's wife," or "friend." None of these roles was a successful avenue to happiness; indeed, this small group of stepmothers was generally dissatisfied both with their marriages and with stepmothering.

The Housekeeper

Some stepmothers described situations where they felt like inter-lopers or intruders in their own homes. They felt caught in relation-ships between their husbands and stepchildren that were strong and exclusionary. They couldn't find their place—their role.

Even after seven years of marriage, Gretta still felt like the house-keeper she had replaced—the woman who had raised Gretta's two young stepsons until Gretta's marriage to their widowed father. After the wedding, the housekeeper was dismissed and Gretta assumed total care for her two young stepsons until six o'clock, when her husband came home. When "Papa" arrived, Gretta was totally excluded from all involvement and interaction with the chil-dren. Her husband went so far as to speak Hungarian to his sons, a language Gretta did not know and which her husband refused to teach her. The hurt and resentment stemming from being shut out of discussions, confidences, and family decisions mounted. Like many stepmothers in this position, Gretta found her resentment shifting from her stepchildren to her husband. A stepmother who is consistently banned from involvement with her stepchildren and husband as a family unit will often withdraw not only from her stepfamily but from the marriage as well.

Dad's Wife

A tiny percentage of stepmothers described themselves as having no responsibility for their stepchildren. This small group totally removed themselves from any emotional interaction with their step-children; their husbands continued to assume all responsibility for the care of the children. These women regarded themselves as their "husbands' wives" and not as stepmothers. They simply acted as though their stepchildren were not part of their daily lives. Such unhappy situations almost invariably resulted in the stepchildren eventually leaving the stepmother's home to live elsewhere.

Friend

Some stepmothers tried to act as friends to their stepchildren, par-ticularly in cases where stepmother and stepchildren were close in age. Stepmothers who are only a few years older than their stepchildren or who live with adult stepchildren frequently experience confusion about their roles. Extending the hand of friendship may seem like the only possibility. However, despite the stepmother's good intentions, the role of friend just doesn't work very well. There are definite and observable differences between the roles of "friends" and the roles of "stepmothers":

- Friends don't generally instruct; stepmothers do.
- Friends have shared interests and/or perspectives about the world; a stepmother and her family may not.
- Friends come together as individuals who have chosen, and enjoy, each other's company; stepmothers and their stepchildren come together in a pseudofamilial manner through a third party, and may or may not enjoy each other's company.
- Friends don't usually live together and are not required to integrate each other's personal habits into their lifestyles; stepmothers and stepchildren must confront and cope with each other's most intimate habits.
- Friendships are voluntary and may be canceled at any point by either or both friends; stepmothers and stepchildren, although they may feel like canceling out, do not have this option.

Suggesting to a stepchild that you be friends opens up the option for the child to decline the offer of friendship and provides the opportunity for hurt feelings all around.

Attempting friendship with adult children who still live at home sets up some very strange family dynamics. A stepmother seeking friendship runs the risk of overidentifying with the "children." She may find herself *becoming* one of the children of the house. Although this alignment with the younger generation may seem like fun at first, the stepmother will eventually discover that her self-esteem, as well as her identity in her marriage, will suffer. Friendship is an unworkable as well as inappropriate role. Most adult stepchildren will be uncomfortable discussing marital issues that concern their father. Stepchildren, despite their age or level of sophistication, generally become uneasy when trying to think about and relate to their father as their "friend's husband."

Further complications arise for the stepmother who is acting in the role of friend, should she and her husband decide to add their own children to the family. These complications are discussed in more detail in Chapter 11.

Stepmothers are not mommies, housekeepers, Dad's wives, or friends to their stepchildren. Stepmothers are just what they are: stepmothers. Yet they seem to avoid the obvious, choosing to remain locked in ambiguity rather than focused and satisfied. Why have they rejected the role of stepmother? In order to define the role clearly and succeed as stepmothers, perhaps it is necessary to confront and banish the negative stigma and fear that have too often been associated with stepmothering.

Understanding the Negative Stigma

Stepmothers have received bad press for a long time. There is a long historical tradition of wicked, cruel stepmothers—a tradition that transcends cultural boundaries. Greek mythology is replete with cruel stepmothers, women who are notorious for plotting elaborate schemes to assassinate their stepchildren. Wicked stepmothers can be found in the folk literature of every country in the world. The Grimm brothers, who are generally held accountable for inventing the wicked-stepmother stories, really should be let off the hook; they did nothing more than collect and dispense about 200 old folktales. Stepmother stories appear throughout time and are absolutely crosscultural. In fact, the very familiar and oft-cited "Cinderella" can be traced to ninth-century China!

Both the printing press and an increase in literacy led to the wide circulation of these tales in the Western world. But these factors alone don't explain the *acceptability* of these particular stories.

Why did the wicked stepmother tales catch on? Why is history so much harder on the stepmother than on the stepfather? Why do the women get to bear the burden of blame?

If you asked my grandmother this question she'd simply have answered with another question: "So what else is new?" Maybe in a real sense, she'd have had a point. Motherhood and fatherhood are different.

Motherhood is more clear and certifiable than fatherhood. In fact, many cultures use maternal lines for determining legacies, names, and, in the Jewish tradition, religious affinity. Such cultures assert that whereas fatherhood may be questioned, motherhood is a certainty. Although a child may fantasize that his parents are not the "real" parents, this fantasy is more difficult to sustain for a mother than for a father.

It is generally agreed that most children and adults find it uncomfortable to voice anger or hatred against their biological mothers. Mother is perceived as a life-giver and life-sustainer. She functions as primary caretaker and is perceived as responsible for her child's very survival and identity as an individual. For a son or daughter to reject the mother is to reject the source of one's own identity. To be abandoned by the mother is to lose part of that identity.

The "wicked stepmother" offers a safe outlet for the natural anger and hatred that children may feel toward their biological mothers from time to time. One psychological explanation for the acceptance of the cruel-stepmother myth is that it allows children a safe method for ventilating negative feelings about mothers while leaving the "good mother" image intact.

This is all very interesting when discussing literature. However, when a woman is trying to foster a real relationship with real, flesh-and-blood stepchildren, the implications of stepmothers as evil and biological mothers as saintly assume chilling connotations. Stepmothers will discover that the best way to deal with the negative connotations of stepmotherhood is directly: If the "wicked" stepmother was created to answer a fear, then a "kind" stepmother can be created to answer a fear as well.

EASIER SAID THAN DONE?

Stepmothers may indeed appear cruel from a child's perspective. Many of the tasks involved in child-care are restrictive and unpleasant by definition. The stepmother will be involved with limit setting, correcting, and reprimanding. This unpleasant side to nurturing is balanced, for the biological mother, by love, affection, and close ties to the child that started long before the child's conscious memory. The child accepts, as a given, that the mother has only the best interests of her child at heart. The stepmother begins her relationship with the child as a virtual stranger. Although she carries out many of the same duties as a biological mother, she lacks the affection and bonding that are needed to balance her demands. Trying to "raise a child" without this balance may cause the stepmother to appear cold and at times, even cruel. The more a stepmother attempts to nurture her stepchildren, the more demanding and cruel she may appear.

In addition to the worn stereotypes of children's tales, stepmothers must deal with very real slights, ranging from insensitivity to out-and-out bigotry. Detractors come from such varied sources as next-door neighbors, teachers, family, and friends. However, the stepmother's worst enemy is her own ambivalence about her role. Stepmothers share the same prejudices and cultural discomfort with stepmotherhood as the rest of the population. Alas, that negativism doesn't always disappear when a woman becomes a stepmother herself!

I have heard stepmothers—almost all, in fact—express extreme distaste over the very terms "stepmother and "stepchild." Cold. Witchy. Evil. Awful. Separate. Wicked Witch of the North. These make me cringe! Stepmothers need to clean up their own act before they can hope to be treated with dignity and respect by anyone else. Stepmothers must refuse to perpetuate the negative mythology that surrounds their role and the unflattering prototypes that spring from the pages of children's stories.

Rules and Tips for the Confident Stepmother

Stepmothers who described themselves as being very satisfied with their role shared a pattern of success. These women seemed to possess an attitude and a system of behavior that can be traced to three simple "rules" and a few not-so-simple patterns of behavior:

- Assume a great deal of control within the family.
- Assume a role as primary parent to stepchildren.
- Do not compete with *anyone* for stepchildren's loyalty.

STEPMOTHERS ARE ADVISERS

Stepmothers who function in the capacity of adviser or guide to their stepchildren report that they feel a special sense of fulfillment and happiness. These stepmothers often select specific goals for their relationship with their stepchildren—activities they have chosen either to teach or to share. Because the goals are concrete and measurable, such stepmothers are able to gauge their success and to take pride in the special reward found in "making a difference" in their stepchildren's lives.

STEPMOTHERS ARE "TRUSTED ADULTS"

Stepmothers are also delighted when they become the recipients of a child's trust. Stepchildren, as a group, have suffered a severe blow to their ability to trust. Divorce or death and the resultant upheaval of the original family shake even the most sanguine child's sense of security and can severely damage the child's ability to trust the world and himself. One of the most important and rewarding components of a stepmother's role is the rebuilding of her stepchildren's often shattered or damaged ability to trust. Such trust is built over time by stepmothers who are consistent, honest, and discreet.

THE CONFIDENT STEPMOTHER: WHAT SHE DOES

Confident stepmothers, who describe themselves as happy and satisfied with their role, point out strategies that have worked for them as they strive to strengthen the solidarity of their new families. A good stepmother, they maintain:

Remains in the Present

The confident stepmother is not threatened by the past. She realizes that discussions of the past are the product of her stepchildren's personal history. The confident stepmother acknowledges, without insecurity, that her stepchildren were not born on the day she became their stepmother; this knowledge may prompt some regret, but it is not threatening.

Plans for the Future

The confident stepmother is always making plans, whether for next year's holiday dinner or her relationship with her stepchildren's babies. Confident stepmothers look forward; this forward-looking approach renews their personal confidence and extends a feeling of optimism and confidence to their stepchildren.

Respects Herself

Confidence and self-respect go hand in hand. The confident stepmother does not expect abuse and does not demean herself by allowing inappropriate or hurtful behavior. The confident stepmother realizes that she is a person worthy of respect and love and wise enough to acknowledge the difference. The confident stepmother expects respect but knows that she cannot demand love.

Commits Herself to Her Stepchildren

The confident stepmother does not wait for her stepchildren to love or accept her before she makes her commitment to them. She knows that her role as stepmother occurred with or without the consent of her stepchildren. She realizes that there is a tremendous imbalance in family power and that she now holds that power. Recognizing that she is the feminine head of the household, the confident stepmother commits herself to caring for and about her stepchildren.

Recognizes Limitations

The confident stepmother realizes that she is capable of *sustaining* a meaningful relationship with her stepchildren. She plans goals and sets her expectations logically, rather than emotionally. The confident stepmother learns all that she can about any situation, projects alternatives, and proceeds to act with an awareness of any inherent limitations.

Accepts Responsibility for Her Own Actions

Confident stepmothers judge only their *own* actions. They come to realize that any individual can only be held accountable for her own behavior, and not for anyone else's. They accept that no one "makes" anyone else do anything. She is responsible only for her half of any relationship.

Is Active Rather Than Passive

The successful stepmother functions from a position of energy and confidence. She takes action rather than languishing about, waiting for things to fall into place. Stepmotherhood often forces a passive woman into a more active stance; this new assertiveness can have positive effects throughout her life.

Accepts the Rewards Gracefully

Through their relationship with their stepchildren, stepmothers come to know the reward of a deep interaction with another human being that is different from any other parenting role, *a relationship free from the psychological entanglements that often complicate biologically determined relationships.* Stepmothers enjoy relationships that are founded upon commitment rather than biology—relationships that are ultimately the products of mutual choice rather than obligation.

In order to begin confidently, a stepmother will need to have a good working knowledge of the various stages of child development. Such an understanding will allow her to focus on her personal relationship with her stepchildren. In order for a stepmother to be successful she must understand her stepchildren as *children* who progress through typical and fairly consistent stages of development and as *individuals* whose reactions will be determined by their own very personal perspective.

CHAPTER 4

Getting Started

If You're Already a Mother

Does being a mother help a woman in her role as a stepmother? No, say stepmothers with children from previous marriages. Although mothers are familiar with the stages of child development and have plenty of experience with the mechanics and responsibilities for daily child-care, they found themselves totally unprepared for the differences between mothering and stepmothering. Nothing prepared them for the confusion and resentment they felt as they witnessed changes in their relationships with their biological children. Expecting that their "mothering" would simply be extended to include their stepchildren, they were often surprised to discover in themselves a different set of expectations, a different level of tolerance, and different feelings for their step and biological children—differences that seriously affected the new family's chances for success and their own chances for personal happiness. What were these differences?

47

Stepmothers found, often to their surprise, that they were stricter with their "own" children—and more demanding. They found that they were quicker to set rules and to enforce infractions with their children than with their stepchildren. They were also quicker to flare up in anger at their biological children. They wondered why. Some speculated that their anger might spring from frustration over failed child-rearing attempts in their new, combined family, and embarrassment over that unexpected failure. A stepmother tends to see her "own" children's behavior as a reflection of her mothering ability, whereas a stepchild's misbehavior, though frustrating, does not make her feel personally responsible.

Stepmothers found that they had vastly different expectations for their biological children and their stepchildren. They found themselves often turning to their biological children to provide emotional support and personal validation when the going got rough, when instant love and an instant family didn't materialize. Stepmothers with children of their "own" were surprised and distressed to find themselves expecting their children to take up the slack in the family, thereby subjecting them to tremendous and unfair pressure.

Barbara, a stepmother of one and mother of two, admits to this pattern of unfair expectations. "If my stepdaughter's room is a mess," she said, "I find myself screaming at my *own* daughter for something as minor as a bath towel draped over her chair." She realizes this causes resentment among the children in the family and between herself and the children. "Sometimes it just seems easier to ask your own kid to do something," Barbara concluded.

Over and over, stepmothers voiced this feeling. But *why* is it easier to ask your "own" son to take out the garbage rather than your stepson? "Oh," claims Debby, "he just knows what I want him to do." "I don't have to go through all those explanations when I ask my daughter to do something," Ann admits.

It doesn't require a Sherlock Holmes to detect that something else is going on behind such statements: When stepmothers don't feel secure with their stepchildren, they turn to their biological children. It's easy to ask someone whom you know, and love, and who also loves *you*, to do favors for you; it's hard to ask someone who doesn't trust you yet. The reasoning behind this is simple: The stepchild's love is conditional; it's still to be earned. On the other hand, the biological child's love is perceived as unconditional. Stepmothers seem to revel in the fact that love and respect do not have to be earned or maintained from biological children. This feeling of the immutability of their love serves as a basis for assuming that all sorts of chores and favors may be demanded, thanks to this reciprocal love between mother and child.

When a stepmother falls into the trap of this false reasoning, she runs the risk of expecting her children to demonstrate far more compassion, maturity, and altruistic feeling than they are capable of. She sometimes runs the risk of losing sight of the flesh-and-blood children she lives with, and of viewing her biological children as "ideal" and her stepchildren as "real"—and therefore subject to more realistic, lower expectations.

What can a stepmother/mother do about these unequal feelings? How can she equalize the pressure on both biological and stepchildren and prevent herself from perpetuating a pattern of behavior that can only harm the new family?

ACKNOWLEDGE THOSE DIFFERENT EXPECTATIONS

First, it is best to acknowledge your feelings, and discuss your expectations with the children. Biological children will have their feelings of worth confirmed; they *are* being asked to do more, but this is a natural result of their already secure relationship with their mother. Stepchildren will similarly feel validated: They will be delighted that more is being asked of the biological child, whom they have probably perceived as favored.

Sharing these feelings isn't always easy. Stepmothers are often uncomfortable when they realize that they don't feel the same way about their step and biological children. Over and over, stepmothers described how they treated both sets of children the same; how they acted the same toward both sets of children; how the rules were the same; and how their responsibilities for both sets of children were the same, too. Yet despite such repeated protestations, most stepmothers agreed that there was an intangible "something" that separated their feelings for their step and biological children. This "something"—an effort to show affection and forgivability toward the stepchild—softened reprimands, criticisms, and anger. This "something" was a strong biological identification and empathy for a mother's "own" child. Once admitted and brought out into the open, this distinction was easier to deal with.

The single mother who marries and becomes a stepmother finds that both she and her children face a number of practical and emotional changes that will affect the ways in which they interact with one another. Facing and discussing each aspect of family life—as it comes up—will help pave the way to a smooth transition.

Mothers who become stepmothers will need to help their children adjust to new homes, neighborhoods, and schools. Any change for a child is a BIG change. Practical changes, such as financial ones, cannot compare in intensity to the emotional changes children confront when they are required to accept their mother's new role as a stepmother.

LOSS OF STATUS

Single mothers often relate to their children in different ways than mothers who are married; there's often a "friendship" component; single mothers tend to *talk* to their children in more sharing ways than married mothers do. The absence of another adult in the home promotes the child to an almost adult level in the realm of receiving the mother's confidences. When a mother marries, she then turns to her husband for adult confidence—leaving the child behind. When that mother also becomes a stepmother, her children are even more likely to resent their apparent "demotion" to one of the mere "children" in the new family.

LESS INDIVIDUAL TIME WITH MOTHER

Single mothers usually have random chunks of time to spend with their children; mother and child may share a bathroom mirror in the morning, chat while getting ready for work and school or for a date in the evening, and spend time shopping for dinner together, or grabbing a quick meal at a fast-food place. Children often substitute for adult companionship; single mothers spend a good deal of their leisure time with their children. When mothers marry and become stepmothers, that intimate lifestyle between mother and child changes, and those precious chunks of shared time come to an abrupt end. Doors are now closed: Time and confidences are shared with the new husband. Leisure time now includes both mother and stepfather or becomes a "family" activity that includes stepsiblings as well.

Many new stepmothers become edgy and uncomfortable when this happens. They miss the lost intimacy and the ease of the mother-child relationship as keenly as their children do.

While Joan lived as a single parent, her life revolved around her twelve-year-old daughter. Joan would take each day as it came; caring for only one child was simple and pleasant. Indeed, virtually all of Joan's time, aside from her work as a commercial artist, was centered on Jessica; taking her to ballet class, helping her with homework, shopping with her each evening for the dinner they'd share. Then Joan married and this intimacy changed; Jessica moved from the center spot in Joan's life to a satellite position. Joan found herself dropping Jessica off at ballet to continue on to her stepson's hockey practice. She did not enjoy hockey; she felt out of place and unappreciated. Her stepsons did not seem to notice her presence, and Jessica began to show less interest in ballet. Joan grew increasingly edgy.

The stepmother who was a single mother to an *only* child may find that she faces a rocky adjustment period both for herself and for her child. The only child has an especially large adjustment to make. That child now has to accommodate to another adult, other children, *and* the sharing of his/her mother in a way that is totally foreign. The mother has to learn how to divide her child-care responsibilities among several children and must quickly learn how to cope with sharing and jealousies, bickering and boisterous play, all absent issues in a single-parent, only-child household. Sometimes, however, a mother's remarriage can signal positive changes for her child or children.

Dorothy was a young single mother who, like many young divorcées, was surviving at just above the poverty level. Her marriage to Don radically affected her children's standard of living. Dorothy and her three children were, as she claims, "pretty good at pinching pennies" before she married. She remembers her children's amazement at their new largess when they all moved into Don's home in the suburbs. While she and Don busied themselves moving in, the children stared at a large bowl of fruit on the dining room table. The children had never seen a big bowl of fruit like that;

in their household there had never been any money for desserts. Dorothy recalled that when she and her children wanted a special treat they would walk up and down the hall of their apartment building and "get fat on their neighbors' fumes"; they weren't sure that the bowl of fruit was real, and when they found it was, they weren't sure it was for eating. When Dorothy and Don assured the children that it was theirs to eat, they pounced on the bowl and ate every piece. Dorothy, like many single mothers, found that her marriage greatly improved her financial situation.

Not all single mothers find that their marriages bring more advantages into their lives. Some new stepmothers, like Hannah, find that they have less money to spend as a result of becoming stepmothers. Hannah had been a single mother with one young son for seven years before her marriage to Rex and had been in the habit of spending money quite freely. She and her young son had lived with relatives, and although Hannah paid a nominal rent and shared household expenses, the remainder of her salary as a high school music teacher was hers to spend—without accountability. Hannah spent most of her salary on her son. Hannah's marriage increased the *amount* of cash on hand, but the *way* in which money was spent changed drastically. Like scores of other stepmothers, Hannah found that handling money in the new family involved new disciplines and a sharing of control: Planning and sharing were the rule, instant gratification the exception. Family living involves more expenses than the single-parent lifestyle—higher food bills, additional expenses for clothing, higher rent or mortgage payments, and insurance bills. Again, stepmothers like Hannah found that adjustment was easier when they faced, and discussed, the changes marriage would bring to them and to their children. They didn't always find this process easy, however, and most of them felt the need for guidance in taking the first steps toward creating a new family.

BEGINNING STEPS

1. Don't Rush!

Going overboard in an attempt to treat stepchildren in the same way as your biological children is just unworkable. Although the new stepmother may have good intentions, she just won't *feel* the same about all children in the family. Pretending that you feel the same way about everyone is just not feasible; mothers nearly always feel differently about their own children. To expect to feel the same way about children you've just met as you do about those with whom you share a biological and historical connection is impractical; such dishonesty serves no one! Your "own" children will feel confused and betrayed by such protestations of instant-equal love and step-children will see such dishonesty for what it is. There is nothing wrong with acknowledging truth.

2. Share Your Time

Sharing is difficult for all children—and most adults, too! Your children are being asked to share their mother with other children and with another adult! It is also a well-kept secret that stepmothers often resent time spent with stepchildren if they perceive such time as detracting from time spent with their "own" children. Even the most well-adjusted stepchild will need extra time and affection from the new stepmother. If the stepmother does not feel that she is "getting anything in return" for her efforts with her stepchildren, she may resent even more keenly the time spent away from her own children.

3. Keep Talking

Encourage children to speak freely, to ventilate their feelings. Each child must have an arena where negative as well as positive feelings can be safely expressed. Harriet, a widow, was very much in love when she married Vincent; she was thrilled that her son, John, would have a "father" and two brothers. Despite Harriet's happiness, John deteriorated during the first five years of her marriage, changing from a smiling ten-year-old who loved school and Little League to a sullen fifteen-year-old who was frequently a truant and more than occasionally high on marijuana; he was unhappy and out of control. Harriet took John to a therapist, who learned, during the first sessions, that John had hated the idea of his mother's marriage from the beginning and still hated his "brothers"! Harriet was shocked; John had always said everything was fine with the family!

4. Maintain as Many Routines as Possible

Children are fearful that they will lose their mothers. This is a deep emotional fear that cuts across age lines. Whether you are dealing with a two-year-old who suddenly attaches himself to your leg or a teenager who plants herself on the sofa for a month like a silent couch potato, the fear is the same. Any change in routine may exacerbate a child's fear that *Mother* is changing!

Sarah tried to be a superstepmommy—and discovered that changing all the routines for her young son and trying to be a perfect mommy, wife, and stepmother backfired! Sarah had been a single mother for most of her son's ten years. She had worked as a nurse from the time Jason was nine months old, and as he matured he assumed many household chores. At the time of his mother's marriage, Jason was a responsible and independent fourth-grader. Sarah was proud of his competence in domestic areas. Sarah's new stepchildren were older than Jason and had no desire or flair for domestic chores. Sarah worried that perhaps she had overburdened her son during her single years and determined to do more for Jason now that she was married and had the opportunity to cut back on her working hours. One evening shortly after her marriage, Sarah tiptoed into her sleeping son's room to put away some laundry. It was 1:00 A.M. and everyone was asleep. Jason sat up in bed, wide awake, and asked, "What are you doing?"

To Sarah's surprise, her independent, respectful, previously calm little boy began to yell, "STOP IT!!! WHAT ARE YOU DOING? I'M SUPPOSED TO PUT AWAY MY CLOTHES! I ALWAYS PUT AWAY MY CLOTHES! I ALWAYS CLEAN UP MY ROOM! WHY ARE YOU CHANGING?" As Sarah held her sobbing son she realized that even positive changes can be very threatening for children.

5. Make Time for Yourself—Alone

It is especially important for a new stepmother to find time to be alone. Too often, in the haste to create a family, the stepmother rushes everyone into an idealized level of intimacy. Stepmothers must remember that they married primarily for *themselves*. Children may or may not be absolutely delighted with their mother's marriage; children may or may not be delighted to be part of this new family. Children shouldn't ever be given cause to feel that they have lost their relationship with their mother, but she, too, must have time for herself.

6. Help Children Understand Your New Commitment

A stepmother must clarify and recommit herself over and over again to all the children in the house. Biological children will need to understand that they are still loved and are still irreplaceable. Some stepmothers, in a perverse approach, try to "prove" their love for their stepchildren by minimizing or disguising their loving behavior toward their biological children. They may stop showing affection to their biological children if they are uncomfortable showing affection for their stepchildren; everyone loses with this approach!

Children will understand their mother's commitment to their new stepsiblings if this commitment is discussed. Talk about fears, get them out in the open; children need support at this time. Children need to understand (which means to be *told*) that their mother's new commitment does not diminish her feelings for them. A stepmother should not minimize her expression of loving feelings for her children; such demonstrations set a positive example of closeness for stepchildren and reinforce her own children's self-confidence.

7. A Different Kind of Love

Most stepmothers feel so guilty about not feeling the *same* love for their stepchildren and their biological children that they overlook the obvious: *People love in different ways*. Mothers certainly do not expect to feel the same kind of love for their children that they feel for their own mothers; stepmothers don't expect to feel the same kind of love for their children as they do for their husbands. Stepmothers easily acknowledge different kinds of love in other aspects of their lives. So, too, they can feel different kinds of love for their stepchildren and their biological children.

If You've Never Had Children

Stepmothers who have never had children of their own are most prone to disaster in their marriages. Inexperience with children often causes stepmothers to be totally unprepared for the impact children have on their marriages and their personal life. Inexperience often prompts stepmothers to underestimate—or *overesti-mate*—the stepchild's contribution to the new family and either to overlook the richness that children bring to any couple's life or to lean too heavily on children to "make the marriage work." These misapprehensions must be exploded before a stepmother can begin.

COMMON FALSE EXPECTATIONS

"I'll Have 'Nice' Stepchildren"

Children are, by nature, self-centered creatures. Children are also, by nature of their immaturity, often not "nice." Children are dependent, self-centered, emotionally and intellectually immature, and overly concerned with their own comfort. Feelings for others must be taught and are not usually felt automatically.

"The More I Give the More I'll Get"

Giving is not usually reciprocated in direct ways by children. Many stepmothers who are inexperienced with child-rearing believe that the more they try, the more they will get in return. Often, such women have been active in the work force and apply inappropriate criteria to child-rearing only to find that strategies which worked beautifully in the office simply bomb out in the home. Children tend to take a lot more than they give. Parenting, by definition, implies that the parent will help "socialize" the child so that the child learns the skills of reciprocating, sharing, and exchanging good feelings.

Not only will children often fail to be "nice" but it will probably fall to the stepmother to teach her stepchildren about "niceness."

"Only 'Real' Mothers Have Power"

Stepmothers often feel that they don't have the right to any authority over their stepchildren. Stepmothers are the adults in the family. Children and adults are not on equal footing. The stepmother, although inexperienced in mothering, possesses a wealth of adult experience and skills that she will share with her stepchildren. This sense of adulthood should encourage stepmothers to become more confident.

"I'll Rescue My Husband and His Children"

Children and husbands are not social-work projects. Many stepmothers enter their marriages as rescue workers. Like so many Wendys in the children's tale of Peter Pan, they fly off to rescue their husbands and stepchildren, only to learn a scary truth: Husbands and stepchildren generally do not feel the need to be rescued by anyone.

"I'll Be Their Real Mother"

Some stepmothers assume that a child is a child is a child; they anticipate that their stepchildren will fill their need to be a mother. It doesn't work that way. Stepmothers with that expectation are susceptible to tremendous hurt. Eager to shower their new children with a love they have been saving up for years, they are often desperately disappointed when they are met with coolness, hostility—anything short of adoring, open-armed love.

"I'll Be a Better Mother Than Their Own"

Stepmothers must refrain from competing with biological mothers. The stepmother who perceives her relationship with her stepchildren as a competition with an adversarial mother is setting herself up for anguish and defeat. Raising children is a commitment and a responsibility, not a competition.

"This New Family Will Replace the Original Family"

There really are no replacements in life; there are only *new relationships*. No one feels this more keenly than a child. Think about a child whose puppy has just been run over. Well-meaning adults tend to rush in and offer a replacement. Their good intentions are usually rejected with wails of "I don't want a new puppy, I want *my* puppy." No loving adult would remind such a child of all the complaints he or she used to have about the departed puppy. Certainly no one would blame the new puppy for the child's rejection. Most people faced with this situation would understand the child's grief: One puppy cannot replace another. Families and mothers are not interchangeable or replaceable, either. Only when the child has completed his grieving for the previous family, and for the absent mother, will he be ready to accept a new family or a new parent.

"They Will Have to Love Me"

Love cannot be legislated. Children cannot be told to love their stepmothers any more than stepmothers can be forced to love their stepchildren. Children will *not* automatically love you because you are married to their father; respect in the form of polite behavior can be required; love cannot. Love must grow on its own.

"Love Will Conquer All"

A woman actually becomes a stepmother at the altar. Caught up in the romance of the moment, she tends to sweep the children along with her prevailing mood. Alas, the wash of romanticism inherent in the new marriage is not the most ideal atmosphere for logic, which would prevent her from assuming that the warm and loving feelings she has for her new husband automatically will be reciprocated by her new stepchildren. She may be shocked to discover that her stepchildren do *not* love her. Even more shocking is the discovery that she does not automatically love them—as she had romantically assumed she would. Love for stepchildren is not conferred with the exchange of marriage vows.

"This Marriage Has Nothing to Do with the Kids; They're His"

Although many stepmothers begin their relationships with starry-eyed expectations of motherhood, others start out assuming that their stepchildren will not affect their lives. Such women begin their marriages with the assumption that they will be able to distance themselves from their stepchildren's lives, leaving their care and responsibility totally to the father. Many such stepmothers have remained childless by design and have conveyed their preference for a childless life to their husbands. They somehow imagine that marriage will in no way change their husband's previous arrangements for child-care: They assume that the husband will continue to manage child-care the same way it was done before the marriage. There is no way this can work. Stepmothers who plan on excluding themselves from their stepchildren's lives while living under the same roof are simply kidding themselves. Living with children without any interaction is, at the very least, "cold." It is unrealistic to expect to maintain detachment from human beings with whom you will be sharing your home and your husband.

WHAT CAN A STEPMOTHER EXPECT?

Becoming a stepmother *will* change your life; it *will* link you intimately with the lives of one or more children. It will *not* automatically ensure your husband's love, imbue you with respectability, or provide you with an instant family. All of *that* is up to you. In the next chapters, we'll talk about how to do it. We'll ask and answer a lot of practical questions, and a few philosophical ones:

- What are some typical behavior patterns that an inexperienced stepmother may discover?
- What common problems impede the beginning of a smooth relationship between stepmother and stepchildren?
- How can she cope with these problems?

CHAPTER 5

Learning About Child Development

The age of a child will greatly influence that child's readiness, ability, and desire to begin a new relationship; each age group presents a different set of concerns, issues, and joys for stepmothers.

The Infant and Preschool Child

Stepmothers are often upset to find themselves in charge of little cherubs who are anything but cherubic. The dream of an adorable child slumbering peacefully in one's arms is often shattered by the reality of a sobbing, sullen, frightened child clinging tearfully to its father's trouser leg.

It will help the stepmother to understand the world of a little child—a world that is limited by thought processes that aren't capable of dealing with abstractions. It will help to understand that the world of a little child is truly a scary place, a place without clear borders—where a new stepmother may represent a threat to the fragile order the little child is only beginning to construct. It will help stepmothers to understand that the sometimes rejecting, hostile, or pitiful behavior of the young child is not personally directed at her; it's a sign of confusion and a lack of comprehension.

The very real pain of the new stepmother must be addressed, too. Most women assume the care of young children with extraordinarily high hopes. It is easy to "fall in love" with a little child and it is all too easy to expect that that love will be immediately returned. It is hard not to be hurt when a young child rejects those early advances; it is hard to know how to approach a child who so obviously wants someone else. However, it is possible for a stepmother to form a close and loving relationship with a baby or a very young child *if* she understands the child's world and the ways she can become part of that world.

HOW DO BABIES THINK?

There's obviously little point in handing a baby a how-to book or writing a baby a letter; a baby's just not ready for such interaction. There are lots of other communication techniques that won't work with babies, either. Stepmothers of very young children will have to shoulder the bulk of all reasoning and thinking simply because little children are developmentally unprepared to reason and think on their own.

Babies don't make plans; they have no understanding of cause and effect. In fact, they're just beginning to figure out that they are separate from the world around them. Babies are entirely dependent upon adults for their most basic physical survival; the extent and richness of their lives, and the way they will grow and perceive the world, is in the hands of those who care for them.

As babies grow into toddlerhood between eighteen months and three years, they are almost entirely involved with the business of exploring their world and the people who inhabit it. Toddlers and preschoolers are naturally wary and skeptical. Language skills improve at this stage and communication with the child becomes a little easier.

Little children will not be able to give detailed explanations either of their feelings or their experiences. They spend much of their time trying to make sense out of their world, deeply engrossed in the effort to meet their own needs. It's not realistic to expect a child to deal with the abstractions of a stepfamily when he or she is struggling with mastery of the fork!

Understanding the way little children begin to think may help stepmothers as they begin their new family lives.

Toddlers Lump Things Together

Toddlers will group things together without any apparent pattern; for example, a "daddy" may become any person who scratches his nose in a way that the toddler's father does.

Words Have an Individual Meaning

You may be saying "Honey," and that means something totally different to your little stepchild. "Honey" may mean something that a child desires, a catchall word for feeling good or perhaps for feeling deprived or sad.

They're Inconsistent

The world is "magical" to a little child; people change identities with their clothing. Toddlers don't "see" each adult in a consistent way. They don't see events consistently, either.

Between the ages of three and five, children begin to give "reasons" for their behavior and try to interpret their experiences; however, their "reasons" may not have much to do with an adult's reasoning. The ways in which children reason at this age sometimes lead adults to believe that they are lying or being obstinate when in fact they are simply thinking things through to the best of their limited ability.

Toddlers adopt one opinion after the other. Don't expect them to like ripe bananas today just because they liked them yesterday!

They Lack Direction

Little children often mix up unrelated explanations when trying to reason through the causes of an event; they don't really know what is relevant to their reasoning. When a little child is asked how a car works, he may respond by naming off all the parts of a car.

Children Lack a Sense of Sequence

Children may reverse the order in which things happened. A child may announce that he lost his fork because he's not eating, for example, instead of the other way around.

Children Don't "Think About Thinking"

If a child is asked, "Where did you learn that?" the response may be "I always knew it"—or a surprised stare.

Children Have Trouble with Relationships

Children have difficulty understanding family relationships, age relationships, spatial relationships. They are just learning how to name individual objects; they haven't mastered the skill of fitting things or people together.

Children Give Meaning to Chance Happenings

Children believe that things happen because they are caused by someone; objects can act on behalf of people or in obedience to them. A little child of this age might wail over a missed plane, then ask, "But didn't it see we were here?" If he tells you about a dream, and *you* don't remember how it turned out, he'll protest, "But you were *there!*"

A cork might be "reasoned" to float not because of any scientific principle but because it is simply "smarter" than the rock, which sinks.

THE ADJUSTMENT PERIOD—WHAT TO EXPECT?

Little children may not be ready to think about the changes in their lives, but they certainly do feel them. They don't have the vocabulary, the experience, or the developmental ability to deal with change. Because of these limitations, they let their actions speak for them. What can a new stepmother expect?

The Angry Child

Three-year-olds, angry about the changes in their lives, may turn the anger inward; they may whine, complain, or chronically boss other children around. They may become self-destructive, pulling their hair, biting their nails, or picking their skin. They may turn the anger outward: Becoming overly aggressive, such children may alternate between being bullies and crybabies, acting out the pattern of pain over and over again by lashing out and then seeking comfort. Such acted-out behavior is easy to spot; however, just as important for the stepmother and stepchild's adjustment are those "too quiet" kinds of behavior.

The Timid Child

Many stepchildren, especially little ones, have been overprotected by their fathers and other loving relatives. Overprotected children will be timid and reluctant to accept their stepmother into their lives. Children need to explore, to grow, and to view the world as a safe place. Overprotection gives children the message that the world is a frightening, dangerous place and that they are not competent to deal with these dangers. The child raised in an overprotected setting will commonly be fearful and will resist trying new experiences. Some children have such a strange view of the world that they may choose to play the "victim" rather than the "hero" in their pretend games.

The Perfect Child

Such children are "little angels." On first glance they seem to have adjusted perfectly to their new stepmothers. However, the child who never misbehaves is usually a very frightened child. Having experienced disorder, he or she is fearful of creating any further chaos.

The Denying Child

Young children often feel that they possess power over situations; their normal egocentricity causes them to believe that their perception or desire can alter the reality of a situation. Denying the presence of the stepmother and the fact that "Mommy" is not coming home may become the young child's reality.

The Fearful Child

Three-year-olds see parents as a concept—a single unit comprising two people. The three-year-old who accepts the fact that her biological mother will no longer be living with her may begin to fear losing other important people as well—and may be particularly fearful of losing her father or new stepmother.

The Self-Blaming Child

Three-year-olds are often convinced that their behavior causes events to occur. A child of this age may believe that breaking a plate has caused it to rain on the day of a planned picnic. Children of this age may assume that their behavior has caused the death or divorce of their mothers or the remarriage of their fathers.

The Babyish Child

When children of this age become very insecure, they seek security by reverting back to a safer time in their young lives. Three-year-olds derive much of their courage from the security provided by their families. Any disruption in this security may cause them to become fearful, shy, and cautious. Thumb-sucking, blankets, bottles, and the need for diapers may reappear.

The Manipulating Child

Little children prefer to have the adults' attention all to themselves; this is a normal phase of young childhood. They may cry and cling to whoever was taking care of them before their father's marriage; they may wail pitifully for Daddy to stay home or for Grandma to come back and live with them. This behavior may be very upsetting for the stepmother.

It is best to realize that a little child takes the stepmother's measure by such attempts. A stepmother must address these fears and not permit the child to manipulate her by crying, screaming, clinging, or sulking. Little children don't have many tools to get what they want. A two-year-old who figures out that separation fears can be used to attain whatever she wants *when* she wants it may quickly come to use such "fears" as a tool. The fears may be real, but if left unaddressed they can become manipulative.

HOW TO COPE

Stepmothers need to be calm and consistent and to understand that "acting-out" behavior stems from the very real fears of the young child. The calm, confident handling of little children will allay the child's fears and quiet the acting-out or regressive behavior.

Distract Babies and Young Children

Babies try to understand situations that are hard for them to comprehend in ways that are familiar to them; sometimes these actions just don't work. A little child may try, for example, to turn on a light by blinking her eyes open and shut, mimicking the light. The same baby may run back and forth to the door calling "Mama" in an attempt to recapture the former home. One-year-olds are into everything; they often attempt things that are way outside their current competence and become easily frustrated. Fortunately, they are easily distractable. Saying "No" won't work with an infant or a very young child, but "No" followed by a distraction—something to take the baby's attention elsewhere—is very effective.

Two-year-olds, asserting their newly discovered independence, dislike being told what to do. Couple this negativity with the clinging and separation anxiety typical of most two-year-olds, and you've produced disaster for a stepmother. Try to avoid confrontations with two-year-olds. They function best when their world is arranged so that they may attempt to do the things they wish to try as independently and with as much of a chance of success as possible.

Learn by Watching Them Play

Stepmothers can learn a lot about children by observing them at play. Very young children use play as a way of making sense of their world. Children talk to—and through—their toys; as they get older, they enjoy imitating, role-playing, and pretending games.

Reality and fantasy are still confused for most three-year-olds. Children of this age mix things up, sometimes imagining that people are living inside the T.V. set, for instance. Little children may need help separating *real* stepmothers from make-believe stepmothers in their storybooks!

Children of this age confront a host of fears, all of which seem very real. In addition, they idealize the adults in their lives and want to be like them. They believe that adults are very powerful; they have no inkling of their parents' limitations. The world, to a young child, is magical. Children believe that inanimate objects have feelings; children believe in retributive justice; and children are confused as to just how their desires interact with what actually happens. Complicating things even further is the child's sudden awareness of sexual differences and the beginning of questioning about birth, sickness, and death. Children typically struggle with severe guilt around this age; Freudians explain such guilt by pointing to the child's romantic attachment to the opposite-sex parent. Others explain this guilt as the beginning of the child's formation of a sense of right and wrong. If you observe the child at play, you will discover which of these common fears plague him. Then you will be able to calm those fears and help the child to feel safe in the world and secure in his new relationship with you.

COMMON FEARS AND CONCERNS

Fear of Unfamiliarity, Separation, Being Startled

A baby's fears center on sudden noises, being startled. As they get older, babies fear separation, the new, and anything unfamiliar.

Fear of New Experiences

A young child's way of coping with his fear of new experiences is to make the new experience a part of his fantasy world. There are problems in this strategy for the little child who really can't differentiate between fantasy and reality in the first place. The child at play is trying to learn about the world, to assimilate reality. New situations and new relationships only complicate this task.

The Scary World of the Three-to-Five-Year-Old

As children begin to mature, their world expands, prompting many young children to begin to see the world as a potentially dangerous place. As the child begins to see the enormity of the world, he begins to have a sense of powerlessness. Beginning at about age three the child becomes curious about birth, life, and death; this curiosity often leads to a litany of worries as the child tries to gain a hold over a world that at times seems filled with danger. These childhood worries include a fear of monsters, the dark, dogs, fire engines, illness, death, injury, and handicapped people.

Signs of Stress

Any good child-care book, or any experience with young children, will reassure a new stepmother that a measure of fearfulness is normal for young children. How, then, can stepmothers tell if a child is unduly tense, fearful, or angry?

Children, like adults, show certain symptoms of tension: Nail-biting, hair-pulling or twirling, wetting the bed, and stuttering are common at this age. Stuttering is often tied to tension; some experts believe that this tension simply springs from the child working hard at language formation, while others contend that stuttering indicates some sort of psychological tension. Nevertheless, most children outgrow stuttering within a few months. Don't try to correct the child's speech or worry about speech training. Try to remove the tension. If there has been too much of a push for talking or correct speech, relax the pressure.

With any of these stress indicators, "let the child alone." Give the child and yourself some time to settle in. If the indicators of stress continue or intensify, seek the help of a family counselor, child psychologist, or psychiatrist.

Comforters

Even if the children are behaving in ways that are personally unpleasant or undesirable to you, the adjustment period will go along more smoothly if children are permitted to retain their "comforters." Babies and young children use comforters to help themselves deal with the stresses of their lives. Comforters such as blankets, thumb-sucking, masturbation, rocking, singing, etc. are a child's way of trying to meet her own needs. Stepmothers should be encouraging about the child's eventual giving up of the comforter, but the wise stepmother will back off until the child feels more secure. Permit the child to sleep with the stuffed animal, toy, or old baby blanket. Remember that children's fears are especially acute until they develop a strong sense of the difference between real and make-believe. Telling a frightened child that the monster is make-believe is *not* helpful. Helping a child to hold onto a favorite toy and compare that toy to the monster is more helpful in assisting differentiation between fantasy and reality.

Dragging a fearful child over to a dog will probably not do too much to end the fear; however, desensitizing the child to his fear of dogs by incorporating such fears into stories, games, or other play may help.

Role-Playing

Children around the ages of three, four, and five delight in role-playing. Such play-acting, in addition to being fun, gives the step-mother a way of understanding a child's point of view quickly, vividly, and with a depth that often outdistances the child's verbal abilities. Role-playing allows even a very young child to reveal his version of reality, which may or not reflect actual events or circumstances. The little girl who "plays" stepmother by frowning and yelling is conveying her perception of the world. The arrival of a new stepmother is an earthshaking event for a little child; it is a grave error to assume that young children will easily accept their step-mothers. The child's inexperience and natural wariness of strangers is bound to prompt initial resistance. Fortunately, young children respond well and quickly to regular routines, consistent behavior, and cheerful attitudes.

Your Love Is Vital

Children desperately need loving caregivers. You will be such a caregiver. Children who are deprived of constant, supportive, loving care become timid, withdrawn, and depressed; these children are often not very lovable. They may not fit the idealized picture of the open, loving, little nursery school cherub.

Children who have been ignored, neglected, or mistreated in their young years especially need the loving care of their step-mothers. Too often, children who have been abused grow into adults with skewed perceptions of the world and recreate abusive situations in their adult relationships as victims or perpetrators. The stepmother who provides loving support and attentive, consistent caregiving can change the course of her stepchildren's futures.

Children count on their parents for leadership, love, and security. They watch their parents and pattern themselves after them. Personalities are formed in this way. Dr. Spock goes so far as to say, "The greatest gift from parents is love, which they express in countless ways: a fond facial expression, spontaneous demonstrations of physical affection, pleasure in their children's accomplishments, comforting them when they are hurt or frightened, controlling them to keep them safe and to help them become responsible people, giving them high ideals."* Stepmothers can begin to provide the loving care that young children so desperately crave—and will find, in the process, that loving a little child *feels good*.

A small child may be a bit problematic at first for a new stepmother. The little girl has "lost" her biological mother upon whom she has modeled herself. The little boy has lost his first love and is left with his psychological rival—his father. The stepmother may not be particularly welcomed by either boys or girls. A little girl may feel guilty over the departure or death of her biological mother, and may resist a stepmother's attentions, resenting the way she has "usurped" the little girl's next-in-line position with Daddy.

Children between the ages of three and five need constant reassurance. How can a stepmother begin to build a meaningful relationship with her young stepchildren?

Commitment

Little children are responsive by nature. Stepmothers must take the first step in beginning a relationship; a little child just can't. The need may be present, but the ability to begin a relationship has not been developed yet. It's up to you.

Build Trust by Being Consistent

Stepmothers will play a great part in a child's ability to trust others and the way in which a child will come to view himself and the world. Children gain trust in themselves by being respected as human beings. The self-assurance a child builds during the first five years of life will help him become comfortable with himself and with all sorts of people for the rest of his life.

Provide Security to Encourage Independence

In order for babies to feel safe enough to explore the world, they must feel that they can return to a "safe harbor." Babies who feel secure will explore, reach out to discover new people, places, and situations. However, these adventuresome babies will want to return to those people who are safe. We have all seen the baby of

* Spock, Benjamin, *Baby and Child Care*, p.45.

this age smiling at the stranger and then hiding her face in Daddy's shoulder.

Build Love and Respect

The love that a child receives creates an ability to give love in return. Stepmothers can help children learn to love by loving them. The love a child begins to feel will affect that child's ability to form and sustain positive relationships throughout life.

HOW TO BEGIN

A Gradual Approach Is Best

Young children respond best to a gradual approach; they will cling to familiar, trusted individuals and be suspicious, frightened, or hostile to newcomers—stepmothers included! Suspiciousness and wariness are normal for little children. The support of your step-child's father is a very important factor. Fathers should try very hard not to hover, and to be cheerful, confident, and unafraid to leave the child with the stepmother. The attitude of those the child already trusts will help or hinder the young child's relationship with the stepmother; the attitude of those trusted adults is perhaps the most powerful initial factor in helping the child into the new relationship.

Spend Time Alone

In order to become a trusted figure and an important person in your stepchild's life, spend lots of time *alone* with the child. You'll know that you have assumed an importance in your stepchild's life when the child seeks *you* out in times of stress or misses your presence when you're out of sight.

The Years from Six to Twelve

School-age children can reason and think, give explanations, and form relationships. However, their thinking and emotions remain very much tied to the "here and now"; their way of thinking is *concrete*. School-aged children enjoy classifying things. They like to make collections.

Children of school age are typically very active, enjoying a wide variety of games and sports. Peers become very important during the childhood years; the grade school years are the time for best friends and buddies, for clubhouses and secrets from the adult world. There is a rigidity to childhood in thought and in emotion; things are right or wrong; there are no mitigating circumstances. Children require "proof," tangible examples, in order to learn effectively or wholeheartedly to accept anything new. Children tend to take each experience as it comes rather than think about a sequence of events in general terms; they use a trial-and-error method in most areas of their lives. This is the age of fun for children and parents alike: games, hobbies, outings, friends, sports, and a wide range of activities.

The rigidity of childhood, the need to see evidence as proof of fact, will preclude abstract conversation and analysis between you and your stepchildren. Children of school age are not yet capable of drawing generalizations from their experience. The world is composed of good guys and bad guys; everything must fit into a neat category. The child will spend a good deal of time trying to classify the people and things of his world; the new stepmother may seem to defy classification. A stepmother can help her child override certain limitations in reasoning skills and emotional maturity by taking the time to learn about a child's world, by entering the magical world of childhood.

HOW TO UNDERSTAND A CHILD'S THINKING

They Don't Generalize

Young children have difficulty making generalizations; in fact it must be noted that the ability to *analyze* and *generalize* requires thinking skills of the highest order. A large segment of the adult population demonstrates difficulty in analysis and generalization. Children are usually incapable of accepting a premise and reasoning from it; they see only a special case without appreciating the need to express a general law.

They Don't See Contradictions in Thinking

Children cannot perceive contradictions; they have difficulty seeing a situation from another's point of view and do not see any reason to relinquish their own point of view.

They Don't "Get" Hidden Meanings

In a proverb, for instance, or a fable, the child will fail to see a hidden meaning but instead will relate some familiar aspects of the story to an experience he already understands. Children do not readily understand sarcasm, analogies, or abstract examples. They are very literal-minded.

They Have Difficulty with Definitions

Children will define something by its use ("a spoon is to eat with"); later on, they begin to be able to generalize by noting an object's use and its relationship to other objects. A stepmother may prove indefinable for children. Stepmothers "act" like mothers, but they aren't. The simple frustration of the child struggling to define the indefinable prompts the common cry of "You're not my mother." Although this disclaimer is especially hurtful for the stepmother, perhaps it should be viewed as the child's attempt to define what *is* in terms of what is *not!*

Names Retain Mystical Significance

Until late in childhood names (like rules) are graven in stone. Few children realize that names were conferred by people and can be altered; children will often assert that names were God-given and as such are unchangeable. A mother is a mother is a mother . . .

Children Explain Every Coincidence

The child's mystical attitude toward rules and names extends to his general feeling about the world. Until late in childhood, a child will attempt to explain every occurrence, not really believing that there is such a thing as a chance occurrence or a coincidence.

They Learn by Doing—Not by Listening

Children find it very difficult to learn from verbal teaching. A new skill or concept will be better learned when connected to an activity that has meaning for the child.

HOW TO HELP CHILDREN THINK

Adults can help children move from one level of reasoning to another. New concepts and difficult relationships need to be explained. Children need frequent opportunities to discuss their actions and opinions in their own words. Helping children to understand their world is an ongoing process—a job that you'll do every day. You can help children give definitions, solve problems, or state propositions verbally by asking them to perform tasks and then to discuss the way those tasks have been carried out. Verbal expressions should be linked to tangible action until it becomes possible for children to make generalizations from similar experiences or to recognize situations similar to those they have already learned to solve and describe in terms that are meaningful to them. Everyday chores and events around the house—doing the laundry, walking the dog, mowing the lawn—are gold mines of experience for the child.

Children Need to Try Things Out for Themselves

Children find it difficult to go beyond the specific information they are given and to try to imagine new possibilities or explanations for events. They have an almost mystical attitude about authority. Until they are about ten years old, they believe that the rules of games are created by their parents. Violating rules at this age is seen as almost impossible. After the age of ten, there is a change in a child's thinking about rules; the child may accept that the "rule" still has a lot of authority, but no longer feels that "everything was arranged for the best" and that the established order must be respected. Children at this age begin to believe in the value of experimenting, though they will still seek the approval of their peer group.

Children Are Very Concerned with Fairness and Concepts of Good and Bad

Children now begin to explore motives and the concept of cause and effect. They begin to believe that actions are worse if damage is greater, but if motives are wrong, and material damage small, that's worse than when motives are right and damage is great. They learn to distinguish "mistakes" from deliberate wrongdoing and are very concerned with the fairness of punishments.

Children try to sort through *why* they don't live with their mother—*why* she died, or *why* she left. The child's need to see one "mother" as good and one "mother" as bad may cause the child's loyalty to leap from stepmother to biological mother and back again.

A caring adult to listen to the day's happenings is essential— someone to be there when a child comes home from school or at least in telephone contact. Be aware of the "push-me-pull-me" quality of children's independence: They need to be autonomous, but they also need constant love, validation, and support.

Around age six, children begin to fall out of love with the other-sex parent as they begin to identify more strongly with peers of their own sex. Stepmothers may find that they have a more difficult time with their stepdaughters than their stepsons because of these psychological and emotional changes. Experts have long claimed that boys have a harder adjustment after divorce because, living with their mothers and "losing" their fathers, they find themselves in flux; if this is true, then probably girls who live with their fathers and "lose" their mothers will suffer similar conflicts. Stepmothers simply add another complication. You'll need a lot of patience.

A FEW TIPS

- Children often shove their feelings underground because they don't want to rock the boat. They may fear antagonizing anyone and, like their younger siblings, may just decide to be "very, very good." Be aware of this false "goodness" and encourage the child to express his real feelings.

- Beginning at about age six, children begin to "cool off" toward their parents. They still enjoy being silly on occasion, or even cuddled for a brief period, but they begin to look to people outside the family for information and amusement. At this stage, children tend to dislike displays of affection. Go easy on the cuddling and be aware of their desire for privacy.

- Children are hugely interested in what other kids say and do. From the age of six on, there's a fascination with secret clubs, cliques, and complicated rules and strategies. The six-year-old may not be permitted membership in the clubs of older children, but he enjoys their attention and is happy to become a "go-fer" for older children, cheerfully running errands, retrieving balls, or doing chores. Do not appear to minimize the importance of these activities; try to show interest in the day-to-day details, if the child is willing to share these with you.

- Children are beginning to pull away from parents; they need support but they will be naturally suspicious of motives and distrustful. Try to be patient and let the child come to you.

- You may have to cultivate a thick-skinned toughness. Children are rigidly moralistic; much of their "cruelty" springs from a need to define relationships and concepts in terms that are familiar to them. When Sandy, a stepson of eight, announced at Christmas dinner that he, his father, stepmother, and two stepsisters were not a "real" family, the assembled guests gasped with embarrassment. Sandy, however, continued to eat his Christmas turkey, unaware of the pain he had inflicted. When he was given a chance to explain his statement later, he claimed that families were one mother, one father, and one child, and that he lived in a *step*family!

- Be a resource person. Children are fascinated by adults; the adult world is seen as powerful and mysterious. Children like to concoct tales and stories to explain the inexplicable doings of the adult world. A stepmother can provide a key to this world for her stepchild. The fact that she is not blood-related may serve as a boon to her relationship to her stepchild, who is trying to gain independence from parents. Since school-age children are trying to break away from parents, a stepmother may be "cool" if she doesn't try too hard to be "Mommy." The children can have their cake and eat it, too: They complete their cooling-off period with their parents and attach to this new person—a trusted adult who is around the house all the time.

- Children don't want to be different. It is helpful for them to realize that *they are not the only ones with a stepmother.* It is just not "cool" to be the only kid with a stepmother. Often children go to great lengths to disguise their stepfamily status. Some

children begin to refer to stepmothers as "Mom"
and pretend to be nuclear families; other children
ignore the existence of their stepmothers and any
stepsiblings. Ten-year-old Maryann simply chose
to ignore *everyone's* existence. When her stepmother visited her school during open school
week, the teacher was amazed at her existence.
Maryann had "forgotten" to tell her teacher that
her widowed father had married; she had similarly forgotten to deliver the notes her stepmother had written to her teacher. Maryann
had explained away her two stepsisters as her
"friends."

You'll find lots of opportunities to be part of your stepchildren's
lives. School-age children are great joiners. There are Cub Scouts,
Brownies, Little League, "the gang." You can satisfy your own need
for closeness and provide real help to your stepchildren simply by
being around—going to games, being a den mother or troop leader,
supplying the cookies or driving in the car pool.

Adolescence

Adolescence is a time of flux. Teenagers are engaged in a struggle
for personal identity and independence from their families. The
stepmother trying to build a family relationship with a young person who is seeking to move *away* from family concerns may find
herself in conflict. Not only is this conflict resolvable but adolescents, because of their sophisticated reasoning abilities and their
increased maturity, may (with luck) provide the stepmother with the
best chances for happiness and success!

Adolescence is a time of exclamation points. It is a time for experi-
encing and testing life. Adolescents tend to analyze and judge
everything, including their parents. Much of the adolescent's
energy is directed toward moving away from childhood and getting
ready to assume a place in the adult world. This need to move away
from the very world he seeks to enter creates conflict.

The adolescent struggles with new physical, cognitive, and emotional skills in a state of heightened self-consciousness. Everything

seems suddenly different to the adolescent. Trying to fit a "strange body" into a world grown suddenly unfamiliar can be scary for any adolescent; for the adolescent with a new stepmother, it can be overwhelming. Some adolescents express their stress by acting out, while others withdraw and become depressed. More commonly, they simply swing from one mood to another.

It is helpful to remember that adolescence is a time of searching for values: Adolescents struggle to arrive at their own unique point of view about everything. They are constantly involved in a struggle to weigh, measure, and decide from the experiences that bombard them. The adolescent is also in the process of developing a recognizable adult personality; he has not yet chosen the primary face he will wear for the world. Adolescents try on great varieties of personalities; additionally, they try on the gamut of emotions. Adolescents, as we used to say, "let it all hang out."

This can be very confusing for the new stepmother who is trying to get to know her adolescent stepchildren—particularly if she is not accustomed to teenagers. A few tips about how teenagers think, act, and react will help the novice stepmother as she approaches her new "job."

HOW ADOLESCENTS THINK

Many adults are fooled and frustrated by the seeming sophistication of adolescents' manner of thinking. They now are able to think on an abstract level and they're capable of a wide range of new and highly developed thinking skills, but because these new cognitive skills are used in conjunction with a lack of world experience and social and emotional immaturity, they may actually impede interaction with others and understanding of events.

The constant exchange and discussion of points of view with their peers leads adolescents to a greater understanding of themselves and of the world. Their constant probing curiosity often causes adolescents to seem intrusive as they seek to find out exactly how others think and feel and ask prying questions. Ironically, they bristle when asked the same kinds of questions by an adult.

The consideration of many viewpoints gives adolescent thinking new flexibility, but this very quality often leads to great indecisiveness. The adolescent seems to consider every possibility for every decision. Again, if the adult seems indecisive, the teenager is quick to call her a "wimp." The typical adolescent has a predilection for gossiping and for heightening simple events into grand-scale dramas. Let the adult "overreact" in return, however, and she's "making a big deal out of nothing."

Adolescents tend to be argumentative about anything and everything. The stepmother who exclaims, "They just want to argue for the sake of argument" may be more correct than she realizes. She had better gird her loins for battle—there's no way to avoid an occasional argument with a teenager. Arguing comes with the territory.

Adolescents can give exhaustive definitions, state hypotheses as general laws which they then go on to test, consider every possibility, and then state the result as a law—a law which will hold good in all similar cases. This new ability to create "laws" may also make the adolescent a rigid and unyielding "world critic." The adolescent is increasingly interested in various social systems, including the ones that operate within his own family. He is critical of his own standards and of the assumptions of the various groups of which he is a member—family, school, the world.

Perhaps it is his capacity to expect to create immutable laws that enables the adolescent to recognize the occurrences of a chance event—one that takes place where *no* law is operating. Then what? This very understanding may lead adolescents to become unduly fatalistic and reluctant to accept responsibility for their own actions.

A Passion for Justice

The newfound ability to think things through gives the adolescent the idea that it is very important to justify the judgments he makes, and he expects others to do the same. It may be very hard for an adolescent to accept another's point of view if he can't follow the train of reasoning that led to the conclusion. Whereas a younger child may answer, "I don't know," an adolescent will test various hypotheses and assert that something "is not possible." Often, only a time-consuming and perhaps stressful explaining process can assure the teenager that the adult has "justified" his thinking on a given topic.

The Beginnings of Empathy

Adolescents can now begin to understand analogies and to apply examples that they have not directly experienced to their own lives.

The adolescent's new ability to see different viewpoints may initially lead her to "overidentify": An adolescent who watches a soap opera may fall in love, while one who takes a first-aid course may suddenly suffer from a score of self-diagnosed maladies. New abilities to think abstractly, compare viewpoints, and empathize with the feelings of others carry with them a sense of confusion and, often, a wariness and suspiciousness of adults. Now, more than ever, communication is important. We can begin helping teenagers over the bridge to adulthood by helping them to clarify their thinking.

Helping Adolescents Think Better

Many adults never attain the level of abstract thinking that most teenagers today attain. Many adults continue to think as children, or to revert to thinking as children, failing to analyze their experiences and to perceive and create general laws in the world around them. One of the greatest gifts a stepmother can offer to her stepchildren is the ability to think more clearly and to enjoy the process of intellectual development.

Providing Concrete Examples

Adults often talk in abstractions; they speak about loyalty and love, respect and responsibility, without relating these qualities to the events of everyday life. Adolescents need definite and clearly understood examples in order to begin to understand what you mean when you use abstract terms. Provide ample opportunity for adolescents to discuss and solve problems. Problems should be presented to adolescents in ways that refer to their own concrete experience. Above all, don't be in a hurry to arrive at a "solution." With adolescents the route from A to B includes a trip through the entire alphabet.

WHAT TO EXPECT

Adolescents cope with life in strange ways, many of them unattractive and unappealing. It helps if you can understand that these common behavior types, while unpleasant to deal with, are necessary coping strategies for the floundering adolescent.

The Challenger

Some adolescents deal with their struggles for identity by challenging *everything*; their vocabulary is charged with antagonism. They compulsively rebut everything and everyone. These teenagers need a combination of patience and limit-setting.

The Self-Defeater

Other adolescents deal with their fear by becoming passive; those who have enjoyed especially close and loving homes may fear competing within the new family. They seek to avoid competition and loss by "withdrawing from the race." Such adolescents may suddenly fail tests, forget appointments, and consistently act in ways that short-circuit their progress and sabotage their chances for success. These teenagers need bolstering and support. They need to hear that they are lovable and are capable of succeeding and that they will not be abandoned or ignored as they grow more capable and independent.

The Rebel

Many adolescents cope with life by rebelling, often fixating on a career, professional goal, or lifestyle that is diametrically opposed to their parents' way of life. These young people seek to find their identity by initially deciding what they are *not*; in most cases the initial decision is to be *not* like their parents. These rebels need to be helped to realize that they actually have the latitude to develop individually without parental disapproval. Often they'll drop the "rebellion for rebellion's sake" and begin to find true independence—but sometimes it takes a while. Again, patience and a certain amount of teeth-gritting may be the stepmother's best strategy.

SETTING LIMITS

What about rules? What about punishment? What about just getting teenagers to behave? Most parents have a difficult time with adolescents and compliance. Adolescents *need* to test and challenge rules; rules are usually perceived as impediments to the adolescent's natural drive toward independence and autonomy.

Setting limits is difficult for the new stepmother; she has no history to refer to, no background of support and coping through the years of childhood. New stepmothers need the support of their husbands and others who are already trusted and loved by their need to create their own relationship with their stepchildren, one that is independent of the other adults in the adolescent's life. A delicate balance in any case, but especially so when the child is already an adolescent when you enter the picture.

The transition to adolescence can be stormy for "old" stepmothers as well. An adolescent who has been parented by a stepmother throughout childhood may, in the way of adoptees, suddenly express a desire to learn about his own mother or in some way change the nature of the relationship he has with her.

The relationship between stepmother and stepchild during childhood is not an accurate measure of their life together during adolescence. Sweet, compliant children who are close to their parents may need to go through an especially tumultuous adolescence, whereas the mischievous child may settle into a relatively uneventful teenage period.

Rules: A Delicate Balance

Unlike children who believe rules to be unalterable, adolescents realize that these rules have been decided by adults; adults are fallible; therefore, the rules are subject to change. During adolescence young people come to realize that their parents are fallible beings. This discovery, combined with the adolescent's natural self-centeredness and lack of experience (or tact), can cause a child to constantly question a stepmother's authority.

Rules Should Encourage Independence

The purpose of rules should be twofold: to shield adolescents from danger and to enable all members of the household to live together amiably. Rules should be designed to help adolescents negotiate difficult situations and to encourage the development of independence. Parents who are willing to be tough guys may actually help adolescents through sticky situations; the adolescent with strict parents can maintain his or her dignity when rejecting a forbidden adventure.

Stepmothers need to balance support and empathy with firm, though flexible, guidelines. Avoid power struggles whenever possible. It is wise to avoid placing yourself in confrontational situations. One way of minimizing confrontation and power struggles is by initiating "house rules." Present these as the rules of the house, not as attempts to change the adolescent or to step in as "Mother." And remember to change the rules as the child grows older. Guidelines appropriate to a twelve-year-old can serve only as rebellion fodder to a teenager.

House Rules

"House rules" refer to the way the stepmother and father have chosen to live. As a member of the household, the adolescent is expected to comply. House rules must be reasonable, and should be based on mutual courtesy. Adolescents can, and will, understand that even bunkmates in camp and roommates in college agree upon certain ways of living.

Common Courtesy

If you want to know where your stepchild is, be sure that all members of the household are in the habit of informing each other, via note or phone call, of their whereabouts. If adults as well as children and adolescents do this, the rule will be seen as a common courtesy—not spying.

Keep rules to a minimum, and make them flexible enough to permit the adolescent to exercise his own judgment in specific situations. Stepmothers can help their adolescents exercise good judgment by supplying the criteria necessary for making wise judgments. Adolescents can be helped to weigh variables, think about possible alternatives and consequences, and enjoy the rewards when a good decision is made.

Katherine strongly objected to her stepchildren attending parties that were unsupervised or where alcohol or drugs would be available. She did not wish to police her stepchildren, or to be in the position of saying "No" to the multitude of inappropriate invitations that came her stepchildren's way. Katherine learned that the simple way out of this situation was to put the responsibility upon the adolescent's shoulders in a positive way. She learned to tell the adolescent *that permission is granted for any party that is supervised and alcohol/drug free*. Telling the adolescent what is acceptable, rather than what is forbidden, sets a friendlier tone. The adolescent becomes responsible for her own compliance, able to weigh the decision and the consequences of disobedience. In this way adolescents learn to become responsible for their own actions and to see rules as examples of common courtesy rather than as punitive restrictions.

Changing the Parental Role

Parents of adolescents often notice that their role shifts drastically during this period: A redefinition is in order. Adolescents no longer delight in the attentiveness they enjoyed during childhood. Family dinners, outings, and "togetherness" are often abruptly shunned in favor of "hanging out" with the guys or the girls. Parents are often confused and hurt; they resent this rejection. Stepmothers may be especially distressed, feeling that such behavior is directed against them. Such distancing, or moodiness, or strangeness around families is the norm for adolescent children. It's a tough lesson to learn, but a necessary one. A few hints may be helpful.

TIPS FOR LIVING WITH THE ADOLESCENT

Remain Calm

Remember that adolescence is a time of incredible highs and lows. Mood swings are so pronounced that some have even claimed that adolescence mimics the symptoms of the manic-depressive. Adolescents are trying to fit a body and a mind into a world that has suddenly grown too large and too unfamiliar. Adolescence is a scary time. Make allowances for tempestuous moods, and don't overreact.

Help Adolescents Find Acceptable Methods of Letting Off Steam

Rebelliousness is a normal part of adolescence. However, as with the exploring two-year-old, parameters of acceptable and safe behavior must be maintained. An adolescent may *feel* like smashing all the lamps in the living room, but obviously such behavior is not tolerable. The adolescent should have the family's permission to *feel*—to be angry, sulky, whatever, in a way that will not cause family upheaval—but not to do destructive things.

Respect the Adolescent's Feelings

Too many adults keep repeating to troubled teenagers that these are "the best years of your lives." This is not true, except in adult nostalgia. Adolescence is tough. As they try to find a place for themselves in the world, adolescents must come to grips with plans for their future and at the same time struggle with strong sexual urges and pressures to socialize. It's not easy. Be prepared to listen and to sympathize. Take confidences seriously and *never* ridicule an adolescent's feelings.

Understand the Need to Separate from the Family

Adolescents need to separate from their parents in *all* ways: physically, by planning on college, or an apartment of their own as soon as they can do so; intellectually, by trying on ideas and ways of thinking that are often exactly opposite to the parental point of view; and emotionally, by distancing themselves from the parents in order to become more independent. This moving away is *normal* and *necessary.*

The period of greatest conflict between parent and child is usually in the early stage of adolescence. As teenagers actually assume and accept their increasing competence and ability to move into the adult world, the need for conflict with parents decreases. Parents need to limit dangerous or unattractive behavior, avoid oversensitivity, and continue to serve as role models for their own personal value systems.

Don't Criticize Their Friends

Having ruled out most of the adult world, adolescents seek the company of their peers. In their haste to find a place for themselves they try to create an entirely new environment, conforming to styles and behaviors of their age group. You may not like their music, clothing, hairstyles, or their values, but it's best not to criticize.

Be a Parent, Not a Friend

Too many stepmothers make the mistake of trying to be a buddy to a teenager. Adolescents do not need stepmothers who are buddies. Too often, stepmothers fear that they will lose their closeness to the child and so are reluctant to set or enforce rules. Stepmothers who seek to avoid their stepchildren's disapproval by rejecting the parenting role will incur scorn and rejection. There is nothing more ridiculous to an adolescent than an adult trying to "act like a kid." One stepmother went out of her way to revamp her businesslike wardrobe: Hoping to move closer to her stepdaughters' sense of style, she bought a closet full of designer jeans and name-brand shirts, only to be greeted by giggles that turned into out-and-out hoots. The girls did not want a forty-year-old friend; they were comfortable with their stepmother as her old-fashioned self. The typical adolescent has quite enough friends, thank you. Parents, on the other hand, are in short supply.

Be Honest

Adolescents are constantly on the lookout for hypocrisy. Stepmothers who are honest about their feelings and opinions may not win a popularity contest, but they will be trusted and ultimately respected.

Be Flexible

Adolescents cannot be expected to remain static. Rules and expectations *must* be modified as the adolescent grows toward adulthood and circumstances change.

Solicit Their Opinions

Adolescents who feel that they have a say in the workings of the house, be it a change in curfew or a change in chores, will be more communicative and will be more likely to comply with rules.

Be Available

Stepmothers should never put off a teen who needs to talk. Personal issues and concerns are often difficult for the adolescent to frame and convey. An adolescent who approaches a stepmother may have spent weeks garnering the courage to do so.

Listen

If you have adolescents who are talking to you, you are halfway home: *Listen carefully.* Conversations about other kids' problems may be their own as well.

Don't Give Hasty Answers: Take Time to Think

Adults often assume that every question must have an instant answer. Not true! Many questions that adolescents ask concern complex issues or problems that the stepmother is not prepared to deal with. If in doubt, wait. There is nothing wrong with putting off decisions; it's okay to listen without giving an immediate response. Adolescents may be delighted to realize that when time passes between a question and its response, the answer is more satisfying.

Respect Their Privacy

Privacy is a paramount issue for adolescents. Because they are so deeply engaged in figuring out their own identities, privacy becomes almost an obsession for them. Snooping through personal belongings is taboo, as is betraying confidences, listening in on phone calls, or "grilling" them about their friends.

Relax Control

Just when adolescents seem to need the most control—when grades are critical for future success, when rooms and laundry and chores seem to balloon, when nothing seems to get done on time or competently—that's the time to BACK OFF. Adolescents build self-esteem by assuming responsibility for their own lives. Permit real consequences to teach responsibility. Adolescents who are permitted to taste the consequences of their actions learn to be responsible faster than those who are lectured; if an adolescent "forgets" to take care of her clothing, let her wear a wrinkled blouse—or iron it herself. A stepmother can then change her role from nag to commiserater.

Encourage Independence: Part-Time Jobs Are Wonderful

Part-time jobs provide financial independence and a role in the adult world. Adolescents need confirmation of their emerging independence; part-time jobs give adolescents a way to feel less dependent on their parents.

Find Something Positive to Say Each Day

Everyone needs to hear positive things. No one needs this support as much, and as often, as a self-conscious adolescent. Find something, no matter how small, to praise each day.

Share Their Interests and Concerns

Whether it involves sitting at a sporting event that you couldn't care less about or defending your stepchild's point of view in a neighborhood confrontation, devote time to your stepchildren. Taking a genuine interest in their lives will create a real and lasting relationship. You needn't be personally interested in the things that interest your stepchildren; you need only be interested in the children themselves. All parents would love to have children who shared their interests and avocations, but that rarely happens. Support sports, clubs, and hobbies; read the books they like. You may get lucky and find yourself *really* sharing those interests.

Be Willing to Negotiate

Rather than playing policewoman, *negotiate*; ask teens what they will be willing to give up, or do, for something they want. Don't listen to aimless complaining and whining; ask teens to list *specifics*. Asking them to list what they would like to change helps them focus their discomfort on something that is concrete and attainable and helps them learn to accept their share in the responsibility for the changes they seek.

COURAGE!

Adolescence is a tough time; so is becoming a stepmother. Although stepchildren and stepmothers may seem at cross-purposes, with the stepmother wanting a family and the adolescent wanting to leave, they may actually have more in common than either can imagine.

The new stepmother seeks to order her new life and develop an identity within the family. The veteran stepmother questions exactly where she will fit into her stepchild's increasingly independent lifestyle. Whether novice or veteran, stepmothers may be surprised to discover that they are engaged in many of the same struggles as their adolescent stepchildren. The stepmother who recognizes these parallel identity crises may be viewed as a breath of fresh air to the teen who really *does* need adult guidance and a listening ear. In turn, stepmothers may be delighted to find compassion from a most unexpected source—their adolescent stepchild.

By now you know a great deal about children in general and your stepchildren in particular. The time for living together is approaching. It is time to begin thinking about building your family. What will you need to think about before you actually move in? Will there be a wedding? A honeymoon? Where will you live? What will you be called? An exciting time is ahead.

PART II

Building a Family

CHAPTER 6

Preparing to Live Together

A stepmother's relationship with her stepchildren begins long before she actually lives with them. Many stepmothers miss the opportunity to get off to a good start because the first meetings with their stepchildren come at the wrong time: either too soon—before there's a plan to become a family—or too late. First impressions do matter.

It's not always possible for a potential stepmother to plan a first meeting with her stepchildren-to-be. These first meetings frequently occur spontaneously, often long before there's a serious involvement. Some women become stepmothers to children they've known for years in other contexts, perhaps as students, neighbors, or as friends of their own children.

First Impressions: Setting the Stage for Success

When I asked stepmothers about their first meeting with their stepchildren, most reported that these first, and usually casual, meetings were successful. The casual nature of these encounters where no one had anything significant at stake, contributed to their success. It was the later meetings—those that occurred after the children had been told of the impending marriage—that needed more careful handling. In order to begin a relationship on the best possible footing, it is important not to dismiss those first successful meetings but to use them as a key to later successes.

REDUCE PRESSURE

The first "real" meeting between stepmother and her stepchildren occurs at a point when the decision to marry and create a new family has been made. At this point, you begin to become a stepmother. Often it is a painful process. In order to enhance the chances for a relaxed and happy beginning, take some hints from your successes at those earlier chance meetings. Although the stepmothers I spoke with met their stepchildren in a variety of settings, their first meetings all shared one important feature: First meetings must be unpressured. Reduce the chances of pressure and tension to as low a level as possible. This means no formal dinners, no grilling, no spilling of too-personal information.

If possible, plan a real activity of some sort for your initial meetings. Nothing is more uncomfortable for children than to be subjected to examination and interrogation or "long boring discussions." Early meetings are best treated in the manner of a "blind date." In order to reduce everyone's nervousness, plan an activity that allows for possible escape!

THE IMPORTANCE OF SPECTATOR EVENTS

Spectator events are particularly appropriate for early meetings. No one has to *do* anything at a movie or a ball game except be there. A spectator event gives the stepmother and her stepchildren a chance to be together without anyone feeling threatened. Even the most hostile teenager or fidgety toddler will eventually relax if not pressured to perform or take part in some required activity or conversation. Aim for an activity that permits, but does not require, some limited interaction. Movies, a television show, a sporting event, a fireworks exhibition—anything that can be watched (or politely ignored) together. It is impossible to fail when nothing is required.

CHECK YOUR PROGRESS

After several casual outings, you and your future husband will be able to gauge the direction in which you are moving. You may discover that you and the children are more and more comfortable together, often chatting away, or you may find that you are returning home in tears, frustrated and weary of trying without response, tired of watching your soon-to-be stepchildren stare silently at movie screens, pick at their uneaten meals, and pointedly ignore you.

BEGIN TO VISIT AT EACH OTHER'S HOMES

After several outings it is important for everyone to get to see each other in their own territory where they can "be themselves." *Take it slowly.* Being in someone else's territory can be uncomfortable and threatening. Everyone should have some time to take in the bombardment of personality that is evident in the home. A short visit, maybe a stopover on the way to or from an activity, is an appropriate and unthreatening way to begin to get to know each other at home.

WHAT ABOUT SLEEPOVERS?

Sleepovers between father and future stepmother complicate an already complex situation. Sleepovers turn the getting-to-know-each-other process inside out. Although the stepmother may hope to speed up the process by this intimacy, it may be counterproductive if its premature. If sleepovers occur in the child's home, the child is forced to accept the stepmother into his or her territory too soon. If the sleepover occurs in the stepmother's home, the child will probably feel displaced. Generally speaking, sleepovers before marriage or formal moving-in are as emotionally unsatisfying to the developing family as one-night stands are to most single women.

WHAT IF NOTHING WORKS?

What should you do if nothing seems to work? The baby still shrieks in fear behind her father? The teenager is still scowling? The nine-year-old is whining? If things have not improved over the course of several nonpressured outings, the time has come to talk. Talking out tension will set the stage for the future. Frightened children don't need lectures, but they do need to know that their *displeasure* is not being ignored. They need to be assured that their unhappiness has been noted and that the soon-to-be-stepmother hopes that they will be able to have more fun next time.

Whatever the words, remember that a stepchild's cool or hostile behavior usually indicates fear rather than hate. Stepchildren need to know that you are aware of their feelings—and that you care.

Early resistance by stepchildren boils down to what used to be called simple old-fashioned testing. Stepchildren have already been abandoned, either by death or divorce. They may or may not have been exposed to other women in their father's lives; often, they have. Many children initially give a potential stepmother a hard time simply because they are reluctant to trust; they have been burned and are often simply afraid to be hurt again. Such children need time.

IF THINGS ARE GOING WELL

After several meetings that involve activities, you are ready for outings with a more personal touch. What you do will depend upon the ages and interests of all involved. This is the time for you and your stepchildren to begin to build your relationship by sharing interests that you really care about. If the relationship seems to be moving along well, you might ask them to help plan the next activity. A good way to get everyone talking is to begin sharing their likes and dislikes. A good rule for these early outings is that each child gets to choose one activity and then to accompany the others on their choices.

BE YOURSELF

In order for any relationship to have a chance at success, all parties must be accepted for themselves. This is particularly true for stepmothers and stepchildren whose relationship is that of a parent and child but with a built-in contradiction: The stepmother and her stepchild begin as strangers! In order to begin to feel comfortable, let your stepchildren get to know you and try to really get to know them—be sensitive to clues about their interests and supply the information they need to get to know you. Don't climb onto a horse if you've always hated horses or expect your stepchildren to be thrilled about the opera when you've already seen the rock posters in their rooms. Don't expect them to be mind readers. They need real information to make up their minds about you, too!

Let them know your likes and dislikes—the kinds of things that make your eyes mist with joy or with hurt. Let them know what kinds of things really drive you up a wall. Nothing hurts or confuses or angers a child more than a phony. Don't smile at muddy footprints on your white carpeting when you really want to scream. Don't pretend an avid interest in football if you're bored to tears by the game.

Be friendly, flexible, and understanding, but most important, *be honest.* You will be living with these children; any pretenses you begin today will remain between you and your stepchildren for years to come!

Common Problems

According to the National Census Bureau, nearly half of second marriages fail. No one likes to think about the possibility of a marriage failing but the statistics can't be ignored. The best way to weather any storms that blow into your marriage is by facing the most common problem areas head-on.

Conflicts between stepmothers and their husbands revolve around these major areas:

- Unequal treatment of children in the family
- The husband's lack of involvement in child-care
- Unrealistic expectations
- Intrusion of the biological mother (See Chapter 10)
- Loss of romance in the marriage

Let's discuss these problems one by one.

UNEQUAL TREATMENT OF ALL THE CHILDREN
IN THE FAMILY

Stepmothers I interviewed who had children from previous marriages often felt that there was unequal treatment of all the children in the family by their husbands. Most stepmothers also felt that they were trying much harder with their stepchildren than their husbands were trying with *their* stepchildren.

Fran put it this way: "Most of our conflicts are about fairness in treating the children. For example, sometimes my husband is quick to ask Maureen, his daughter, to assist him by handing her a screwdriver and showing her how to use it when my little son is standing right there and could just as easily be taught how to use tools." Fran, like many stepmothers, finds herself getting increasingly upset over such inequities. Obviously there's something more going on here than who gets to wield the screwdriver.

When a stepmother feels that she is "bending over backwards" to be fair and equal in her treatment of her own children and her stepchildren, such small inequities may quickly escalate to intolerable proportions.

Many stepmothers reported that they were resentful or disappointed by their husbands' lukewarm reception of their children from previous marriages. These same stepmothers, however, were even *more* upset when their husbands showed a lack of involvement with their *own* children—leaving a double burden of caring and responsibility on the shoulders of the new stepmother.

HUSBAND'S LACK OF INVOLVEMENT

Many a stepmother is shocked by her husband's lack of involvement with his children. Although these daddies were often perceived, during courtship, as actively involved in the care of their children, much of this caring seems to disappear after the vows are exchanged. The gap between the stepmother's anticipation and the reality of her husband's day-to-day involvement and hands-on responsibility is often huge. Most women who married men with children thought they were marrying a "new breed of man"— thoroughly modern fathers who had a deeply ingrained sense of commitment to their children. The discovery that such men were not as "maternal" as they'd anticipated comes as a tremendous shock to most stepmothers. This disappointment often translates into a feeling of being duped or betrayed, of being "snookered" into a situation where the father takes the credit for raising his children as a thoroughly modern daddy while the stepmother takes on the bulk of responsibility for the actual day-to-day care.

UNREALISTIC EXPECTATIONS

Most stepmothers assumed, before their marriages, that their husbands would continue to function as both mother and father to their children. These women were disappointed to discover that the husband's interaction with his children did *not* replicate a mother's feeling and responsibilities for her children. If the stepmother was a biological mother as well, this resentment sharpened. Stepmothers discovered that mothering and fathering are different—that a father's sense of commitment and responsibility for his children translated into a far different kind of behavior from what they had anticipated.

This difference between expectation and reality was perhaps the most difficult aspect of a new marriage for stepmothers to accept. Most found that they were expected to have a much higher level of involvement with their stepchildren than their husbands had—just as a matter of course. These stepmothers did not always resent the amount of responsibility that they were expected to assume, but all were stunned by the lack of appreciation for their efforts.

Most stepmothers were amazed at the casualness with which family members—grandparents, aunts, uncles, friends, husbands, and stepchildren—expected that they would assume the care and maintainance of the family as a natural part of their new marriage. The disappointment they felt in the husband's lack of responsibility for the stepchildren, the unrealistic expectations both on the stepmother's part and by others *toward* her role, combined with a lack of appreciation caused many stepmothers to feel resentful and unhappy. If left uninterrupted, this cycle of resentment can spiral a stepmother directly to the divorce court.

A new stepmother can begin the cycle at any point. Most often it starts because she *feels unloved by her stepchildren.* She *seeks support* and *is criticized by her husband* either for being "insecure" or for "complaining." Her *anxiety escalates*. She *increases her involvement in child-care responsibilities*. To decrease her anxiety she draws closer to her stepchildren. At the same time, she tries to prove to her husband that she is not insecure. If her *efforts are rebuffed, her anxiety mounts;* her *increased effort leads her to seek appreciation;* the *lack of appreciation discourages her.* She *takes desperate measures* in an attempt to win love, appreciation, and respect. Now, her *efforts are criticized by her husband as being obsessive.* Her anxiety and frustration reach intolerable levels.

CYCLE OF RESENTMENT

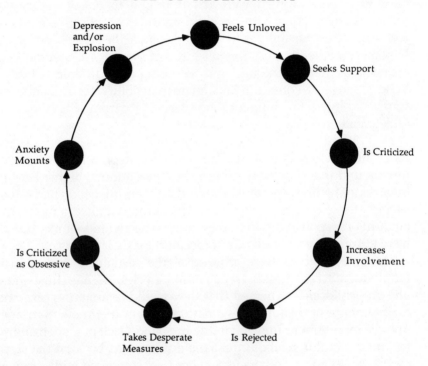

BREAKING THE RESENTMENT CYCLE

Take some time alone to figure out just what is bothering you. *Be specific.* Take paper and pen and list your specific goals and specific problems.

When you've clearly defined your problem, it's time to attempt a solution. You might ask yourself at this point, "What do *I* need to do to make this better?" Once you've pinpointed a problem and begun to think about what will really make you feel better, you *will* feel better. The very process of sitting down and thinking about feelings in specific, concrete terms may even end the problem.

More often than not, a stepmother will discover at this point that the "who" in your question "Who can make this better?" is . . . "You!" If the solution does lie within the stepmother herself, the process ends with her feeling of relief and of being much more in control. Her heightened sense of control will serve to help her through the next little crisis. If she realizes that her husband is part of the problem, or part of the solution, then she will tell him so. Too many wives expect their husbands to magically intuit their needs. Don't expect such acts of clairvoyance outside of a nightclub routine. Husbands are not particularly psychic—they must be told specifically what the problem is and what you need from them.

INTRUSION OF THE BIOLOGICAL MOTHER

A stepmother must really understand and come to grips with the fact that her stepchildren's biological mother will be a very real presence in all their lives—whether she is living or dead. There are practical issues that must be addressed: in the case of the absentee mother, questions of visitation, telephone contact, school conferences, sharing children's activities, and special events. If the mother has died, discussions of death, visits to the cemetery, and maintaining contact with the mother's relatives are important tasks. In addition to these and many other practical issues, children must ultimately reconcile a host of complicated emotions in order to come to terms with their relationship (or lack of relationship) with their mothers. The task of helping children sort out these difficult and confused issues often falls to the stepmother. (See Chapter 10.)

LOSS OF ROMANCE

One of the primary killers of romance is children. Children make privacy difficult; children bring out conflicting viewpoints; children change a family's priorities. Keeping romance alive is vital for the happiness of both husband and wife. The stepmother who feels that romance has gone out of the marriage will more than likely blame her husband; the husband will more than likely blame the stepmother; both will blame the stepchildren. The best way to prevent the loss of romance—or to nip it in the bud—is to function as a team with your husband from the very beginning.

Forming a United Front with Your Husband

Unequivocally, the relationship between you and your husband is the most important factor in the success and happiness of your new stepfamily. Stress, unhappiness, tension, and ultimate failures of stepmother/stepchild interaction are usually directly traceable to a nonsupportive husband. The stepmother, plagued by insecurity, often stung and confused by the seeming rejection by her stepchildren, needs the daily support of her husband to survive. Often, she has to ask for this support and demonstrate her need for it.

The oft-cited statistic tells us that almost 50 percent of marriages break up due to "problems with the husband's children." The real fact is that these marriages break up due to problems between the wife and the husband with *regard* to problems with his children! Too often, stepmothers find themselves in a terrible bind, expected on the one hand to accept responsibility and act as "mothers" to their children, while at the same time expected to refrain from overreacting to inappropriate or hurtful behavior. These stepmothers find themselves accepting responsibility for problems they did not create in order to refrain from reacting in ways that might displease their husbands. This double bind reflects a dangerous lack of communication and cooperation between the new couple.

The happiest and most successful stepmothers are those who enjoy mutually supportive relationships with their husbands. Stepchildren behave better and are eventually happier and more secure when the family is headed by a securely coupled pair.

PUTTING THE MARRIAGE FIRST

You can't "rescue" the family; you can't replace or erase the memories of the original biological family; you can't become the children's "mother." You *can* deepen and enrich your new marriage by assuming responsibility for sharing the care of your stepchildren and all the problems that arise. You *can* share your life with a man who has chosen to accept the responsibility for raising his children despite the trying circumstances of his life. His marriage to you is a testament to his belief in the institution of marriage despite the frustrations, hurts, or tragedies of his previous relationships.

SEPARATE CHILD-RELATED PROBLEMS FROM MARRIAGE PROBLEMS

Stepmothers react sometimes to problems with their stepchildren as though they were marriage problems. For example, a stepmother who can't stand her stepdaughter popping her chewing gum at the dinner table may lash out at her husband for his lack of support rather than telling her stepdaughter to get rid of the gum.

Don't be reluctant to approach your husband with problems or be afraid to discuss problems for fear of seeming incompetent, complaining, or nagging. Many stepmothers reported that they were loath to spoil the honeymoon phase of their marriages with complaints, or that they were reluctant to discuss any problems with their husbands for fear of damaging a good relationship.

Too many stepmothers do not really talk to their husbands until they are ready to explode. They bottle up the hundreds of little irritations, slights, annoyances, and major hurts until they are at the breaking point.

Why do so many women wait until it is too late? Stepmothers are afraid of being compared. Their husbands have already suffered one or more losses; they have survived marriages that ended in divorce or death. No stepmother wants to be compared unfavorably with an absent mother who is perceived as incompetent or with a deceased mother whose memory is idealized by the family.

These fears are easily put to rest by communicating. Stepmothers who enjoy a strong and mutually directed couple relationship will not fear comparisons. You can sidestep such comparison by emphasizing your own relationship with your husband.

SHARE GOALS AND RESPONSIBILITIES

In order for a stepmother to have a united front with her husband, there has to be a strong sense of partnership. You and your husband should share the same short- and long-term goals and enjoy heading toward them together. The successful marriage has a plan— sometimes a specific one, such as "In five years we will change our careers and open a flower shop"; sometimes one as philosophical as "We will simplify our life and surround ourselves with only loving and friendly people." A strong couple will agree on their goals. This unified perception of the world will help the couple to remain focused on each other during any stressful periods.

Stepmothers rarely complain about the breadth or depth of their household responsibilities, but they do, almost with a single voice, complain about their lack of validation, appreciation, and pats on the back. They need recognition for what they do. Take the time and make the effort to agree about who is responsible for what. Do this early on in the relationship and modify these responsibilities when necessary. When stepmothers assess what they are responsible for and what their husbands are responsible for, they may see that the real issue is not the number of chores (although these can seem overwhelming) but rather their feeling about carrying out some of these responsibilities. Again, paper and pen are helpful: List all your responsibilities in one column; list your husband's in another. Talk to him about trade-offs if you feel overwhelmed or particularly uncomfortable or resentful about some of "your" particular tasks. And don't forget to include some responsibilities that you and he will do *together*.

SET ASIDE TIME FOR ROMANCE AND FUN

We've been discussing the importance of sharing family concerns, problems, and issues; these are undeniably important. However, it is equally important to *stop* talking and thinking about problems each day. Some stepmothers, in a misguided attempt at being "good mommies," become little more than drones: They turn *too much* of their attention toward family problems. Such women find, to their ultimate confusion, despair, and anger, that this overinvolvement with family issues is rejected by their husbands. When issues of child-raising eclipse the couple's marriage, everyone in the family will suffer. Strong families need a strong, loving couple at the helm.

In order to keep the marriage alive and viable it is imperative that the couple have some time alone. Time alone means just that: *alone!*

Husband and wife; man and woman; adults only. The focus of this time alone may be romantic, sexual, or recreational, but it *must* be characterized by the sharing of adult interests. (Remember dating?) Discussion of children or family concerns should *not* take place during such times. Alone time does not have to be exotic or expensive. Alone time may consist of nothing more than sitting in a room that has a door that can be shut behind you and your husband.

One couple got into the habit of "parking" each day: They sat in the car in their garage, tuned the radio to their favorite station, and just talked for a half hour. Another couple took to having late lunches together. Still another had a cup of tea together each day when they came home from work. Time alone may be as simple as walking the dog or sitting on the front stoop, or as luxurious as a planned weekend getaway. Short periods of time alone each day are vital to keeping the couple intimate, connected, and in touch with each other.

Some couples like to plan activities that they enjoy together: skiing, fishing, bowling, cards, hiking, dog-training classes, an opera series, or season tickets to a particular sport or series of plays. *What* you do together is inconsequential—enjoying regular planned time together *is* critical. Stepmothers have found that planning something for the kids to do during these times helps erase resentment. During the times that the couple is doing "their thing" together, the children might be doing something they enjoy, whether it's their own activity or something as simple as having pizza on the evening when their parents go out for a romantic dinner *à deux*.

THREE SIMPLE RULES FOR CREATING A UNITED FRONT

1. The couple comes first.

If possible, the couple should have time to see and/or speak to each other alone before dealing with the crises of the day.

2. No unilateral decisions.

The husband or wife will make no decision without talking it over first. Crisis situations that call for immediate decisions are subject to review. This prevents the children from finding the "softer" touch or playing off father and stepmother against each other. (In our house, the children refer to us as "the Congress.")

3. *Allow children to strengthen your marriage.*

The presence of live-in children actually solidifies a good marriage. Stepmothers and their husbands find that children give a marriage a permanence and an increased sense of time that childless marriages do not have. Stepmothers and their husbands often feel that they have been together for far longer than the calendar reflects; their child-related experiences seem to give them a different time perspective.

Consider Sandy and her husband, Al. Al brought two children to the marriage—a girl of ten and a boy of twelve. Sandy brought an eleven-year-old boy. After five years of marriage, Sandy and Al had been through their own *two* weddings (one a private ceremony and one with a large reception), two Bar Mitzvahs and one Bat Mitzvah, a Sweet-Sixteen party, five school graduation ceremonies (two elementary graduations, two junior high school graduations, and one high school graduation), and had seen their oldest boy through the college admissions process from applications to acceptance to seeing him settled in his out-of-town dormitory.

Sharing the experience of watching the children grow from childhood through these various rituals gave Sandy and Al the feeling that they had been together since the beginning of the children's lives. As couples truly begin to share a family history with their children, their actual time together begins to blur. Although others often treat them as newlyweds, Sandy and Al feel as if they could be celebrating their twenty-fifth rather than their fifth anniversary.

Children and the experiences they bring to a family are tremendously enriching, but remember that the marriage comes first. In order to keep a family healthy, the members of that family must retain their individuality. A family must not become defined by its problems.

THE GOOD NEWS

Most husbands want to be supportive, but they need to be shown how. Most husbands want their marriages to work, so they often find it difficult to look below the surface of a stepmother's complaint. Most men are more direct than abstract; they seem to function more effectively in the here-and-now. In order for you to really have a united front and good communication with your husband with respect to child-rearing, you need to be *specific*. "Modern" men try to be understanding, empathetic, and analytical, but most of them haven't had the years of conditioning and practice at communicating at an emotional level that women have. *Be patient.* And *always* remember to separate "a problem with a child" from "a problem with the marriage." By defining the problem that way at the outset, you'll prevent your husband from getting on the defensive and assuming that you're blaming him.

A fresh, sullen, withdrawn, hostile, depressed, hyperactive, silly, giggling, rude, mischievous, spiteful, horrible, and/or manic stepchild is a *family* problem. This is simply a matter of perspective. The stepchild who acts inappropriately is everyone's concern. But what happens when Grandma or Daddy or Auntie comments, "But they're such sweethearts with us. They never . . ."

The confident stepmother does not accept inappropriate behavior as "her" problem. Children who are acting out or unhappy in any situation are both the father's and the stepmother's problem. In the same way that the stepmother would acknowledge that a child was in trouble who was acting out in school, a father will acknowledge that a child is in trouble if he or she is acting out or unhappy with his stepmother! When the problem is defined (by *you*) as "our" problem—not "his"—it's much easier to solve it as a team.

In order to create a united feeling, use the word "we" whenever possible. It is amazing how such a simple tactic can turn around a couple's perspective. Let's imagine that Andrea, a young stepmother, has been having a terrible time handling her two-year-old twin stepsons. Most of her day is spent running around cleaning up after the toddlers' tantrums.

See the difference in presentation:

1. Vincent, I can't take this anymore. Your sons are destroying our house. I can't have anything nice! WHAT ARE YOU GOING TO DO?

   or . . .

2. Vincent, we have a problem. The boys broke our flower pot. Remember the one that Aunt Jane

and Uncle Elmer gave us for a wedding present?
What can we do?

No one enjoys being criticized. Husbands are not a unique breed on the subject of criticism; they usually do not enjoy hearing "Your son did this" and "Your daughter did that." Such criticisms only serve to alienate your husband: He feels attacked. As an unpleasant side effect, the constant repeating of "your" son, "your" daughter, "your" children only serves to separate you from your stepchildren and further diminishes both your sense of connection with the children and your power and authority in the house. Problems properly defined can be solved by thought or by additional information. Ask yourself: Why are you posing this problem to your husband? What do you want him to do?

ASK FOR HIS HELP

Rather than criticizing, try asking for your husband's help in understanding, analyzing, or figuring out a solution. This is the time for "I" to come out of the closet. You are not criticizing. You are asking for help with something that bothers *you*. Again, be specific both in stating the annoyance and in soliciting help. What do you want from your husband? A kiss? A word of encouragement? Actual intervention? *Be clear:* "I need a hug" is friendlier and more productive than "You don't love me."

SUPPORT HIM

Do not criticize, demean, put down, or in any other way diminish your husband in the eyes of the children. Unfortunately, many stepmothers seem to try to exercise power over their husbands when they feel a *lack* of power over their stepchildren. This is wrong! It is important for children to see mutual respect between their father and stepmother. Subjecting your husband to criticism or to anything less than unflagging support in front of the children will cause resentment in your husband. He may retaliate in kind by being disrespectful and unsupportive, or he may withdraw. Dissension between stepmother and father will cause stepchildren to escalate their struggle for family power. In a word, if you want support, give it!

ACCENTUATE THE POSITIVE

Keep the fun in your marriage! Find something to smile about each day. Share something silly or happy. Say something pleasant to your husband. Compliment his clothes, his hair, his after-shave, or the good way he smells after a shower. Drop him a note; remember silly anniversaries of personal importance. Surprise him with a night of uninterrupted sports-watching or a backrub. Buy him a silly card.

Shared interests, mutual goals, good communication, time alone for romance and fun, mutual support in a noncritical atmosphere: The sustenance of such elements forms the basis for a united front with your husband. Keeping these elements alive in your marriage is fun and exciting.

A SUCCESS STORY

Jane and Jonathan are a professional couple in their late forties, a happy stepfamily with a combined group of six children for the past seventeen years. In speaking with Jane and Jonathan, both individually and in tandem, I learned something interesting: Their conception of success was based on the *achievements* of the members of their family rather than on the way everyone *felt* about everyone else. I heard about one boy who was in law school, another who had won a swimming tournament, a daughter who was on the honor roll. As our talk continued, Jane and Jonathan casually alluded to problems that would have knocked the socks off other stepmothers: One of the boys had returned to his biological mother for a semester; one of the girls had spent her adolescence sulking that she didn't have a "real" mother. I marveled that such emotional stress did not have an impact on Jane's perception of herself as a successful stepmother and her family as a happy stepfamily.

Jane and Jonathan have an important lesson to share: Family success can be gauged in nonemotional terms. Obviously a warm greeting card or a bouquet of red roses will mist the eyes of all stepmothers. However, "mushiness," hugs and kisses, I-love-you's and You're-wonderful's are not the only indications of success!

One of the best ways of gauging success is by setting specific goals and time frames, and reviewing them later. When the goal has been met, celebrate! If the goal is still outstanding, renew it! Is this goal still important? If not, revise your time frame and your approach.

Some women become stepmothers at the altar; others become stepmothers by design, or by surprise, sometime after their marriage. Still others find that after years of marriage, situations or circumstances change and they become responsible for older children, adolescents, or even adult stepchildren. Whatever the timing of the event, *all* stepmothers will need to think through their feelings and to find ways to announce their new family to their friends and relatives.

CHAPTER 7

The Wedding:
Announcing the
New Family

Weddings call up all sorts of romantic illusions. The concept of a couple's public proclamation of love and commitment is one of the most cherished of human rituals. When a woman marries a man with children, this ritual often embraces a large cast of characters, some of whom may respond in negative ways.

Stepchildren as Participants

Stepmother brides may find that they confront many other problems along with wedding day jitters. The most common of these are stepchildren who refuse to attend the wedding; stepchildren who you wish would have stayed home because they choose the wedding as a stage for acting out or otherwise inappropriate behavior; and stepchildren who choose to attend only to refuse to participate.

THE RESISTERS

Many stepchildren resist the idea of their father's marriage. This disapproval is more likely to reflect the children's conflict about their father's remarriage than any personal dislike of their stepmother. Such resistance is found in children of all ages and may appear in a variety of forms: crying toddlers, sulking nine-year-olds, teenagers who refuse to dress up, college students who can't find the time to come home for the wedding.

THE PANICKERS

Some children suddenly panic over their place in the soon-to-be formed family. Panic appears most commonly in children who seem to have been welcoming the new marriage and have not really shown any evidence of problems. Their panic seems to drop from the skies; it strikes both the stepmother and her new stepchild.

Such panic is not unlike that of the vaudeville virginal bride of yesteryear, who locked herself in the bathroom on the eve of the marriage. Stepchildren may suddenly become overwhelmed with the changes their lives are about to undergo, and may simply become immobilized with fear or seek to stop the proceedings by refusing to cooperate.

Carolyn describes a typical example of this panic. Michael had been a happy and relaxed eight-year-old in the months that preceded Carolyn's marriage to his father. In fact, so enthusiastic was Michael that Carolyn had dubbed him her "assistant." Michael helped select the color scheme for his dad's attendants, helped Carolyn plan the wedding reception menu, and was given free rein to choose special desserts for guests under age ten. The entire planning process had given Carolyn an especially warm and tender feeling about her soon-to-be-stepson. And so when Michael panicked at the ceremony, Carolyn was both upset and confused.

"We had a beautiful and elegant wedding and luncheon. The only negative was Michael. He didn't want all the pictures taken. He began to cry and refused to sit still. Out of the fifty or so pictures that were taken, his teary face ruined all but one!"

Michael, like many stepchildren, just panicked. Unsure about how his life would change, unsure about his new role in the family, feeling suddenly pressured and insecure, Michael simply dug in his heels and refused to be photographed.

JEALOUSY

Weddings are typically the "bride's day." Some stepchildren have difficulty accepting this special attention graciously. So do some stepmothers, who are embarrassed to admit that they had a little trouble sharing their special day with their stepchildren.

Most stepchildren will naturally feel anxious about the possibility of losing their father and about their place in their family amid all this romance. The wedding, and the limelight shining upon their new stepmother, may be enough to exacerbate their jealous feelings.

Stepmothers may be embarrassed to admit their jealousy about sharing their wedding day with their stepchildren. These feelings are common—and easy to overcome when you face them head-on.

Tracy told me that her wedding was just about ruined because her stepchildren "were always around their father. They even opened most of our presents," she said.

Diane added that her stepdaughter almost ruined her wedding with her pouting because she wasn't part of the wedding ceremony. As Diane put it, she "really was too old to be a flower girl, and besides it was OUR day."

Martha asserted that her actual wedding day had no particular problems, but she did add that she was annoyed with her husband because they had only one day to themselves for a honeymoon— and he insisted on calling home to check on his young son several times during that one day!

And then there was Laura, who began her honeymoon with the screams of her stepdaughter ringing in her ears. The six-year-old had been a lovely flower girl, had danced with her father and her new stepmother in a "family dance," and had fully expected to go on the honeymoon; this little girl had to be taken away forcibly in tears from the reception by a family friend.

STEPCHILDREN IN THE WEDDING PARTY

Most stepmothers reported that their stepchildren, regardless of age, were included in the wedding party. Stepchildren functioned as ushers, attendants, flower girls, best men, and bridesmaids. Even the youngest children often participated.

Some stepmothers incorporated the stepchildren in the wedding vows; Marge and Larry, Marge's daughter from a previous marriage, and Larry's son all had the judge ask them to hold hands as they accepted one another as a family.

Still other stepmothers used the wedding as an occasion for the clergyman or judge to ask the guests to accept, bless, or welcome the new family.

Enjoy Your Wedding

MINIMIZE CONFLICT BY CAREFUL PLANNING

Everyone has heard tales of family feuds that began with a wedding "slight." Hurt feelings in families are painful; hurt feelings among family members living under the same roof can be intolerable! Obviously everyone will not be able to be accommodated; however, stepchildren should be given preference.

How to avoid problems? *Lots of talking and meticulous planning are essential.* Most people become uncomfortable around weddings because they simply don't know what is expected of them. The size of the wedding or the ages of the stepchildren are fairly irrelevant to this issue of preparation. Rehearsals, either actual or talk-throughs, are absolutely necessary for ironing out potential problem areas. Stepmothers need to have backups and alternate plans for everything!

Marie's wedding day was ruined by poor preparation. Her two young stepchildren, both under age five, were seated in the front of the church. As the organ began to play the children started sobbing and continued to cry quietly until the ceremony ended. On reflection, Marie realized that her little stepchildren had not been prepared adequately for her wedding to their father. Two months prior to Marie's wedding, the children's mother had remarried and almost literally dumped them on their father's doorstep; they hadn't seen her yet and were still very confused about *why* they couldn't live with her any longer. It's hard even to speculate about the fears these little children had about their future after *this* wedding.

You will find that your wedding day is much smoother if you discuss and resolve the following issues:

- What is expected of the children?
- Will there be an exchange of vows?
- Are the wedding-day outfits purchased, fitted, laid out, and agreed to be worn? (Be sure everything is tried on—an itchy shirt, a too-starched dress, or shoes that pinch may create havoc when the big day arrives!)
- Have the children a ride to the wedding, either with you, their father, or a trusted relative or friend? (Many stepchildren do not make it to the wedding when mothers of maternal relatives are depended on.)
- If there will be a honeymoon without the children, do they have a place to stay with a person who is supportive of the new marriage?

Stepchildren shouldn't be bullied or manipulated into participating more than they wish. On the other hand, if a stepchild desires to participate, create a role if need be. The key is to try to anticipate and avoid any problems before the wedding day.

THE STEPCHILD WHO DOESN'T WISH TO ATTEND

Participation may be optional, but it's difficult to see how the same child who refuses to attend a wedding will be able to live with a stepmother and father after the ceremony. All children will probably experience some sort of discomfort and/or nervousness as the wedding day approaches, but the child who actually refuses to attend the wedding should receive professional counseling *before* moving in with his or her new stepmother.

OUTSIDE INTERFERENCE

Many stepmothers reported that their weddings had suffered sabotage attempts by the mothers of their stepchildren, who refused to permit the children to attend. This refusal to grant permission was an odd but common feature of the stepmother's wedding—especially odd when the biological mother was aware that the children would be living with the stepmother. Despite this awareness, and despite the mother's past or projected contact with her children, she frequently went out of her way to try to keep the children from the wedding, either directly by not returning them from a visit or through psychological pressure.

Gina spent the early hours of her wedding day pacing her wedding suite as her fiancé, Tony, consulted with his attorney; Gina's soon-to-be stepchildren were being prevented from attending the afternoon wedding by their mother, who had decided to take them for an unapproved overnight visit. The attorney intervened, and the children finally made it to the ceremony.

Unfortunately, a wedding day sabotaged by the biological mother seems to serve as the kick-off day for a game that will play itself out over a long period of time. In order to minimize this unpleasantness and tension, it is best to ensure the presence of stepchildren by having the children spend the night before the wedding at home with their father or with a trusted friend or relative.

HAVE A GOOD TIME

Weddings cannot be "done over." At some future point, the individuals who have been thrown together *will* coalesce and become a family, and for the sake of that future family, *all parties* who will be members of the family should be present. For the sake of the family they will become, make every attempt to record a wedding that you'll someday look back on with fondness as the beginning of happiness.

Telling the World

Some stepmothers elope. Perhaps they do not wish to use their wedding as a "family" affair, believing that a couple gets married, not a family. Some women become stepmothers several years *after* their marriage. *All* stepmothers need to announce their new family at some point.

There are no stepmother showers. Although stepmothers are parents to their stepchildren, the formation of the new family usually receives no fanfare. Stepmothers and their stepchildren are not welcomed into the fold of the family and community with the pleasant rituals that attend a birth or even an adoption.

No rites of passage assist the new stepmother in the assumption of her important life role. In fact, of all the stepmothers interviewed, not one remembered that becoming a stepmother was celebrated or acknowledged in any way. Stepmothering is probably the only life event that the general public chooses to acknowledge by ignoring it.

DO STEPMOTHERS REALLY NEED RITUALS?

Do we need public acknowledgment of our new responsibilities? Do we need a line of greeting cards? Do we need "Steppie Showers"?

In a word—yes.

There is a good reason for the rituals people perform and enjoy. Rituals surrounding birth, marriage, death, and various other rites of passage help us move from one stage of life to another. The rituals of our human existence assure us that many others have passed through these same experiences; they help soothe our fears and give us strength and confidence.

Becoming a stepmother is a life-changing event. Stepmotherhood affects a woman's personal lifestyle in a far more profound and dramatic manner than marriage itself does. Those daunting statistics rear their head again; nearly fifty percent of second marriages fail because of problems with the husband's children. Rituals imply acceptance and public acknowledgment. Acceptance, support, and validation for stepmothers provide a sure way to address the complexity of the stepmothering role.

Rituals can also help others in their relationship to the stepfamily. Too often family and friends aren't quite sure how they are supposed to react to the new family. Rituals can help establish the existence of the family and clarify the depth of the stepmother-stepchild relationship.

Many people are uncomfortable with stepmothers. Friends, family, and community may be unsure about what the new stepmother should be called, what titles are used within the family, and how the new family functions. Even people who are close to the new couple are unsure about their relationship to the new family. This discomfort and unfamiliarity may actually prevent a good relationship from blossoming.

ANNOUNCE THE NEW FAMILY

People are accustomed to being notified of various life changes: We announce engagements, marriages, births, graduations, professional practices, and the like. Stepfamilies need announcements as well. Announcing the family members and their new relationship is an excellent way of stabilizing the family.

Creating an announcement for your new family will help you and your husband confront new family roles in a practical way. One stepmother questioned me about announcing these roles "so early" in the formation of the new family. "What happens," she asked, "if those roles change?" The question implies a lot about what is wrong about stepfamilies. Stepfamilies seem to want to adopt a wait-and-see attitude when it comes to thinking about "who" they are in the new family, rather than identifying specific roles and goals and committing themselves to doing the best job they can. Waiting won't work. When a woman gives birth she doesn't decide what her role will be, depending on "how it goes" with the new infant; she is a *mother*. When a woman assumes responsibility for her husband's children, she is a *stepmother*. Since the world can't figure that out, you'll have to tell it.

You won't find printed announcements at your local stationery store. Your announcements may be hand-written or designed and printed professionally. Style is a matter of personal preference; the purpose of the announcement is of primary importance. Announcements will include the names of the couple and the names of the children—but more important, the titles and relationships of all the members of the new family. Because the husband and wife in this new family will, by definition, have different relationships to the children—either step or biological—a general announcement will have to clarify whose children are whose.

Let's consider the mythical Hamilton family consisting of Jonathan Hamilton and his two children, Brett Scott and Cori Hope Hamilton, and Samantha Smith Hamilton and her two children, Jessica Lynne Smith and Josh Seth Smith. The following announcement would be appropriate:

Samantha (Smith) and Jonathan Hamilton
announce our marriage and
are proud to introduce our new family:

Brett Scott Hamilton	(November 6, 1984)
Cori Hope Hamilton	(January 19, 1982)
Josh Seth Smith	(December 26, 1981)
Jessica Lynne Smith	(May 3, 1983)

HAVE A PARTY

Celebrate the occasion! Have a party! The nature of the party will be as individual as your particular family, whether you choose a catered affair complete with printed invitations and a six-piece band, or a backyard barbecue. Have a party that introduces the children to your family and friends, and your family and friends to your new husband and stepchildren. This gathering should be totally separate from the wedding. Invitations may be as informal as a telephone call or conveniently included as part of your wedding announcement or invitation.

INTRODUCE THE CHILDREN TO FAMILY "SECRETS"

Tell your stepchildren anecdotes. Describe family members they have not met because of circumstance, distance, or death. Bring your stepchildren up-to-date on their new extended family. Extended families can be great disappointments or joys for you and your stepchildren. (See Chapter 9.)

The day does arrive when you and your stepchildren will begin living together. Together you will confront a host of practical and emotional issues. Recognizing and coping with nervousness, unrealistic expectations, and hopes for the future are exciting challenges. Setting up house, coping with privacy issues, integrating different lifestyles, and accepting and delineating house rules and consequences for misbehavior all have to be accomplished without damaging anyone's self-respect or enthusiasm for the new "family." A tall order? Absolutely.

CHAPTER 8

Moving In

Setting Up House

Okay, so the day has arrived. The moving trucks have come and gone, or you've simply packed up your suitcases and arrived. The day everyone has been thinking about is here; the family begins. The first few days—even the first few *moments*—are important; they set the tone. Start at the very threshold, and take each step carefully.

UNPACKING

Depending on the age and interest of the children, unpacking can be a family adventure or a disaster. It is important that children do not feel overcontrolled or overwhelmed. Everyone should be responsible for finding and putting away his own possessions. Even the younger members of the family will enjoy "finding" their toys. Definite chores give everyone something to do and help children feel less uncomfortable. Participating in the moving-in process helps everyone feel a real stake in the creation of the new home.

There are no awards given out for quick unpacking, but to listen to many stepmothers you would think they were involved in an Olympic competition. The first day together, spent unpacking, sorting, and trying to establish some beginning sense of order, should be as relaxed as possible. First impressions are created that first day and the frazzled stepmother who seeks to get everything looking picture perfect will more likely be remembered for her short temper than for her quickly arranged rooms. RELAX! The goal for the day should be easily attainable and should set the stage for further successes. Plan on readying a place for everyone to sleep that night, and make sure there's food for breakfast the next morning. Anything more that gets accomplished is "icing on the cake."

CELEBRATE THE FIRST DAY AS A FAMILY

Remember that this is the day stepchildren will remember as the beginning of their life with you. Make it as pleasant for yourself, your husband, and your stepchildren as possible. Don't set impossible standards that can only fail. Set a time limit and then stop working and celebrate. Eat dinner out, or order in a pizza. Be creative. Think of something fun. Have little surprises— housewarming gifts. Take pictures (even of the mess!). Have fun that first evening. Try to think of something memorable to do. If you must put away the pots and pans, try to have fun. Play Geography while you work, or sing, or toast marshmallows in the fireplace or on the kitchen stove. It's not hard to have fun with children. Enjoy the evening and try to smooth over any immediate problems or fears that may have otherwise been overlooked.

KEEP AWAY FROM RULES/MAKE ONLY NECESSARY DECISIONS

The moving-in night is not the time for rules, regulations, and long-term decisions. School-aged children should be aware that this is a "special night" and that there will be plenty of time later for deciding exactly how everyone will live together.

WHO SLEEPS WHERE? MAKING A PLACE FOR EVERYONE

The best way to handle critical decisions, such as who gets the bedroom nearest the bathroom, is to take time with them. It is difficult to make decisions before everyone has really settled in and gotten to know one another. It's important to understand that little is permanent during the first months together. If possible, and if the ages and temperaments of children permit, allow the children to have a voice in where they would like to sleep. Don't assume that children want to remain in their old rooms; don't assume that children want to move into new ones. Don't assume anything. If the child is old enough to speak, ask for his or her opinion: Shoulder shrugs and "I don't know" get no vote. Room changes may be made temporarily, say for one week, at which time the family can reconvene and decide whether or not they want to switch. Be especially sensitive about suggesting that children double up and room together!

WHAT TO EXPECT

Stepmothers will find that their stepchildren's ages will affect the way they react to moving in.

Small children may be totally confused and frightened by their new surroundings; the hustle and bustle may simply be overwhelming. If there has been a change in custody and the children are not used to sleeping at Daddy's, there will probably be a sleepless night or two. Be very careful about events of the first night. If the children are restless, they should be comforted *in their own room.* Avoid like the plague taking a little child into your room or your bed. The concession of the first night will become the pattern of the first month!

Little children are very fearful about any sort of change. To calm their fears be sure that as many of their comforters and familiar toys are beside them. School-aged children may actually have fun moving. Being treated in a "grown-up" fashion and given special tasks to perform may help the school-aged child feel that he or she has a real stake in the new family.

Adolescents will be more concerned with their own interests. Allowing an adolescent the personal time to settle in by providing telephone time, privacy, and perhaps the freedom to listen to his "own" music will help calm everyone's nerves. Permitting adolescents free rein that first day is a gift.

Stepsiblings

Stepmothers are often biological mothers as well, bringing children from previous marriages to their new families. They often find that juggling the needs and well-being of two "sets" of children is initially unsettling.

Almost all the stepmothers I talked to reported that their children were negative at first about their potential stepsiblings. It seems to be easier for children to accept the idea of their parents marrying than it is for them to accept the fact that there will be additional children in the family.

Mothers and fathers who have fallen in love hope their children will also love each other and will help create a happy family for everyone. Because children are by nature self-centered, they are often unwilling or unable to suspend their own interests for the sake of others' happiness. Stepsiblings do not usually dislike each other inherently as individuals, but they are bound to be wary, at least at first.

DON'T EXPECT INSTANT LOVE OR INSTANT "FAMILY FEELINGS"

Family feeling grows as children have the opportunity to experience living together. At first, children have no commitment to one another. They are committed only to their respective parents and biological siblings. Stepsibling relationships will grow and deepen based upon many contributing factors including the ages of the children involved and the opportunities for growing together through shared experience. Many parents make the mistake of trying to do everything together in an attempt to create a feeling of family. Don't forget that in a typical family children form a subgroup apart from their parents.

BITE YOUR TONGUE . . .

Many parents, while proclaiming a desire for a "normal" family, really aspire to some mythical, fairy-tale family life where all the children play happily and quietly under the benevolent smiles of their parents. Real families are colored with a bit more human emotion; they are often noisy, subject to rapid changes, and involved in power struggles and identity crises. Real families exhibit jealousy and competition as well as quick-silver flashes of rage and unexpected shimmers of kindness. Real families, when defined in real terms, begin to sound a lot more like—stepfamilies.

In order for children to grow together, they must be permitted to develop their own relationships without parental interference. Children need to understand that short of dangerous physical violence, their altercations will *not* gain the sympathy or intervention of either or both parents. Children need to be given the opportunity to experience things together, whether it's walking to school together, united in their "status" as the new kids, or being shipped off to the same summer camp. Parents need to find ways to ensure that their children share experiences apart from parental intervention.

Sally and Robert married and decided to send their four children to the same school for their first year of marriage. Because the children were in different grades, Sally and Robert needed a school that would include grades two through high school. The only convenient institution meeting this criterion was a parochial school noted for its academic excellence but also for its unrelenting strictness. Sally and Robert debated the advantages and disadvantages of such a rigorous academic climate for their children, finally deciding that they favored letting the children meet the challenge of the parochial school together rather than splitting them up and sending them to different schools in different parts of the community.

Sally and Robert's decision proved to be wise. As expected, the children, accustomed to the more relaxed atmosphere of public school, were not happy with their new school. However, this dislike actually turned out to be a plus: "Suffering" through this experience together gave the children something to complain about to one another that had nothing to do with their parents. United in their common hatred of the school rules and the dress code they quickly became close. Years later, they still reminisce about their shared experience at what they fondly remember as the "School of Horrors." The experiences stepsiblings share that are separate from those of their newly married parents tend to promote development of quick bonding.

WILL THEY GET ALONG?

Whether or not all the children will get along with each other is probably the biggest question on any mother's mind when thinking about marriage and stepchildren. If by "getting along" you mean happy children playing together before the fireplace, exchanging whispered secrets and shared giggles, the answer will most likely be "No," at least not for a long while. However, if you want to know whether a real family will develop, a family based on the give-and-take of shared values, interests, and occasional disagreement, the answer is a resounding "Yes." Stepsiblings *do* get along as well or in some cases markedly better than children who are biologically or legally related.

After an initial period of adjustment, most stepmothers find that the children settle down to typical sibling difficulties revolving around the issues of sharing, competition, and jealousy. Many stepmothers were greatly warmed by signs of closeness among the children in the family, and spoke lovingly of times when children defended one another against a school bully or stuck together during a crisis, such as a family illness.

COMMON PROBLEMS

Sharing

The most prevalent problem for stepsiblings is sharing—sharing possessions, sharing rooms, sometimes sharing friends. Underlying all the hundreds of items to be shared is one that is hardest of all to share: parents! Sibling rivalry is nothing new to any family with more than one child; stepsiblings just use different ammunition. A blood-related brother might shout, "I wish you weren't my brother!" whereas a stepsister will shout, "You aren't my sister!" Such statements grate on a parent's ears, but a wise parent will try to avoid responding and will simply wait for the minor tempest to blow over.

Different Parental Styles

Children now have to adjust to different ways of doing things and witness different interactions among family members. If the stepmother is less than thrilled with the manner in which her husband

and his children interact, she'd better discuss this matter before she decides to move in. The day-to-day demonstration of behavior that the stepmother finds unacceptable may prove intolerable if she believes her own children will be affected adversely.

Visitation

If both sets of children have living, noncustodial parents, they will all have to deal with visitation. The different patterns of visitation will affect the entire family. Stepmothers with children from a previous marriage reported that their children visited their fathers on a regular basis and enjoyed a good relationship. Most children spent frequent weekends and holidays with their biological fathers. Most stepchildren did *not* visit with their noncustodial mothers, however. This disparity left stepmothers in a strange predicament: their "own" children were leaving for a visit with "Dad" while their stepchildren would remain at home. These stepmothers lose out on the "breaks" from child-care they had previously enjoyed as single parents. This lack of relief, combined with existence of an uncooperative biological mother, was responsible for a good deal of resentment and stress.

Stepmothers whose children continued to enjoy good-to-excellent relationships with their noncustodial fathers seemed particularly stressed when their stepchildren could not enjoy the same relationship with their noncustodial mothers. Claire is such a stepmother. She states that there is no comparison between the children's relationships with their respective biological parents. "My ex is genuinely involved with his children. There are never excuses why he can't see them. 'She' does her best not to include her children on holidays. She has never even seen them during a vacation."

"Late-Arriving" Children

It is very difficult for children who have been previously "visiting" to become incorporated into the daily routine of family life. "Late-arriving" stepchildren—those who come to live with the family because of a change in circumstance—usually are uncomfortable and unsure about their role. Stepchildren who have previously visited their fathers, stepmothers, and stepmother's children may need to redefine their attitudes and feelings about the family before they can adjust to living with the family on a full-time basis.

Visiting a home is vastly different from living there. The step-mother needs to demarcate carefully the difference in the new routines and responsibilities and the difference between "visits" and living at home. Additionally, most "late-arriving" children are already into their adolescence, most commonly a stormy adolescence at that. Such teenagers seem determined to break away from rules of any sort. Late changes in custody are often prompted by some sort of problem that has cropped up in adolescence: drugs, truancy, or some other form of emotional distress. The stepmother with children of her own may fear and resent the influence her troubled stepchildren will have upon her children. Adolescents often come to live with fathers and stepmothers as a result of deviant behavior, or due to an inability to get along with their mother's new husband. Sometimes the mother's situation changes; she becomes unable or unwilling to care for the children on a full-time basis. Whatever the circumstances, children who move in "after the fact" feel strange and unsure of themselves. Stepsiblings may exacerbate these feelings as children try to find their new place in the family. If the late-arriving children are older or younger than the residential children, there may be a feeling that age-related status needs to be reordered; the oldest child in the family may suddenly become the middle or youngest child, the "baby" no longer the baby. Late-arriving stepsiblings change the dynamics of the family. If the father or stepmother is less welcoming of the late-arriving child, professional help or mediation should be sought to avoid the sense of family disruption.

Coping with Privacy Issues

Privacy, what the pop psychologists like to refer to as "personal space," is essential for most people. In a new family, everyone may have the strange and uncomfortable sensation that they have "no home." Home is now strange. Home is now peopled by unfamiliar individuals, furnishings, and ways of being and acting. Because everything seems strange, the need for breathing space and the need to keep a sense of personal identity may be paramount. The need for privacy may be the most apparent symptom of this need for familiarity and personal integrity.

Stepmothers and stepchildren may expect these privacy needs to escalate to almost obsessive proportions, especially during the moving-in period, a time when everyone feels more or less off-balance and insecure. Such uncomfortable feelings may cause a heightened sense of possessiveness in regard to what is known and stable. A stepmother who is unsure of her role in the new family may cling to old habits as a lifeline. Stepchildren who are feeling displaced or uneasy about their futures may cling to worn-out teddy bears and outgrown clothing with a passion that is desperate.

The slightest intrusion upon personal space may be perceived as an intolerable and unforgivable onslaught. In order to give everyone the sense of personal space and breathing room needed to build a new family, it is essential that everyone get a chance to express what it is that he and she regard as sacred. It is then absolutely important that these desires be respected. Whether it is the stepmother's need for an undisturbed bath, or a small child's desire to watch "Sesame Street" curled up with a favorite blanket. Such desires must be honored.

LIVING TOGETHER: IT CAN AND DOES WORK

Stepmothers were surprised time and time again by the adjustment of children to one another after an initial period of vying for a "place in the family." Once children find their place, they are usually able to begin to relate to each other on a personal level. Children can and do get along. They form relationships based on fair treatment, shared interests, and shared history. Stepsiblings can and do form close and enduring relationships.

GENERAL TIPS

- Make sure children have time ALONE with their biological parent.
- Make sure children have time ALONE with their stepparent.
- Institute acceptable ways of disagreeing and consequences for unacceptable behavior.
- KEEP OUT OF KIDS' ARGUMENTS; most arguments will stop if you remove yourself from the middle.

Establishing an Atmosphere for Communication

Communication: that great catchall term of modern-day life! "Talk to your family," say the counselors, the books. Your heart says it, too, and yet for a stepmother who faces the chilling shrieks of a preschooler squirming out of her arms or the indifferent shrug of an adolescent, such advice may seem unworkable.

Good communication is not a pie-in-the sky dream. Communication is the transmission of one's feelings, attitudes, opinions, or information to another person. There are many different ways of establishing an atmosphere where communication can take place.

STEPS TO GOOD COMMUNICATION

One-Sided Conversations

Communication may be one-sided, especially at the beginning of a relationship. One-sided communication may at first seem a misnomer. Only one side speaking? That isn't communication. Everyone knows that communication occurs in a fragrant kitchen, sitting around the table holding mugs of something hot and talking earnestly, or perhaps chatting over icy drinks on the front porch. These pretty illusions materialize occasionally, but they are not the rule when talking about beginning a relationship with real children! It might help the stepmother to keep in mind that she is beginning a *parental relationship,* and as such she can use the model of the biological mother, who begins talking to her baby long before the infant is capable of speech. She doesn't sit around waiting for the baby to start a conversation or to answer her. Similarly, stepmothers should begin talking *to* their stepchildren. Do not wait for them to speak first. Stepmothers, as parents, can and indeed should establish the relationship, and one-sided conversing is a good way to begin.

Building Trust

In order for a stepmother to have any type of secure relationship with her stepchildren, she must first establish herself as a person who can be trusted. That means stating her feelings with honesty, not snooping, and not disclosing personal secrets without permission. Good communication only occurs between people who feel safe and secure with one another. Good communication necessitates an environment where individuals feel protected and self-assured enough to voice opinions and feelings, hopes, dreams, and confidences.

Children living with stepmothers will have already suffered a major personal loss in their young lives; the loss of their original families. It is very important that stepmothers remember that the past cannot be changed. A stepmother may have to wait out and override the hurt, resentment, and negative expectations about family relationships that stepchildren have accumulated along their journey to her.

Be Yourself

Stepmothers must try very hard not to pretend. The stepmother who tries her heart out may *cry* her eyes out in the very near future, summarily rejected by her stepchildren who perceive her as a phony. Children of all ages are particularly sensitive to phoniness; to a child phoniness is one of the most serious of adult offenses. By virtue of their physical, financial, and emotional dependence, children must trust the adults in their lives; phoniness threatens this trust. For a stepmother to be branded "phony" is to damage seriously the possibility of having a happy or successful relationship. It is better for a stepmother to be deemed cranky, picky, or downright mean than to be dismissed as a phony!

Express Yourself

Stepmothers must be willing to risk expressing their own wishes, hopes, dreams, expectations, and needs. Stepchildren cannot possibly meet any stepmother's expectations if they do not know what they are! Stepchildren need to learn about their new stepmothers. They need to know those things that simply drive their stepmother up the wall. They need to know those things that make their stepmother smile. To withhold such information from children is truly cruel. Again, this may seem one-sided—but it's a beginning.

Listen

Stepmothers need to listen actively to their stepchildren. Be interested. Some new stepmothers may find a child's life, and the long stories the child tells, a little boring. The finger painting may look just like all the others the child has brought home, but to the child it is especially interesting and unique. Listen to children, and not just to the words: What the child actually did or saw is not as important as how the child perceived the experience—how the child describes that finger painting, or tells that long story.

Listen to the silences as well as the shouts. Try to hear the feelings behind the words, the words behind the sighs or tears or strained smiles. A good stepmother is a bit of a psychic, a bit of a detective. She needs to listen and then to provide a quiet place where a child can feel free to talk.

Be aware of nonverbal communication. Looks, touches, smiles and frowns, body language, and nervous habits all indicate how people really feel about one another. The wise stepmother realizes that hugs, touches, small smiles, and chicken soup for a sniffle convey feelings as well, if not better, than the words she says. The wise stepmother both gives and receives these nonverbal signals.

Set Limits

Once the child begins to talk freely, a whole new set of problems may emerge. Some children and stepmothers are filled with such hurt, anger, resentment, anxiety, or other negative feelings that their negativity explodes. Fair talking limits must be set up in order to avoid hurts that could derail the possibility of communication for long periods of time. Words can hurt more than any slap; verbal abuse has no place in a family. Inappropriate language, sarcasm, or insults guised as "honesty" have no place between family members.

Time-Outs

If and when communication gets out of hand—when one or both parties feel that they are not getting anything but hurt out of an exchange—it is time for a "time-out." A time-out means stopping a discussion. If the child insists on continuing, the time-out is enforced by the stepmother; she ceases to respond to the child. Ask the child to leave the room for a little while. If the child refuses, you leave. If necessary, reschedule the discussion for a specific later time.

No Talking Behind Backs

Communication can only occur between parties who are present. Third party conversations are to be avoided at all costs! "My mother

always says that you . . ." or "Grandma doesn't see why you can't
. . ." Although it is tantalizing to grab for the bait and begin a grand
argument, stepmothers must acknowledge that it takes two to argue
and it is impossible to argue with a "ghost." Taking the bait of such
statements leaves the stepmother with the option of playing out an
adult argument with her stepchild. Not fair, not profitable, and
easily avoidable! You can deal with such baitings quite simply. You
might calmly respond *by not responding*. A simple "that's interesting," or something equally noncommittal, lets the stepchild off the
hook. He or she has conveyed the information and you've defused
the power of the statement. You might use this opportunity to learn
more about your stepchild by turning the question back to the child.
The child who says, "My mother says . . ." might then be responded
to like this: "That's interesting, What do *you* think about it?" Avoid-
ing third-party conversations is very important if you are to feel a
sense of control and if the child is to be spared an uncomfortable
situation. Children should not have to be engaged as judges in
popularity contests.

Raise Issues

Sometimes it is easier for stepchildren to agree or disagree with
their stepmothers than to raise issues themselves. There is no need
to wait for a child to get around to formulating and expressing a
problem. If a stepmother notices that a child seems gloomy she
might say, "I can see that you're upset. If I were you, I'd probably
feel gloomy, too." By validating negative feelings, the stepmother
will often find that the stepchild is also able to begin talking comfortably.

Paula had been "rejected" by her stepson Bobby for weeks. She
cooked his favorite dinners; he picked. She drove him to baseball
practice, asked him about his games; she got shrugs and silences in
response. She bought him tickets to a hockey game and found them
torn and wet in the bathroom sink. Paula began to assume that
Bobby resented her marriage to his father and her presence in his
life. One day she decided it was time to clear the air. On the way
home from practice, Paula stopped at a local park and asked Bobby
to walk with her. It was an autumn day and he walked beside her, a
chubby twelve-year-old, his eyes riveted on the leaves he crunched
underfoot. They walked in silence for many minutes before Paula

said, "If I were you I'd probably hate me, I'd probably want to just wipe me off the face of the earth, for complicating my life." Bobby stopped and stared at his new stepmother in undisguised astonishment. His eyes softened and locked on hers. "I don't hate . . . I could never hate you . . . I'm just scared."

Paula and Bobby could have gone on for years, trapped in a relationship that would never have had a chance. If Paula hadn't decided to clear the air by stating her interpretation of Bobby's behavior they would never have had an opportunity to develop any relationship; Paula would have continued to misinterpret Bobby's withdrawn behavior as hatred and Bobby might have interpreted Paula's continued silence as yet another rejection. Paula opened the doors to communication by simply stating what she thought was wrong.

The Pen Is Mightier

Sometimes writing is easier. Written language enables feelings to be expressed that might be difficult to speak. Little notes can be used to show affection and long letters often provide an easier vehicle for discussing complicated issues than long discussions. Writing provides a way of assuring yourself no interruptions: A written statement can be read, reread, thought about, and saved. Many relationships that were initially awkward are smoothed over by writing. Stick a little note in a lunchbox, slide a little letter under a bedroom door. When talking seems tough, writing often seems easy!

Open up the doors for communication. Express your feelings. Set your goals and create an environment where ideas can be exchanged respectfully. It doesn't matter if you begin by talking to the air—sooner or later you will get an answer and then get ready to listen!

Delineating Responsibilities

Most stepmothers feel that their responsibilities mirror those of typical custodial mothers. Stepmothers assume the bulk of child-related duties and responsibilities.

Janice is a stepmother to two young children. She defined her responsibilities as "to clothe, shelter, and feed them. To provide personal and medical attention, to help with homework. All the same responsibilities I would have if they were my own flesh and blood."

Andrea buys the food, cooks dinner, does laundry, visits dentists, doctors, and teachers, coordinates visits to maintain family relationships, drives to and from social activities, plays mediator to erupting arguments, dishes out chores, and decides on the consequences of unacceptable behavior.

Denise felt that she had had a lot of responsibility "dumped" on her. Like most stepmothers who felt that they had been delegated to shoulder the load of responsibility, she felt resentful. Denise felt that her husband had automatically surrendered all responsibility for his three young children when he married her. Denise discovered (after her marriage) that her husband felt that children were "women's work." She cared deeply for her stepchildren; she could not simply refuse to care for them just because her husband would not pick up his share of responsibility. Denise felt caught in a situation that seemed very unfair.

ACCEPTING BY DEFAULT

Too often, deciding "who" will do "what" evolves into a lopsided child-care arrangement. When stepmother and father "discussed" child-rearing, the husbands frequently claimed discipline and limit-setting as their contribution and left "the rest" for stepmothers to pick up. Most stepmothers were dissatisfied with "mutual discussions" that left them with the bulk of child-care.

Many stepmothers assume total responsibility for child-care because it seems as though no one else will. Some, such as Hillary, claimed to feel more competent at handling parenting responsibilities than their husbands. Hillary "took on all the responsibilities of mothering because their father isn't very good at it. Many times the weight and frustration of what my heart told me to do and what was acceptable to the little girls really blew my mind. I never felt sure about how my caring and reprimands would affect the girls and it took almost two years until I began to feel comfortable."

Bonnie similarly did not feel that there was any choice in caring or not caring for her three young stepchildren. Bonnie spoke for many stepmothers when she confided that "it was mostly a choice between swimming or drowning. Things had to be done in the family, the children needed to be cared for, spoken to, *raised*. Someone had to do it and I was the one!"

Most stepmothers felt that their stepchildren deserved more than they were getting. Most decided that someone (themselves) had to care for the children. Although they might resent having to shoulder the entire burden alone, they made the decision to do it anyway—because nobody else would.

THE RELUCTANT GO-BETWEEN

Many stepmothers married to divorced fathers found themselves saddled with an unwelcome responsibility: Their husbands felt that their divorces had severed all need to communicate with their children's biological mothers and so this task fell to stepmothers as part of their "mothering" duties. In all but a tiny proportion of cases, this interaction was distasteful and anxiety-producing.

Some stepmothers found themselves accepting responsibilities that actually made them physically ill. Katherine's husband refused to drive the children to visit their mother, who lived in another town. The mother also refused to come to their town to visit with them. Feeling that the children were suffering from this stalemate, Katherine took it upon herself to drive the children to their visits. This task, and the unpleasant reception that awaited her on both ends of her trip, made her anxious. For days before the scheduled visits, Katherine would be nervous, jumpy, and easily startled. On the drives to the next town, her heart would pound and her palms grow sweaty on the steering wheel. When she would arrive the children would race from the car, the mother would rush them into *her* car, and Katherine would be left to drive home alone. Often Katherine would feel so nauseated and dizzy that she would be forced to pull the car off the road until she regained her composure. When she arrived home, her husband, Tom, would greet her frostily, announcing that he thought it was "stupid" that the children's mother couldn't find her way to town.

Although she is still not comfortable about it, Katherine continues to make her periodic drives. Occasionally she tells Tom that she needs a "break" but that is only rarely. Like many stepmothers, Katherine overrides her personal discomfort and continues to drive the children. Why? As Katherine puts it, "I feel like I'm not being supportive if I don't do it."

Eleanor is a stepmother of three teenagers, one boy and two girls. During the eight years of her marriage to her husband, Ted, Eleanor has found that she continues to assume more and more responsibility. At the present time, she feels that she does "everything" that needs doing for her stepchildren. The extent of her involvement has made Eleanor feel very close to her stepchildren, but she good-naturedly warns other stepmothers to "be careful what you do. Once you do something one time, it will become 'your job.' "

STEPMOTHER'S CHOICE

Stepmothers who actively chose to assume the lion's share of child-related responsibilities seemed to feel more in control of their family than those who did it by default. Obviously this sense of control and satisfaction was related to the husband and stepchildren's acceptance of the stepmother as a primary parent in the family. Beware of accepting responsibility blindly or by default without making a choice. That way leads to resentment.

The "New" Daddy

Many stepmothers thought they were marrying a "new breed of man"—men who had opted for custody; widowers who had been able to rear their children alone; men who had cared for their children for years before they married again. These women expected that such fathers would be more involved with active parenting than the stereotypical daddy. Certainly, fathers who had been functioning as the sole residential parent had assumed responsibilities that far exceeded the typical tossing of a ball or glancing at a homework assignment. After all, these were "modern men." These men would *understand* what it meant to center a life on the needs of a child. These men would be actively involved, interested in the minutiae of their children's lives. These men would be sensitive, insightful, even motherly. After all, hadn't women been told for the last decade or so that it was opportunity and interaction rather than gender that made a nurturing parent? These men were certainly nurturers. Right?

Wrong.

"TRADITIONAL" DADDIES

The report was that most fathers were *not* nurturing. They functioned in a very conservative, traditional capacity. Even if they had attempted to go through the rituals of nurturing behavior while they were single, they were clearly happy to stop such behavior when the stepmother came on the scene. The responsibilities and duties of fathers fell with startling frequency into very traditional quarters: Fathers were responsible for discipline, financial providing, overseeing leisure activities for boys and sports activities for both boys and girls. Less frequently, fathers were described as overseeing chores and homework.

Susan's husband, Freddy, is typical of many fathers. Freddy's involvement with his children centers on discipline. Freddy, like most of the fathers we heard about, carries out the discipline because the kids will listen to him but sometimes not to Susan. Susan and Freddy don't always agree about Freddy's brand of discipline (and that, too, is common): Susan often feels that Freddy lets things slide that she would not let the children get away with. Sometimes Freddy even does the children's chores himself rather than asking the children to do them. Susan finds that she resents Freddy's lack of involvement. After all, as Susan says, "They're his children and he needs to enter into the 'hard training' part as much as I do."

Some fathers were even less involved with their children. There seem to be three oft-cited reasons for this lack of involvement:

- long working hours;
- feeling that raising children is "women's work";
- feeling that children do not require such active involvement.

"WEEKEND DADDIES" ALL WEEK LONG

Many fathers were noncustodial ("weekend daddies") before they married. As such, they had never been responsible for primary parenting. As full-time fathers they often had different ideas about what parenting involved than their wives.

Many stepmothers, such as Allison, stated that their husbands didn't spend enough time with the children. They noted that when their husbands did spend time, they seemed more like buddies than fathers.

For men who are accustomed to being weekend daddies, it will take time to adjust to having children around on a full-time basis. Weekend daddies are notoriously poor at limitsetting; Many weekend daddies are accustomed to providing gratification for their children in terms of material goods or entertainment. When the relationship between parent and child is limited to short vacation or visitation periods, the tendency is for discipline and/or limit setting to go out the window. Unfortunately, too many new full-time fathers many continue their pattern of weekend daddying into the new family situation.

THE DADDY WHO ALWAYS HAD "HELP"

Many fathers who lived with their children enlisted the assistance of women to help them raise their children. Some full-time fathers moved back to their parents' home so their children could be raised by "Grandma." Wendy's husband lived with his parents before their marriage. His mother cared for the children from the time he left for work until he returned; she became the children's surrogate mother. Both grandmother and grandfather were a great help. When Wendy's husband came home from work, he fed the children dinner and made sure their homework was done.

Now that Wendy and her husband and stepchildren live together, Wendy wishes that her husband would get more involved with the children. She, like many stepmothers, would enjoy building a more solid family. Wendy often feels that she knows her husband's children better than he does—an issue that was echoed by stepmother after stepmother.

Deedee resents the fact that her husband, Pat, doesn't seem interested in raising his daughters. The girls, now ten and twelve, never spent much time with their biological mother, even during the years that they lived together. When she and Deedee's husband divorced, the girls were only three and five. After that Pat and the girls lived in his mother's home and Grandma virtually raised the girls single-handedly. When Deedee married Pat, she felt as though she had just "picked up where his mother left off." Deedee was very angry about this, but she has kept it to herself until very recently. It took years for her to gather the courage to talk to Pat about her resentment. Pat's response was surprise; he hadn't recognized Deedee's anger. His feeling was that the "job always seemed to just get done."

Other fathers, who did not receive help from their families, hired housekeepers who either lived in or came to the home on a daily basis. Many stepmothers resented the fact that such domestic help was dismissed immediately following their marriage—without their consultation and without regard for whether or not the step-mother worked outside the home.

Many stepmothers felt that children were closer to them than to their husbands! Ilene's husband seemed to feel that "children should be on automatic pilot." Stepmothers who had been married more than a few years began to see that their increased involvement and interaction with their stepchildren evolved into a much closer type of relationship than the relationship the children had with their fathers.

DREAM DADDY

A discussion of family responsibility would not be complete with-out a "success story." Ann and Richard are such a couple. They prove that dreams can become reality. Ann's love and admiration for her husband, Richard, shine through her words.

"He's an above average father. He does more than any man I've ever known. He's very into housework; he even loves doing the laundry! Yardwork is a joy to him. I tell him he does too much and unfortunately, because of his nature, his children have never become very well versed in the duties around them. However, he's always very supportive of me and how could I not be satisfied? He'd do everything if I let him."

Amazing? Even more so, when Ann adds that her husband, Richard, is a paraplegic and walks with the aid of crutches and braces. His handicap does not keep him from doing anything he sets his mind to. Ann and Richard are united in their goals for the family and in their commitment to each other.

Common Problems for the New Stepmother

Stepfamilies are different from biological families. A stepmother's family must integrate a number of different and sometimes conflicting lifestyles under one roof. Some things will be subject to compromise, others will not. The challenge lies in deciding which is which, making compromises wherever possible, and realizing which lifestyle components will just not bend.

For example, a family might compromise on the subject of dining together—or not. Margaret had always envisioned family dinners like those enjoyed in the "Father Knows Best" television shows of her childhood. However, when she married Bill, a widower with three teenagers, she was shocked to discover that "Dad and the boys" had "always" eaten together in front of the evening news. Since this pattern had happily gone on for the past ten years, Margaret realized that she had little chance of successfully winning her campaign for family dinners in the dining room with quiet conversation. More to the point, Margaret realized that her husband and stepsons actually enjoyed their evening meal. Rather than engage in a power struggle, Margaret compromised; dinners were moved from the playroom to the dining room and so was the television set!

Sheila found that she was faced with a situation that defied compromise. Shortly after her marriage, her twin stepdaughters came down with a terrible head cold. The six-year-old girls were so stuffy and miserable that they looked as though they were constantly crying. When their colds did not disappear after a week at home and in bed, consuming gallons of chicken soup and hot lemonade, Sheila took the girls to their pediatrician. "Where's the cat?" immediately asked the doctor. The twins had a severe allergy to cats; Sheila's seven-year-old-Persian, Commander, had to go.

You can choose your roommates, you can choose your husband, you raise your own little babies from birth, but you can't choose your stepchildren. Stepmothers often have to learn to live with children they didn't choose (and perhaps would not have chosen), and to try to integrate lifestyles, values, manners, and personal habits that are worlds apart from their own.

TABLE MANNERS

It is incredible how often the issue of food surfaces. When asked about their stepchildren's most irritating feature, many women mentioned table manners before anything else. There is something primal about the sharing of food. It may not be an exaggeration to suggest that the table is the primary arena by which stepmothers gauge the success of the family in general and their individual relationships with their stepchildren. It would seem that in today's world women would have better measures for their success or failures than the dinner table, but the stepmother's responsibility for the table seemed to be hers whether or not she worked outside the home! Indeed, a stepmother's outside job just made her a bread*winner* as well as a bread*server*.

PRIVACY ISSUES

Lack of privacy is the most frequent personal complaint among stepmothers. This lack of personal space has two components: real and psychological. Let's deal with the real; children and teenagers DO have a tendency to make noise, litter, knock on doors at inconvenient moments, break things accidentally (or worse, intentionally). Children and adolescents do fall ill or otherwise require attention at inopportune moments. They often make it difficult for their father and his new wife to enjoy those warm feelings that usually characterize a new couple's relationship. Sometimes stepmothers find it difficult even to feel sexy when sharing the same space with those breathing, moving, talking, testaments to the existence of her predecessor.

Romance and sex often suffer from a stepmother's sense of insecurity and vulnerability in her new family. Many women, beginning to feel resentful and powerless, seek to address these issues in the bedroom. Often this is not a conscious effort; however, it *is* difficult for many stepmothers who feel insecure, unappreciated, resentful, picked on, shut out, and constantly reminded of a past they weren't part of to turn on the charm in bed.

DÉJÀ VU? BACK TO THE GRIND?

Some stepmothers described an unpleasant sensation of "returning to the past." Many stepmothers who were previously married described their current marriages in terms of "returning"—returning to the daily demands of marriage, to full-time parenting, to housewifely responsibilities. They spoke of going back to the "hectic life of wife and mother" as though they were returning to work after a nice long vacation.

The sensation was not always pleasant.

LOSS OF PERSONAL TIME

Diedre seems headed for trouble; her life has simply "changed too much." Before Diedre married and became a stepmother to two girls ages seven and eight, she was a very athletic individual; she had a sport for every season of the year. Now, after only a few years of marriage and stepmotherhood, Diedre finds that she doesn't do *any* of her former activities—neither sports nor the crafts and hobbies she used to enjoy.

Diedre, like too many stepmothers, has given up too much for her new family—in a very real sense she has given up *herself.* This surrender has taken its personal toll. "I have always enjoyed doing things for the family but I realize now that I am suffering by not allowing time for *me*," Diedre puts it.

"I feel so old," she says. Diedre is twenty-seven.

FEELING "OLD"

Like many stepmothers, Diedre is neglecting her own needs in the service of her family. Many women immerse themselves in their new families because they are unsure about exactly what they are supposed to be doing. Stepmothers who are overburdened often feel older than their age, as Diedre does. Many feel older because of a sense of time pressure, a feeling of trying to cram more experiences into the present so that the past may be overtaken and eventually erased. There is also a practical explanation for "feeling old": A stepmother often cares for children who are older than her biological children (or the children she "might" have had). This creates a time-warp feeling for stepmothers; they often feel as though they are operating outside their own biological clocks.

Rules of the House

Discipline, as defined by the stepmothers surveyed, refers to the ability to set limits on behavior in a way that works for the smooth functioning of the family. In no way should discipline include physical, verbal, or emotional abuse of any kind. The line between discipline and abuse must be made clear quickly and simply.

Discipline ends in *order;* abuse ends in *hurt.* Similarly, although stepmothers as all parents will develop and use their own styles to enforce such limits, the question of "discipline" is never related to corporal punishment. Corporal punishment, whether administered by biological parent or stepparent, is always inappropriate except perhaps in a life-threatening situation.

Stepmothers almost unanimously described situations where they had consciously chosen to create and/or enforce certain basic rules of living—with varying degrees of luck. Let's try to learn from their experience.

CHILDREN NEED LIMITS

Children need structure in order to feel secure; adults need structure in their lives in order to be able to plan and manage a household. In order for any group of individuals to live together, there must be some general agreement about the way they are going to live.

Some experts advise stepmothers to leave the discipline up to the biological parent, but the "real" experience of stepmothers flies in the face of such advice. Someone who does not discipline is seen as powerless, an outsider and yes, even unloving. Many stepmothers mentioned trigger events, arguments that were provoked by their stepchildren and that forced them into blowing up and/or disciplining, forced them to stop "walking on eggs." Many stated that after such incidents their relationships improved markedly.

Early discipline should involve nothing more than setting down some basic ground rules for living—not a bombardment.

BUILDING RESPECT

The children must perceive their new stepmother as clear about her *own* goals and values. In order for stepchildren to perceive you as a credible individual, worthy of respect, you first must see yourself that way. This means no "wimping out"—no running off to your husband at the slightest problem. Authority is assumed as often as granted. No one can be "made" the boss who does not assume the role. Children do not like to see weakness in adults who are in charge. Just look at the horrible time children will give to a red-faced student teacher or an ineffectual camp counselor. Children are not by nature perverse; they simply need to feel safe. Wishy-washy people who are unsure of their own role are not safe to be around.

Put this into adult terms for a moment. What kind of faith would we have in a President who got on the air and announced, "I really don't know what my job is all about or whether or not you're going to trust me. I really love all of you and I hope you'll help me." Such a President would make us all, regardless of political affiliation, very uncomfortable. As adults we want our leaders to be competent and in control; children are no different.

Pat, a forty-year-old stepmother of three school-aged girls, spoke from the heart when she expressed her views on discipline: "Truthfully," she said, "I didn't really feel as if I was being authoritative, just making sure that the girls knew that whenever they were confused there would be one basically constant, basically honest, and absolutely loving person they could rely on to set some boundaries as a safety net."

STUMBLING BLOCKS TO SUCCESSFUL DISCIPLINE

Husbands Who Resist

Mary is the stepmother of two girls, ages eleven and nine, who came to live with the family a year and a half ago. Although Mary is a teacher who has been trained in early-childhood education and a mother herself (with two boys, ages ten and seven), she is having a difficult time adjusting to her stepdaughters. She describes her stepfamily as "struggling," and describes her inability to discipline her stepdaughters. "When I discipline them," she says, "my husband intercedes and they get away without punishment."

Children Who Resist

"You're not my mother": This is the most common refrain from stepchildren resisting discipline. It is thought to be a powerful statement. The way a stepmother responds to this statement will set the tone for all future power struggles. "You're not my mother" might very well be responded to with a simultaneous affirmation and dismissal of that fact: "That's right. Now go ahead and clear the table." It is important to clarify your own position and authority. "I'm not your mother, I'm your stepmother and now please clear the table as I've asked you to." Stepmothers need to clarify their position and authority. "That's right I'm your stepmother" is a clear and straightforward way of expressing that.

Outside Interference

Susan is a corrections officer. With her experience on the job it is ironic that she is having trouble in the arena of discipline. However, Susan, like many other stepmothers, often feels that her efforts are not supported by her husband. In addition, her authority is questioned by those outside the family unit. Her husband thinks that she is too hard on her stepdaughter, who then complains to her biological mother whenever Susan attempts to enforce any of the family rules she has established. Susan feels, and rightly so, that her authority is being undermined.

Legal Resistance

Many stepmothers find that their authority and their inclinations about the best interests of their stepchildren are overridden by the dictates of the court. In fact, the court may be seen as another parent in situations where stepchildren have to comply with legal orders. Time and time again, stepmothers described court decisions that seemed to fly in the face of all logic and reason. They told of situations where stepchildren were required to visit with biological mothers in clearly inappropriate and at times dangerous circumstances. It is important that stepmothers acquaint themselves with court decisions *before* their marriage. It is extremely difficult and frustrating to attempt to change custody decisions. The decisions that were made before the stepmother's marriage will most likely be the ones she will have to learn to live with.

Stephanie was thirty-three when she married her husband and added his two preteen children to her new family along with her own eight-year-old son. Stephanie had been divorced for seven years and was accustomed to an easy relationship of visitation between her son and his noncustodial father, who picked him up at her home every other Friday and returned him before dinner on

Sunday night. Stephanie assumed that her stepchildren would visit their mother on the same weekends. She looked forward to alternate weekends alone with her new husband.

Stephanie was not prepared for her husband's "agreement" with her stepchildren's mother or the woman's rigidity. The agreement placed uncomfortable restrictions on their weekends—the lack of freedom began to haunt Stephanie. The agreement began to dominate Stephanie's thoughts and affect her weekends in a very real way. The agreement specified that the children had to be driven to and picked up from their mother's apartment. This translated into a two-hour drive each way, each weekend! Stephanie was further stunned to learn that her husband was also responsible for taking the children to any of their weekend activities, back in their own neighborhood. If the children were to continue playing team sports, there would have to be three or even four round trips between home and their mother's apartment each time they visited. This hectic schedule destroyed Stephanie's dreams of quiet, romantic, solitary, weekends with her new husband.

"Difficult" Situations

If a potential stepmother and father cannot agree before marriage on child-rearing issues, professional assistance should be sought. If one or both parties is not willing to seek such assistance, then the marriage should be postponed.

Jeanette and Norman met ten years ago when they were both in their late forties. Both had been widowed at relatively early ages and each had three children in their early teens. Jeanette and Norman discussed the various problems of combining their families and the feasibility of raising six very different teenaged personalities under one roof. They came quickly to a mutual decision: They postponed their plans for marriage until the children were "on their own." Because they enjoyed each other's company, they decided to continue seeing each other on an exclusive basis and now, with the wedding of Jeanette's youngest daughter, they are planning their own wedding. Both Jeanette and Norman realized that because their children had such strong ties to their deceased parents, and because their individual families were quite set in their ways (and because neither of them could envision beginning to cope with six teenagers) they would continue to be in love but would postpone their marriage.

In situations where there is no agreement on child-rearing or a marked distaste or ineptitude for sharing child-rearing by one or both members of the couple, it is better to postpone or cancel wedding plans than to plunge into an unhappy situation.

Regina is an outstandingly attractive woman in her early fifties who fell in love with a man who was fifteen years her junior. They enjoyed a fiery love affair and married within several months of their meeting. At the time of their marriage, Regina had three girls living at home; an older daughter was already married. Regina's young husband came to the marriage with five children—whom Regina had never met. Although the flames of her passion continued to burn, she was neither prepared nor equipped to deal with the demands of eight children ranging in age from three to sixteen. Regina quickly came to resent the intrusion of her husband's children. Because she feared seeming incompetent in his eyes, and because she strove to maintain the high romance of their courtship, Regina was isolated with the problems of her new large family. In less than a year's time the marriage ended.

Regina's need for control manifested itself in arbitrary and heavy-handed ways. She admits making such "welcoming statements" to her stepchildren as "I'm the one who's in charge now and you'd better accept this fast." The more she attempted to force control over her stepchildren, the more they acted out. Through poor preparation for stepmothering, her lack of familiarity with her stepchildren, her inability to communicate with her husband about child-rearing issues, and her own frustrated expectations, Regina paved the way for the dissolution of her marriage. Biting the bullet is *not* a good solution.

HOPE FOR STEPMOTHERS

Stepmothers do not have to feel overwhelmed, nor to fear the loss of their marriages along with their sense of self. It is possible to set effective guidelines that will enable a new group of individuals to begin functioning as a family. Running a stepfamily is a matter of figuring out what is important to you and deciding how much you're willing to give to attain your goal. Setting up a stepfamily is a little like the childhood game of Tropical Island. Perhaps you recall that the premise of this game was that a group of individuals was stranded on a tropical island and needed to create a new society from scratch and separate from any others. One of the first necessities for this new "civilization" was a set of rules and consequences. It is the same for stepfamilies as it is for a fantasy Tropical Island. In order for a group to function there must be a common set of rules and consequences. Take a deep breath and follow along . . .

GUIDELINES FOR ESTABLISHING DISCIPLINE

Clarify Personal Needs

Many stepmothers run into trouble with their husbands, stepchildren, and ultimately themselves because they simply are not clear about what they really want and believe in. Feelings of discomfort and anxiety quickly turn to resentment as they wait—and wait and wait—for their stepchildren to begin to "do what they're supposed to" and for their husbands to "back them up." Stepchildren cannot "do" what they do not know and husbands cannot "back up" what is left unsaid. Stepmothers need to give some active time to clarifying what it is they need to live comfortably.

Start by writing a list of *nonnegotiables* and *negotiables*. The list will have two columns and must be limited to concrete actions rather than feelings. Do not worry if the things on this list seem "silly." Everyone is entitled to her little personal quirks. Once you've made this list, look it over carefully. If there is anything on it that you *can* learn to live with, or overlook, add it to the column marked "Needs that *are* negotiable." (Perhaps you really could learn to close the door on your stepchild's messy room.) When you have finished, put your list away. During the next day or two add or delete any needs that come up in your day-to-day living.

Discuss Needs with Your Husband

When you feel comfortable with your list, find some time with your husband to discuss it. Ideally, he will be willing and able to add some of his own needs to this list. Discuss this combined list, then find a time to discuss it with the children. It is very important that this list be presented and discussed as a joint effort: The children can add their needs to the list, too. Remind them that the needs on the list are to be separated into negotiable needs and nonnegotiable needs.

Limit Discussion to Specifics

All family members should try to keep their needs concrete and unemotional. Needs must refer to definite actions rather than feelings. Such statements as "I just want everyone to be happy and get along" or "I want everyone to leave me alone" don't belong on the list.

Listen to Each Other with Respect

Respect each other's nonnegotiables. Remember that although some of your stepchildren's needs (and even your husband's) might seem frivolous, these needs are important to *them*. In order for a stepmother to have her own needs respected, she must be willing to listen and attempt to comply with the reasonable needs of her stepchildren.

Develop Family Rules and Consequences

Based upon the needs of all parties, the father and stepmother should now be able to set up family rules and consequences for misbehavior. These family rules need to be agreed upon (by stepmother and father). If there are severe stumbling blocks in values and conflicting approaches for consequences that cannot be resolved privately, father and stepmother should seek professional help.

Inform the Children

Once the stepmother and father are firm in their agreement of basic rules and consequences, it's time for the children to be told about them. At this point there should be no discussion. It is important that the children see that their parents have discussed their concerns together.

Keep the rules and the consequences to a minimum so that the family is not overwhelmed. Impress upon the children that these are nonnegotiable household rules. Explain the rules and the consequences clearly; do not get into rationalizing or defending your decisions. Deal with negative remarks calmly: "I know this is new for you," or "Thanks for your opinion, but these are the rules."

Stick to Your Guns

Get ready to enforce your rules. Be prepared to have them tested. But if at any point in the formation of family rules and consequences you realize that you have made a mistake or have changed your position on something—CHANGE IT. It is better to give in or give up on a particular rule or point if you are not going to be able to enforce it wholeheartedly.

Paula, a bright thirty-five-year-old stepmother of a teenage girl, found that she had grown increasingly uncomfortable with her stepdaughter's spending habits. Paula had imposed what she thought was a generous limit of fifty dollars per shopping spree. However, Paula came to realize that she herself had created a "Frankenstein Shopping Monster" of her stepdaughter. When she and her husband married, her stepdaughter had been a ten-year-old tomboy with a wardrobe of faded T-shirts and worn jeans. Paula taught her everything she knew about fashion—a considerable body of knowledge. She took her to the finest stores and instructed her in the benefits of natural fibers and custom styling. Now, at fifteen, Paula's stepdaughter will wear *only* designer clothes! Paula's rule about fifty dollars was impractical in consideration of these tastes. She had to reevaluate her stepdaughter's clothing allowance in view of the fact that she had given the girl very conflicting messages by steering her to designer labels and shops. This was difficult, because her husband, who had recently become quite successful in private business, *enjoyed* spending his newly accumulated wealth by "spoiling" his daughter. Now, Paula and her husband had a new problem to solve: how to steer the course of their daughter's values so that she didn't become too materialistic. The best rule to follow is: Be firm—but be flexible. You'll have to revise your list of negotiable and nonnegotiable needs as the children grow older and their needs change. Be careful that your list does not become outmoded!

You're finally all moved in, you've begun establishing a basic sense of order and taken some important steps toward becoming a functioning family. Now it's time to face the fact that your new family embraces a much larger cast of characters than those living under the same roof. Stepfamilies have complicated extended families that may include several sets of grandparents, aunts, uncles, and multitudes of cousins. These numbers both increase and threaten the possibility for future support and happiness.

CHAPTER 9

The Extended Family

We tend to idealize extended families, seeing them as groups of people beaming at one another around perennially gleaming holiday tables. Each face reflects their obvious genetic connections; each exchanged glance is imbued with a glow that forgives little indiscretions.

More often than not, it's not quite like that; the idealized extended family is usually only an illusion. Family differences, competition for love and affection, and values that conflict with the established "family" doctrine are frequent occurrences.

Stepmothers often discover, to their dismay, that they must integrate their own complex extended family with their husband and stepchildren's families, creating, perhaps, an overextended family. The possibilities for joy and togetherness can be diminished as well as enlarged through the newly complicated family structure.

Begin with the Children's Grandparents

It is important that the stepmother be aware of her stepchildren's relationship with their grandparents, particularly the maternal

149

ones. If the stepchildren have a close and loving relationship and have been accustomed to having their grandparents as part of their lives, there will be little for the stepmother to do except get to know the grandparents, assure them of her support, and hope for their support in return. Remember the obvious: The maternal grandparents are the parents of your stepchildren's mother, and they're going to remain loyal to her. Even when they are pleased that their grandchildren have a loving stepmother, their allegiance to their daughter—or to her memory—will prevent most maternal grandparents from welcoming the stepmother to what they perceive as their daughter's place in their grandchildren's lives.

Most grandparents fear that a stepmother will affect their relationship with their grandchildren. Maternal grandparents seem to feel this fear more keenly than paternal grandparents do. The fear is real. It may be difficult to establish and maintain a relationship in the face of conflicts in loyalties in the case of divorced biological mothers, or unfinished grieving if their daughter has died.

It is imperative that you do everything in your power to see that this relationship is in no way damaged by your arrival. The children have already suffered too many losses by the time you enter their lives. They have weathered the storms of divorce or dealt with the trauma of death. They do not need any more losses, dissension, or confusion.

If the stepchildren have *not* had a good or active relationship with grandparents, and if the grandparents seem to want one, you might try to foster a new closeness. Sometimes a stepmother can mend a relationship that has been fragmented, or help build a new one.

Lorrianne was one such stepmother; when she became a stepmother to Alana and Chad, ages four and eight, Lorraine felt that the children should get to know their grandparents. Alana and Chad had not seen their biological mother—a drug abuser—for three years when Lorrianne became their stepmother. Lorrianne fondly remembered her own grandparents; she felt that it was her duty to contact her stepchildren's grandparents and reestablish contact. Lorrianne's story had a happy ending. It seemed that the grandparents had been staying away because they were ashamed of their daughter's addiction and because their daughter had told them that the children had a "new life" that totally excluded them. Mr. and Mrs. B. were thrilled about the prospect of getting to know their grandchildren. Photographs were exchanged, regular weekly phone calls were made, and last Christmas Mr. and Mrs. B traveled to Lorrianne's home for the holidays.

WHAT TO EXPECT

Most stepmothers reported that their stepchildren had limited or no contact with their maternal relatives, either before or after the step-mother's entrance into their lives. Although a few stepmothers reported improved relationships between their grandparents, aunts, uncles, and cousins due to their efforts, most reported that even the limited contact their stepchildren had with these relatives ended with the new marriage.

Typically, if the stepchildren had been living with their father before the marriage they had limited or no contact with relatives on their mother's side. If the children had lived with their mother, the stepmother usually found that the children had maintained a relationship with their maternal relatives and that a change in custody, not easily accepted, tended to end the contact.

Julie felt threatened from the very beginning of her marriage. Her little stepson's maternal grandparents did everything in their power to prevent her from assuming responsibility for the boy. They went to great lengths, both in the courts and by waging an unpleasant campaign of personal harassment that could have threatened Julie's new marriage. She decided not to give in to the unpleasantness. Instead, she took charge and turned this potentially catastrophic situation into a success story.

When Julie married her husband, Joey was little more than a toddler. Joey's maternal grandmother actually tried to kidnap him! Says Julie, "She hated me for taking her daughter's place and was afraid that because of me, she'd lose Joey." Julie continued to call Joey's grandmother each week. When the woman refused to speak to her or to the child, she sent weekly letters and photographs. When the grandmother realized that Julie was going to continue to encourage a relationship between Joey and herself, she began to warm up. Finally, she agreed to drop her custody suit and began to speak with Julie about her grandson. Finally, the two women discovered that they need not compete for Joey's affection. Now, they

spend time together as a family and everyone is much happier—
especially Julie's husband.

Susan decided to facilitate the good relationship that her stepchildren formerly enjoyed with their maternal grandparents. "From
the beginning, the grandparents sent cards and letters. Then they
didn't write to us for a while. We never heard from Grandpa—just
Grandma. After a year or so I called and said that the children really
missed them. Grandma said she was so glad I'd called: Her daughter had told her I wouldn't allow the children to see their grandparents. I told them it wasn't true and that they could see their
grandchildren any time they wanted to! They sent two airplane
tickets and the boys stayed with them for two weeks last summer.
Contact has been reestablished! They plan to come out this spring to
visit the children—and us."

TAKE IT EASY

On the other hand, if grandparents or older children resist meeting
or forming any sort of relationship, it's best to back off and let things
be. Too often, a well-meaning stepmother may push a relationship
that is in no one's best interest. Stepchildren do not need any more
complications. Children who are genuinely adamant about not visiting grandparents are best left alone.

IN-LAWS

Most stepmothers reported very good, close relationships with
their in-laws. Many paternal grandparents had played a very
involved role in their grandchildren's lives prior to their son's new
marriage. In a number of cases, paternal grandparents had
assumed a majority of responsibility for the care of their grandchildren; many stepchildren lived in their grandparents' home prior
to their father's new marriage. Once these grandparents felt confident that their relationship was not threatened by the new stepmother, things usually went very smoothly. In fact, in more than a
few cases, the relationship between stepchildren and their paternal
relatives markedly improved as a direct result of the stepmother's
intervention.

Of course, there are always those cases where only the strength of the human spirit permits a person to carry on. Katherine is such a woman. Katherine married a man who had been the subject of the town's most notorious scandal—a man whose wife "ran off" with another man,—the teenaged father of the baby she was carrying. When he and Katherine married, the girls were still in diapers. In addition to suffering the challenges all stepmothers face, Katherine became a veritable pariah to her family and friends. Her marriage to a divorced Catholic brought severe criticism from family members on both sides. Both families felt that Katherine's husband should not have married. Katherine thought that time would soften the harshness of both families' feelings, but it didn't. She raised both girls in the town where she had been born and raised herself, shunned by church and friends. Katherine maintained at least a "holiday contact" with both families for the sake of her stepdaughters and the son who was born in the fifth year of her marriage. The situation never did improve in the extended family, but Katherine has managed to build loving and close relationships within her own family. Last year Katherine's elder stepdaughter married, and Katherine has just received the news that she will soon become a grandmother. Katherine has continued to take from her family and in-laws the best of what they could offer, and to give what she can in return. After nineteen years of marriage, she *is* a testament to the powers of perspective. Katherine has managed to retain the "family" feeling that was so important to her.

YOUR IN-LAWS AND YOUR BIOLOGICAL CHILDREN

Some stepmothers mentioned feeling a little hurt and resentful about their in-laws' cool treatment of their own children. They were disappointed that their in-laws didn't try to accept the stepmothers' biological children with the same effort that they, as stepmothers, had made for the in-laws' grandchildren. Other stepmothers groaned about being subjected to seemingly endless recitations of "past history." For some, it became increasingly difficult to sit through stories and photo-sharing sessions that predated their existence. Other in-laws seemed to have little difficulty accepting the stepmother's children into their lives. Careful handling can make a real difference.

Your Side of the Family

Almost all stepmothers were satisfied with the relationship between their own relatives and their stepchildren. For the most part, they found that after a short period of awkwardness their relatives welcomed their stepchildren into the family. Time and time again, stepmothers stressed their satisfaction when their families proved able to treat their stepchildren as "real" members of the family.

Surprisingly, stepmothers also reported that their own relatives seemed to be able to treat biological children and stepchildren equally. Only a tiny percentage mentioned that their relatives treated their stepchildren and biological children differently. When they did, their behavior drew prompt comment from the stepmothers, who made the unacceptability of such favoritism known in no uncertain terms. More than one stepmother mentioned that she had decided to forgo family get-togethers when she felt that her stepchildren were ignored or hurt by her family's markedly unequal treatment of her stepchildren and her own children from a previous marriage.

YOUR STEPCHILDREN AND YOUR FAMILY

Stepchildren were generally eager to become part of their stepmother's family, quickly coming to accept them as their own family members. Any coolness between stepchildren and (step) grandparents was more likely to result from the adults' reluctance to foster a close relationship than from the stepchild's ambivalence.

What Do You Need?

Stepmothers need support from their relatives on both sides, their own and their husbands. Support means sensitivity—in all the little ways.

Like gift-giving. One stepmother said, "Relatives should not show partiality. It's cruel, and children pick up on it. My in-laws will either completely disregard my son when it comes to gift-giving occasions or give him a token gift that's worse than none at all.

While my stepsons got Reeboks for Christmas, my son got Keds. For sixth-grade graduation my stepson got a computer, my son got a card and a ten-dollar bill. I've gotten to the point where I don't even want their gifts at all."

SENSITIVITY

Stepchildren who have been abandoned by death or divorce by their biological mothers need special sensitivity; such children should not have to tolerate any additional "rejections." Sensitivity may mean removing photos of the stepchildren's biological mother or at least adding some current photos to the display. Sensitivity may mean trying to talk more about "recent" history at family get-togethers.

SOME TIPS FOR GETTING ALONG

Don't Let Yourself Feel Left Out

Stepmothers can help everyone by setting the tone for the new family. Instead of sitting around feeling helpless and resentful while the family talks about the past, try to add something from the present to the conversation, or something from your own past.

Give It Time

If you truly want your own parents to be involved with your step-children, try discussing your feelings, then step back to give a relationship time to evolve. This relationship, like all others, takes time to grow. It helps if your relatives are given an opportunity to get to know stepchildren on a gradual basis, and preferably one at a time!

Familiarize Family Members with One Another

Introduce new family members to each other before they meet. Write letters, exchange snapshots, talk on the phone.

Don't Push New Relationships

If you would like your stepchildren to call your relatives Grandma and Gramps you might suggest it, but do not push! It is better to *discuss* preference with various family members. Many times step-mothers are needlessly hurt by family members who are perceived as cold when they are really only hesitant about their new roles. Talk it over!

Be Upbeat

Many times, stepmothers unwittingly damage chances for a successful extended family relationship by prematurely sharing complaints with family and in-laws. It is difficult for your family to accept stepchildren, whom they may perceive as problems for you, and it is likewise difficult for your in-laws to accept you or your children if you are griping about their grandchildren or their son! Be pleasant and calm when initiating new family relationships.

Give It Time

Make sure that stepchildren have a chance to get to know your relatives and that your new in-laws have an opportunity to get to know any children you may have from a previous marriage. You cannot force these relationships but you can provide the opportunity for children and their new families to share experiences together. Again, the first steps may fall to the stepmother and her husband: Open your home as well as your heart if you desire a close family. Like any other relationship, these relationships will mature over time. One cannot wave a magic wand and wish a relationship into existence, as many stepmothers try to do and fail. Relationships are not legislated by wedding vows, desire, or demands—they develop in time.

The extended family member that seems to cause the most difficulty for a stepmother is her stepchildren's biological mother. Whether she is living or dead, involved or absent, her impact upon the family will be keenly felt. A stepmother must confront a host of both practical and emotional issues that revolve around her stepchildren's mother. The following chapter will tackle those issues.

CHAPTER 10

Your Stepchildren's Biological Mother

*"I have come to the realization that evil really does exist.
I've met her."*

—A frustrated stepmother

Ask a stepmother about her stepchildren's biological mother and prepare to be deluged by a torrent of pent-up rage, resentment, and frustration. Greedy, self-centered, vain, materialistic, spiteful, vengeful, egotistic, hedonistic, perverted, insane, ghoulish, and "controlling my life from the grave" are some of the more repeatable ways stepmothers use to describe their stepchildren's absentee mothers.

The bad feeling that exists between stepmothers and biological mothers springs from both practical and emotional issues, all of which can be handled by a change in perspective.

The stepmothers I spoke with were in no way prepared for the impact their stepchildren's mothers would have on their lives. Somehow, they seem to have expected those women—now dead or divorced—to stay in the past, but that assumption was a grave error: The biological mother kept reappearing, even though she sometimes did so as a ghost.

These women linger in the background of the new stepmother's lives. Their presence, either actual or in memory, poses a threat to the new marriage—a threat that surprised most of the women I spoke with. They simply had not anticipated how difficult it would be to incorporate another woman, living or dead, into their marriage and family life. Nor had they anticipated the reluctance and clamming-up of their new husbands when they tried to describe and discuss the difficulty they were having coping with the problem.

The Noncustodial Mother

Many stepmothers married to divorced fathers sought to keep their lives in the present, disassociating themselves from their stepchildren's absentee mother. Such stepmothers tried not to delve into "why" their stepchildren lived with their fathers. There seemed to be an unconscious form of naïveté at play here, with stepmothers accepting the most casual explanations for why stepchildren lived with their fathers rather than their mothers. Courts are still very conservative, and custody still overwhelmingly favors biological mothers. Hence fathers with custody more often than not signal an "unfit" biological mother or a "problem" child. The complexities involved in mothers living apart from their children make it almost impossible for stepmothers to form any sort of meaningful dialogue with their stepchildren's biological mothers.

Many stepmothers reported feeling like nothing more than glorified babysitters. "Motherhood" is theoretically a privilege and a responsibility, yet many stepmothers felt that this role had been split, with the biological mother claiming all the privileges and leaving all the responsibility to the stepmother.

Stepmothers can realistically expect to feel aggravated, frustrated, jealous, and angry with their stepchildren's biological mothers at some time during their marriages. However, having said this, let's also assert that stepmothers *can cope* with these confusing emotions. Once the emotionalism has been explored and removed, stepmothers supported by their husbands, can deal effectively with the issues presented by their stepchildren's biological mothers.

WHAT TO EXPECT

Changing Circumstances

"Oh, my stepchildren haven't seen their 'mother' for *years!*" This common quote is rued by scores of stepmothers who discover later that circumstances can and do change. Even biological mothers who have left "forever" sometimes return.

Your Stepchildren's Relationship with Their Mother

Most stepmothers misgauged the level of closeness between their stepchildren and their biological mothers. Some stepmothers anticipated a high degree of involvement by the biological mother, which would leave large chunks of free time for the stepmother, her "own" children and her husband; often they found that this did not happen.

Other stepmothers anticipated a low level of involvement, which would permit the stepmother to have uninfringed authority and "significance" in her stepchildren's lives. This, too, was often not the case. Both sets of expectations were frequently incorrect.

Mothers without custody generally maintain little *direct* contact; therefore, the stepmother is usually responsible for unrelieved child-care. Many stepmothers with children from previous marriages found that they were responsible for the care of their stepchildren *all the time*, while their own children frequently visited their fathers—periods which had previously freed them from child-care.

Even when there is little direct contact, stepmothers quickly discover that a child's biological mother is a vivid presence in a child's life, even if that mother left home right after the child's birth and has not reappeared since! The *concept* of "mother" lives within each child and the desire to know and resolve this relationship is a driving need for many children. Stepchildren who have not seen their biological mothers in many years demonstrate some of the same behavior patterns as adopted children, yearning to "find" their biological mothers and resolve their personal histories.

You Can't "Escape"

It's uncomfortable to have someone in your life whom you may never have seen and may not like when you finally meet. As a stepmother you must learn to incorporate the existence of your stepchildren's biological mother into your life. It won't do simply to ignore the mother's existence. Denial never works, and can only serve to inflate the intrusive quality of the biological mother when she does appear. Stepmothers often resent being forced by their husbands or stepchildren, either directly or indirectly, into contact with a woman they would not, under normal circumstances, choose to have in their life in any context whatsoever. But in order to keep your sanity, you will have to learn how to integrate this woman's existence into your life.

Facing Difficult Issues

Stepmothers and stepfamilies want to be normal more than anything else. The very fact that children are living with their fathers suggests something abnormal to many people. It is still widely expected that in the event of divorce children will remain with their mothers. Biological mothers generally seek, and are awarded, custody of children except in extraordinary circumstances. Although many fathers are becoming nurturing, primary parents, most mothers who live apart from their children do so because of unusual circumstances including physical or mental illness, substance abuse, or abandonment.

A stepmother may find that she is forced to learn about, to confront, to cope with, and to explain uncomfortable life issues: alcoholism, abandonment, bisexuality, drug abuse, neglect, or some other form of aberrant behavior on the part of her stepchildren's mother. Noncustodial mothers are generally painted with an unflattering brush by full-time stepmothers. The objectivity of stepmothers on the topic of their stepchildren's mothers may not be without question; however, confirmation of many of these perceptions springs from a surprising source—noncustodial mothers themselves.

A study undertaken by Patricia Pasckowicz reported the feelings of one hundred women who are noncustodial mothers.* The issues of nurturing ability and desire for full-time mothering were raised by both absentee mothers and stepmothers, surprisingly with many of the same conclusions. Absentee mothers often demonstrated a lack of nurturing ability or a desire to play a mothering role. Ms. Pasckowicz reported that the majority of noncustodial mothers in her study had had some history of mental illness. Boredom, inadequate finances, a need for self-actualization, and rage were some of the reasons mothers gave to explain their absence from their children's lives. Some mothers were sensitive to their own inability to

---

* *Absentee Mothers.* (New York: Universe Books, 1982.)

manage the stress of child-care; these women feared that they might pose a danger to their children if they had to be full-time mothers. In such cases mothers felt that leaving their children was a responsible act of love.

Poor Support Systems—or None

Rhonda is an office manager in her early fifties. Ten years ago, she married a widower with three children. Rhonda had four daughters. Shortly after her marriage, Rhonda was shocked to discover that her husband expected her to assume all responsibilities for all the children. Like many men of his generation, he genuinely believed that raising children was women's work. This belief system also explained his unwillingness to take any responsibility for his children's poor behavior. Rhonda wilted under the demands of seven children, two different religions, and tremendous interfamily conflict. Her grievances were summarily dismissed by her husband, Frank, who expressed disappointment that she "wasn't the woman he thought she was when they married." Rhonda's frustration is evident. This is how she speaks of her stepchildren's mother: "I wish that she had never died and that I had never met her husband!"

Stepmothers often operate under great stress, without support. Friends and family may be either too uncomfortable or unfamiliar with the stepmother's particular problems to be genuinely helpful. Stepmothers typically do not know any other full-time stepmothers; the necessary network simply isn't there.

Prejudice in Favor of "Mothers"

Stepmothers are often expected (or required by the courts) to relinquish part-time care of their stepchildren to a mother who may be unbalanced, incompetent, or even abusive—a person who, if not for the "accident" of birth, they would not permit their stepchildren to have any contact with. Stepmothers must balance their distrust of an actual unreliable mother against their own built-in reverence for the sanctity of motherhood as an abstraction. A stepmother may find that even her closest friends or relatives are unsupportive of any criticism she may level at her stepchildren's mother—no matter how well deserved it may be.

Compounding her frustration and jealousy about the general

respect the world accords to biological mothers may be her own prejudice in favor of motherhood. Stepmothers' psyches, like everyone else's, were shaped by the same cultural biases we all share. Many stepmothers spoke of finding themselves in the strange position of feeling uncomfortable about breaking the taboo and speaking out against a biological mother. Sometimes they found themselves actually protecting undesirable, neglectful, or even abusive mothers.

Children who have been abused, neglected, or otherwise mistreated by their mothers need their stepmother's help in order to come to terms with their ambivalent feelings about their mother. A stepmother can provide a stable home and a listening ear, but for serious issues of abuse (either past or present) seek out the services of a qualified professional who will be able to bring an objectivity to your stepchildren's problems that is out of your grasp. (See Chapter 14.)

A Rock and a Hard Place

It's hard to be in a no-win situation—expected by husbands, family, and friends to act as a "real" mother and yet chastised by these same people for any criticism of the biological mother. Stepmothers are expected to identify and care for their stepchildren as nothing less than their own, yet at the same time to yield all claims to *real* control to the biological mother. Dealing with this situation will require a heroic measure of tact, forbearance, courage, and—most difficult of all—patience.

THE GREEN MONSTER

Most women, outside of harems, are not brought up knowing how to integrate their husbands' prior mates into their marriages. Stepmothers are often called upon to do exactly that. It is an accepted psychological precept that jealousy blossoms in an environment of insecurity; stepmothers are often notoriously insecure in their relationship with their stepchildren and husbands and therefore especially susceptible to jealousy of the prior intimate connection represented by the stepchildren's mother.

Biological mothers often succumb to jealousy of stepmothers. This jealousy seems to spring from a feeling that the stepmother has usurped her place; such jealousy often has no connection to the biological mother's past or present feelings for mothering, marriage, or the children's father. Such jealousy often results in an apparent campaign to remove the stepmother from the picture. Jealous mothers may seek to damage the stepmother's marriage, her relationship with her stepchildren, and her self-esteem. Some of her weapons are sharp indeed.

Provocative Behavior

Biological mothers often act in seductive and manipulative ways. Stepmothers report frequent phone calls to speak with their husbands about personal matters, asking for favors, loans, or advice. Frequent reminders of shared personal history—anniversaries and other special events—make stepmothers very uncomfortable. Some women are a bit more blatant, dressing inappropriately in negligées or otherwise seductive outfits when husbands drop off or pick up children.

Bad-Mouthing of Husband

Where some mothers are jealous or critical of the stepmother, others seek to befriend her. These women seek to ingratiate themselves with the new stepmother, though their motives are not always immediately clear. One young stepmother was pleasantly surprised when her teenaged stepchildren's mother approached her with an offer of friendship. It took this young woman about six months to realize that her new friend's confidences about her former husband's countless affairs and inadequate sexual performance were really anything but friendly.

"Pumping" or Bad-Mouthing to Children

Some biological mothers use their time with their children to "pump" for information about the stepmother's life, her spending habits, her personal idiosyncrasies. This can result in an insecure stepmother's spending lots of unnecessary time making up rules and testing her stepchildren's loyalty. The good news is that the pumping cannot last forever: Even the youngest child will quickly grow bored with visits that focus on snooping. Stepmothers need to learn to act graciously—no matter what. A little imagination helps when you feel as though you're being attacked. If you can imagine that you are a grand "Lady of the Manor" in whose mouth butter wouldn't melt, you will be less likely to be drawn into combat. As a child you were probably advised not to "sink to the level" of taunters, and this advice still serves. Adopting a gracious and cool role in answer to the volcanic eruptions of an unreasonable woman will make you feel better about yourself and set a better example for your stepchildren.

No Brownie Points from "Her"

Most mothers without custody either surrendered it willingly or did not contest their children's desire to change living arrangements. Despite that fact, most stepmothers felt that those mothers never considered them as anything more than temporary caretakers of "their children." This feeling also is probably responsible for much of the rage stepmothers feel. And it's not just their imagination. One of these mothers actually verbalized what the stepmother had assumed she felt all along: "She can raise them, if that makes her happy. They'll come to me when they're all grown up."

Coping with Inconsistency

Despite the lack of actual onstage presence in her children's lives, the biological mother is often an active "presence," orchestrating her relationship with her children from the wings. The biological mother's level of involvement is also generally sporadic. Only a few of the surveyed stepmothers reported that their stepchildren visited with their mothers on a regular basis. It was more common for there to be no contact whatsoever than for regular visitation. The most typical involvement is a random pattern of telephoning.

Mothers who had been totally absent from their children's lives often reappeared shortly after the stepmother's wedding. Often this increased involvement was short-lived; the pattern that predated the stepmother's appearance tended to resume within time.

When Debbie married and became a stepmother to Theresa, the eight-year-old had not seen or heard from her biological mother in seven years. Her only contact from her mother was the card she received on her birthday each year. However, within five months of Debbie's marriage, Terry's mother resurfaced, moved back to town, and began exercising her legal prerogative for weekend visitation— seeing Terry every other weekend. After six months of rather strained visits, one day she failed to show up. She did not reappear for the next six years.

Most cases are not as extreme as Debbie's. Michelle's case is more typical. When Michelle married, Brian and Steven, her two step-sons, had no weekly meetings with their mother, though she lived nearby. Their contact with her was limited to occasional holiday visits and two weeks in the summer. However, when Michelle became a stepmother, the boys' mother sought to replicate the visitation schedule that Michelle's daughters had with *their* father: If Michelle's daughters saw their father for dinner each week, she wanted to see Brian and Steven for dinner; if Michelle's daughters spent a weekend with their father, she wanted Brian and Steve. After several weeks, dinners began to be canceled. Months would go by when she would see the boys only at an occasional school sporting event. Visitation has now returned to the pattern that predated Michelle's marriage.

Stepmothers struggling to build a relationship are upset by such inconsistency. Changes in patterns of visitation make planning difficult and threaten a stepmother's sense of control within her new family. Women who are struggling to adjust to major changes in lifestyle and increased child-care responsibilities may find that they have little patience with biological mothers who rearrange visitation for personal convenience, jealousy, or whim.

It's Hard on the Kids

Except in the cases of very young children, stepchildren were often ambivalent, apathetic, or apologetic about their relationship with their mothers. These attitudes can make it difficult for stepmothers and fathers to help them through this troubled period. In addition, stepchildren may sense or imagine that positive feelings for their mothers are unacceptable to the new family. Faced with the choice between rocking the boat in pleasant waters or braving the hostile territory of a rejecting mother, many children retreat. Stepmothers reported that children were frequently apathetic or reluctant to talk about their mothers. Many times children chose to move away from any relationship at all with their mothers, refusing visits and needing to be coaxed to the telephone to receive her calls. Often they would throw away or quickly hide letters or cards their mothers had sent to them. Trying to avoid trouble or painful emotions is understandable in a child; for the stepmother, it is a danger signal she must recognize—and respond to.

Stepmothers were eloquent in their descriptions of the "push-me-pull-you" tactics of their stepchildren's mothers—and the children themselves.

The Telephone—a Handy Weapon

The telephone was the most often reported vehicle of harassment. Many stepmothers spoke of telephone calls—sometimes numbering twenty or thirty a day—that were either unpleasant in nature or hang-ups immediately when the stepmother answered. Telephone calls at inconvenient and intrusive hours, in the middle of the night, in early morning hours, and at other times when the intent of the call was obviously to harass rather than communicate were frequently reported. Such harassment cannot be handled in the ways available to the general public. Stepmothers cannot hang up when they hear *her* voice or change to an unlisted phone number; biological mothers are usually entitled by law to have telephone access to their children. Similarly bothersome to stepmothers is the scenario where the mother ignores her existence, hanging up when she hears the stepmother's voice or asking for the children or the husband without even giving her a cursory "Hello."

Susie's stepchildren are both of preschool age. Susie finds herself growing increasingly uncomfortable as her husband continues spending his evenings listening to her stepchildren's mother complain about her poor sex life over the telephone. Susie is beginning to grow resentful as she continues her nightly ritual of bedtime reading while such conversations are taking place!

In one extreme case reported, the biological mother is actually in prison! She uses her allotted phone calls to harass her children's new stepmother, Linda, speaking directly to Linda about "the children and what they need and what their father doesn't provide for them." It is not difficult to understand why Linda would like to tell this woman to "butt out."

Betty, a teacher in her thirties, is frustrated by attempts to undermine her authority. When she married almost two years ago her husband's two girls, aged nine and seven, joined her own two boys who were then eight and five. Betty states that initially her relationship with her stepdaughter's mother was "great." The mother had left the family to "find herself" (a la Kramer vs. Kramer). Then, suddenly, she seemed to become threatened and began to cause trouble by undermining Betty's authority with the girls through constant phone calls. Although this mother has stated repeatedly that she isn't the mothering type and that the girls *are* better off with Betty, she continues to intrude in Betty's relationship with the girls. Betty speaks for many stepmothers when she says, "Be a mother or let me do it."

AVOIDING THE TRAPS

Sensing their lack of power and control, stepmothers may risk becoming obsessive about their stepchildren's biological mothers if they are not careful. Beware of tactics that don't work:

Denial of Her Existence

Some stepmothers try to cope by ignoring the biological mother's very existence. This only serves to exacerbate the tension when the mother does resurface; denying her existence is untrue and erodes the stepmother's control and credibility. On the practical level it means that each new reappearance necessitates a new readjustment—and that is very wearing.

Bottling Up Feelings

Hiding feelings doesn't work either; the tension is still there even when the reasons for the "vibrations" are hidden. Husbands react negatively to this tension, and stepchildren are especially attuned to the stress that their stepmother feels. Resentment, disapproval, anger, and other negative emotions are hard to disguise and rarely hidden. Meredith thought she was doing a good job putting on a good face until her two teenaged stepchildren confided to a family member that their stepmother would have "cleaning fits" whenever their mother telephoned.

Pretending

Many stepmothers feel that they must maintain a civil or even pleasant facade to a woman for whom they harbor no pleasant feelings. Many feel that they must tolerate or even encourage relationships that are nearly impossible for them to maintain in the face of their strong negative feelings. Such stepmothers often feel isolated, angry, resentful, frustrated, and overwhelmed, and run the risk of suffering extreme stress. It's better to admit that you don't like your stepchildren's mother and limit your efforts to bare-bones politeness.

Nora is a thirty-eight-year-old stepmother. She and her husband have been married for nine and a half years and have raised Nora's son from a previous marriage. During the course of their marriage, arranging visitation with Bill's sons was always a problem. The boys lived in another state, and the logistics of arranging convenient times and accommodating the boys on short notice were always problematic. The visits were problematic, too: Bill's boys were destructive and had a different set of values concerning property and lifestyle than Nora's.

Six months ago one of Bill's sons, who was the same age as Nora's son, decided to live with them. Actual problems have been minimal, but Nora is feeling a tremendous amount of stress because she's been trying to hide her negative feelings toward the woman who brought up her stepson so badly. Her anger is barely contained. "I think she's the poorest example of motherhood, of womanhood, of humanity that I've ever come across. Her existence has caused more chaos, grief, and upset in my marriage than anything else. She has affected my life emotionally, financially, and psychologically. She has created trauma for the children and for my husband. . . . But I *can't*," continues Nora, "*ever* speak badly about her in front of the children, although I choke on having to be polite to such a woman."

Nora won't find relief from stress as long as she forbids herself to express her negative feelings. Like Nora, many stepmothers suffer from extreme stress when they try to act in ways that run counter to their deepest convictions and perceptions. Stepmothers almost unilaterally agree that they should try to avoid saying negative things about their stepchildren's mothers. In some cases these attempts border on the ludicrous, such as when Ellen states, "She is a horrible excuse for a human being," then adds quickly, "but I would never express these feelings to my stepchildren." Stepmothers confronting the challenge of coexisting with the mentally ill or socially deviant mothers of their stepchildren try to avoid discussing unpleasant circumstances—such attempts include the same type of impossible irony as asking Mrs. Lincoln, "But aside from the assassination, how was the play?"

The Urge to Overprotect

Sheila, an attractive woman in her early forties, has decided to help her two stepdaughters have a happy childhood. She makes up stories and "covers" for her stepdaughters' mother, an alcoholic who is consistent only in her inconsistency. Sheila describes how she tells scores of white lies to protect the girls from disappointment, even pretending to receive phone calls from the girls' mother explaining her inability to arrive for visitations. For the past six years, Sheila's stepdaughters have never had a birthday that their mother remembered *but, they don't know that:* Sheila has shielded the girls from this disappointment by sending cards and presents in their mother's name. Sheila's dark eyes flash as she states that "her stepdaughters are going to have the best mother possible. Even if I have to invent her." This scenario needs no comment; Sheila should know better than to try to deny reality. Such covering up only prevents the girls from developing the skills they will need to cope with their mother as she really is.

No one would suggest that stepmothers give license to their personal resentment or insecurities and lash out at their stepchildren's mothers. On the other hand, it is vital that stepmothers be advocates for their stepchildren. To stand idly by, not saying anything when a mother behaves badly, just because she is the mother, gives unwarranted power to a title and further confuses the child by validating the mother's inappropriate behavior. Somewhere, somehow, a stepmother must strike a balance.

WHAT TO DO?

Sometimes, Nothing!

What can you do about inappropriate, provocative, frustrating, or otherwise maddening behavior? Nothing. Nothing can be done to change someone else's behavior. You can gain a tremendous amount of relief by letting go of the things you can't change and taking charge of what you can: Your own behavior! Don't use your problems with your stepchildren's mother as a convenient "hanger" for anything else that's going wrong in your life or your marriage; being obsessed with someone else's behavior diminishes your control and sidesteps important issues, including the issue of how your stepchildren and their mother will build their *own* relationship.

Given the anger and hostility many stepmothers expressed, you'd almost think they wished there were *no* relationship between their stepchildren and their biological mothers. Although a few step-mothers did fantasize about a complete severance of all contact, most had very different hopes in mind: They wanted noncustodial mothers to learn to be more consistent in their affection; they wished their stepchildren could receive consistent love and support; they strongly desired visitation that was constant and dependable. Stepmothers also hoped those mothers would eventually be open to receiving regular communication and be competent enough to answer the tough questions children posed about their behavior. In a word, stepmothers wanted the mothers to act responsibly.

Stepmothers wanted the children to have a solid, sane relation-ship with their mothers, even when this conflicted with their own personal emotions and interests. Stepmothers seek happiness for their stepchildren; and if this happiness involves contact with their biological mothers, so be it.

Stepmothers have learned, through their commitment to their stepchildren, that it is possible to love different people in different ways. There is plenty of love to go around: More love for the child's mother does *not* mean less love for the stepmother.

Long ago Judge Solomon decided that the true mother was the woman who had the best interests of the baby at heart—but *you* are not a judge. You may have the best of intentions when you decide to foster the mother's relationship with her children, but *beware*: you cannot assume control for someone else's actions. You cannot *give* your stepchildren a good relationship with their mother. You can only be truly responsible for your own relationship with the chil-dren. The success or failure of the mother's relationship with her child is *her* responsibility.

The bottom line is this: *Do* take charge of your own behavior, but *don't* try to play God—or judge—toward others.

Take Charge of Your Own Life

Karen, a thirty-five-year-old former bartender, is an extraordinary example of the damage that passivity can cause. Karen became a stepmother to *two* sets of stepchildren. She didn't know that the second set was coming to live with her new family until two months after her marriage, when her husband said he "must have forgotten" to tell her. Karen's four stepchildren, a girl and three boys, range in age from five to thirteen. When she married, the two oldest children were in their father's custody because their mother is mentally ill. The two younger boys arrived unexpectedly because *their* mother "just couldn't handle them" and had a boyfriend who didn't feel like having children around. Karen often feels like a warden to her stepchildren—or a servant. Her stepchildren call her by her first name or refer to her as "the stepmother." There is an almost eerie sense of detachment and resignation running through Karen's responses. She refers to her stepchildren's mothers as "Wife Number 1" and "Wife Number 2," or "The Mothers."

Although Karen has total responsibility for all child-care, she is told what she may and may not do by Wife Number 2 and receives no help from her husband who is, in her words, "usually not home." Karen talks to the mentally ill mother every morning on the telephone. Although these calls are time-consuming and often unpleasant, and are of no benefit to the children, Karen seems unwilling to take charge and make changes in the routine.

To make matters worse, Karen has been told by her husband that she may not have a baby as "she has enough children already." He recently gave away her dog because one of the children didn't like it. He gave away her parakeet because he didn't like its chirping. Karen was sad, but she said nothing.

Karen is an example of the extremes that passivity can lead to. If a stepmother is to be happy and successful in her role, she must take charge of her own life.

Don't "Take Over" for Your Husband

Stepmothers need not agree to perform their husband's unpleasant tasks. Many stepmothers reported that, despite their own personal feelings, the task of communicating with the children's mother often fell to them, either because they were simply more readily available due to personal schedule or because communication between the mother and father was impossible—or unwanted. Whatever the reason, acting as a liaison with the biological mother is usually uncomfortable and stressful for a stepmother.

One woman stated, "My husband doesn't feel it is necessary or appropriate to talk to her." This husband probably speaks for many men who assume they are demonstrating their commitment to their new marriages by totally alienating their children's mothers. This is a well-intentioned gesture. However, we all know what road is paved with good intentions. The stepmother who is forced to serve as a go-between for her stepchildren and their mother can also expect to build a tremendous amount of resentment.

Another stepmother spoke of being required to drive her children to meet their mother in a town two hundred miles from her home because her husband refused to even "look at the woman" and the mother didn't "feel like seeing anybody in the old neighborhood." The children would look forward to their "sleepovers" and Toni could not stand to see them disappointed by their battling parents. Toni felt that she really was in a no-win situation. If she didn't "volunteer" to drive the children to their visit, she would have to tell them they couldn't go; yet the stress involved in these trips was eventually too much to handle.

Toni was given explicit instructions by the children's mother, who didn't want to have to "look at her face"; she was told exactly where to park and precisely what time to arrive at the meeting place which was changed each weekend. Instructions were delivered early in the week and revised and repeated during subsequent endless telephone conversations until the weekend arrived. Toni found herself spending weekend after weekend hovering in a series of parking lots, waiting with her two young stepchildren for the sight of the mother's silver sports car. When the car was spotted, the children would leap from the car and run to meet their mother before she would have to look at their stepmother; the children, at ages five and seven, thought this was all great fun. Toni drove the two hundred miles home alone, only to return the next evening to repeat the process in reverse, welcoming two invariably red-eyed and silent children. One day, on the lonely return trip, Toni broke her grueling routine and did not go straight home. Instead she spent the day walking along the shore—and thinking. By the end of the day she had made some critical decisions about her future: she decided to stop assuming total responsibility for those trips. She and her husband entered counseling and began to deal with the visitation in a way that did not threaten their marriage and Toni's self-esteem.

Stop Competing for the "Mother" Title

Some stepmothers are engaged in a never-ending battle; they resent the unconditional love granted the biological mother regardless of her actions or attitudes. Let it go! You're the one who's on the job each day. Take charge of *your* relationship with your stepchildren—concentrate on that.

Accept Unequal Financial Responsibility

Sometimes stepmothers must tighten their belts because of the large alimony payments their husbands make. Often they resent the fact that a husband is required to pay child support for children who live with the biological mother, whereas the mother has no financial responsibility for her children who live with their father and step-mother.

The inequality of financial responsibility goes hand-in-hand with the imbalance of responsibility for child-care. Stepmothers are often frustrated by the courts' failure to review the noncustodial mother's financial responsibility for children. Although the law provides for both parents to assume financial responsibility for children, it is rare for a noncustodial mother either to assume or be required to provide any sort of financial contribution.

Unless the stepmother wishes to devote a good portion of her time and finances to "fighting the system," she must accept the unpleasant fact that such issues are outside her control, step away from the problem, and concentrate on enhancing her own role within the family.

Focus on the Present

What is happening *now*? Certainly no one is suggesting that you try to wipe out the past, but dealing with the present is more productive, though sometimes more difficult. Perhaps your husband was an "ostrich," ignoring inappropriate behavior in his former family. So what? Soap operas are popular with the general public for a good reason: They are titillating. It's fun to follow a stormy story, day by day. You may be tempted to succumb to the soap opera of your husband's past life, but it's far healthier for you to continue asking yourself, "What does this have to do with life *now*?" Remember: *You* are more likely to be able to keep the past in perspective than he is. One of the reasons men marry again is for a new start: Unless past behavior directly affects what you're doing now, help your husband to "retire" his past and to live more happily in his new present—with you.

Callie was thirty when she became a stepmother to three preteen children. A social worker by profession, she was certain that she could successfully integrate her three stepchildren into her life and that she, her husband, and the new baby who arrived a year later could form a new family. Callie was unprepared to learn that her stepchildren had been sexually abused by their mother throughout their childhoods. Callie was protective and supportive of her stepchildren's disclosures to her; she welcomed their trust and set about getting therapy for all the children. Callie found that her condemnation of the mother's behavior raised uncomfortable questions about her husband's role. Why, she wondered, had her husband failed to recognize the signs? Why didn't her stepchildren confide in their father at the time?

Callie began to live in her husband's past. As she became increasingly familiar with the specifics of the children's abuse and their fears, Callie began to question her husband's lack of intervention. Although he owned up to his responsibility and apologized to the children privately and in family therapy, Callie's respect for him was seriously threatened. Her obsession with his past began to erode her marriage and spill over into her relationship with her stepchildren. Callie grew increasingly unable to deal with present situations and to accept her husband as a caring father and husband who had changed from his former role of absentee father. Although he had changed and was now eager and able to be a much better parent, Callie's obsession with his behavior almost destroyed a perfectly functional marriage and stepfamily. Callie, and all other stepmothers, must learn to "let go of the past."

Set Your Own Limits

Stepmothers *can* control the manner in which they will be treated by others, biological mothers included. There is no excuse for wimpiness. In order to receive respect from others, you must be self-respecting. One needs only to remember Toni and Karen, and other stepmothers like them who subjected themselves to humiliating dictates by unreasonable women who were probably only testing the waters. You must learn to take charge of your own behavior and set limits on the kinds of behavior you will—and will not—accept from others.

So You've Married a Widower

A stepmother whose husband is a widower must deal with a completely different set of concerns from those faced by women who marry divorced men. First they feel a confused mixture of emotions in reference to their departed predecessor, secretly perceiving her as an unassailable competitor. Often, stepmothers are plagued by guilt and discomfort or shamed by their inexplicable feelings of resentment and jealousy for a woman who is no longer alive. Because of social or religious taboos, stepmothers often feel uncomfortable about voicing their negative feelings.

The death of a mother does not end her relationship with her children. The stepmother must confront the "presence" of the biological mother every day as she deals with the children. She must, in addition, deal with her own feelings about mortality and ritual as they relate to her new marriage, and she must confront the challenge of helping her stepchildren—and perhaps her husband—through any unfinished grieving or unresolved issues.

Any stepmother, by nature of her role, is bound to feel a bit shaky. For stepmothers who have married widowers, the climate for insecurity is ripened. When a woman marries a divorced man she can calm her insecurity with the very real knowledge that her husband's presence implies his choice of her as a partner, no matter who initiated his former separation. Marrying a widower is different; stepmothers are often plagued by the nagging and unanswerable question, "Would he have ever married me?" The practical answer to this question is probably no. A stepmother usually follows a marriage that was viable. If her husband's marriage was a happy one, she may need to accept his reminiscing without feeling threatened. The stepmother must not plague herself with questions about what would have happened if "she" had not died, but should try to live in the present and look forward to the future.

WHAT TO EXPECT

A certain natural idealization takes place when a loved one dies. Stepchildren, husband and many of the people who now inhabit the stepmother's world may idealize the biological mother.

LIVING WITH A SAINT

Many stepmothers in this situation believed that they would have had an easier time of it if their stepchildren's mother were still living. Stepmothers described time and time again how difficult it was to live with the notion of a departed "saint."

Miriam, a twenty-nine-year-old federal security guard, has been a stepmother for almost three years. Her stepson and stepdaughter are now fifteen and nineteen; their mother died six years ago. Living in the shadow of a "deceased mother" is a discomfort for Miriam, a deeply religious woman. The stepdaughter is away at college but her behavior during vacations is causing Miriam to dread her visits. The moment the girl arrives home she inspects the house for any "changes." If something has been moved, she flies into a rage, reminding Miriam that her mother "worked hard to buy a house and nice things for her kids." Miriam understands that her stepdaughter misses her mother and is having a hard time adjusting to her father's marriage, but she is beginning to resent the tension her stepdaughter brings home with her. Miriam's husband is a mild-mannered man who tells her just to go ahead and do what she wants with the house. But when the shouting starts, he has a way of disappearing.

Miriam illustrates the plight of many stepmothers who try to respect their stepchildren's fond memories without going underground themselves. Despite her best intentions, she is still hurt and frustrated by her stepdaughter's unrelenting disapproval. Miriam lives like a shadow in the house of her predecessor, working to contribute to the mortgage payments, fearful of changing so much as the faded bathroom wallpaper. Miriam's resentment grows.

What Miriam hasn't realized yet is that this is *her* problem. Her stepdaughter is managing to get on with her life; she is doing well in college and plans to move to her own apartment when she graduates. Miriam's guilt and discomfort get in the way of her living *her* own life, and making her home her own, both literally and figuratively.

Houses are a big issue for this group of stepmothers. Houses are repositories of memories and commitments and providers of physical reminders of the departed mother. Stepmothers are sensitive to the nostalgia of their stepchildren and their very real pain. However, there is a middle ground between enshrinement of the family home and throwing everything in the trash. Stepmothers can help their stepchildren shift their attention to items that are portable and movable and can become real keepsakes of their mother's memory.

Stepchildren need to believe that their mother's memory is not being erased. Children who have lost their mothers are typically very resistant to change of any kind. Any proposed substitution of furnishings or decor may seem to be an attempt at total erasure of their mother. You can help your stepchildren and yourself come to terms with the past by striking a balance between retaining the memories of the past and moving forward into the future.

LOOK FOR THE SIGNS—AND READ THEM

Your appearance as a mother figure can trigger all sorts of discomfort and unfinished business in your stepchildren. Those who were ten or older at the time of their mother's death may have failed to go through the grieving process. Older children frequently are not given an opportunity to grieve when their mothers die. Such children typically assume a "responsible" role for their father and other family members. Many children lose their "childhoods" with the death of their mother, as they assume adult responsibilities. It is not uncommon for children, especially girls, to undertake the care of the home and younger children. Such a child may resent the appearance of a stepmother and the loss of her own adult role in the family. The wise stepmother can be instrumental in giving one of life's greatest gifts to this child: She can give back the child's stolen childhood by lifting those inappropriate adult responsibilities from the child's shoulders.

WHAT TO DO?

Build a Present History

When a stepmother can share her own history, she becomes more comfortable about accepting her husband's and stepchildren's history, which includes the history of the deceased mother. Unlike the living noncustodial mother, she does not have to be made a villain in order for the family to function smoothly. Nor does she have to be canonized as a saint.

When a stepmother can make the deceased mother part of her own history by learning about her, by listening when others speak of her, she will feel more in control and more secure in her relationship with her new family.

When You Can't Confront "Her" . . .

The biggest problem facing the stepmother is the societal taboo against speaking negatively of the dead. Stepmothers will probably find a friendlier ear and an easier conscience if they speak about their own feelings and reactions. A stepmother who has just been told by her mother-in-law that "Lois always baked the loveliest cookies for Thanksgiving" might confide that she feels hurt when always being compared to Lois. Such a stepmother might find, to her surprise, that the mother-in-law had not intended to make a comparison. Because stepmothers are afraid to speak out, they often find themselves living in someone else's past instead of their own present.

Help Your Stepchildren Deal with Their Grief

You cannot erase the past, but you *can* modify it. You can be of enormous help to stepchildren who have had to deal with death at an early age. These children have suffered an unparalleled trauma. The person with whom they shared the closest of human bonds, and in whom they probably placed the bulk of their trust, suddenly and irrevocably vanished from their lives.

Many children harbor unresolved feelings of grief for their mothers. Older children may have been too "busy" and responsible to grieve; younger ones may never have been given the opportunity to talk about their mother and to grieve for her. Relatives and well-meaning friends are often uncomfortable with the pain of children and choose to shield them from sadness. Sometimes they mistakenly assume—or hope—that the children are "too young to understand." Your younger stepchildren may have been told a bunch of euphemisms: Their mother "went to sleep" or "went to live with God" or "went away on a long trip." Most young children are not taken to funerals or urged to partake in any of the traditional rituals attendant to death in our culture—rituals which were designed, in part, to help us cope with the death of a loved one. You will inherit the results of this lack of grieving. Simply put, your presence confirms the fact that "Mother is *never* coming home."

Assume Responsibility Gradually

Some stepmothers seem to have an easy time of it—at least at first. Stepmothers must be careful that they do not find themselves imprisoned in the good intentions of their stepchildren. Charlotte was such a stepmother. Later in life she married a man with teenage daughters. After months of visiting the girls and her fiancé at his home, she was certain that their relationship would be smooth and problem-free. However, Charlotte soon discovered that she was treated as a visitor after her marriage as well as before. Charlotte was not "permitted" by her stepdaughters to assume any responsibility in the home. She was not "permitted" to cook or arrange furniture—even the flowers her husband occasionally brought to her were whisked away and arranged by one of the girls. Any suggestions Charlotte made about redecorating, meal-planning, or possible vacation trips were greeted by polite silence. It quickly became clear to her that she had moved into a shrine created and maintained by her stepdaughters. If she had not taken matters firmly into her hands, gradually making her place known, she might still be living in her "gilded cage."

Encourage Conversation

A stepmother can help make her husband and children of all ages comfortable by including conversation about the deceased mother as part of everyday talk. Encourage your stepchildren to share their memories and their history. You can help your stepchildren overcome the feeling that their mother's life is being "erased" by encouraging the cherishing of personal keepsakes. Furniture that the stepchild desires can be stored away, but only when the child is ready to part with it. Sometimes a stepmother can help by weaning an attachment for large household items to smaller personal items—for example, from a dining room set to "Mother's candlesticks."

Share the Memories

Stepmothers can take their children to the grave site, suggest they write a story about their mother, take them to church to light a candle or to synagogue to say a memorial prayer, or help them to go through any other rituals that encourage them to experience the grieving process they may have skipped.

Doreen has a close and loving relationship with her four step-children. She has been a stepmother for the past eight years and appreciates the gratifying results of her stepchildren's loving child-hood. Doreen would love to meet the woman who gave birth to these wonderful children. As the years go on, she often wishes that she could have known her stepchildren's mother. Doreen has found a way to integrate the memory of this woman into her own life as a sort of "guardian angel."

Living with the memory of the children's mother is much more practical than spending time and energy pretending she didn't ever exist.

Do Not Compete

Obviously it is impossible to compete with someone who is no longer living, but many stepmothers try to do just that. Try to avoid any attempt to replace or replicate a departed mother. There is no sense in competing. Children can, and do, come to love their step-mothers deeply and with real and deserved affection. Spoiling this genuine affection by comparison with an idealized mother can only bring disappointment and frustration for everyone.

CHAPTER 11

The New Baby

What does a stressed-out, overworked, and in many cases over-whelmed woman need? A baby!

Stepmothers described a powerful desire to add a baby to their family. Why? Some had never had a child before; of course they wanted one now! Some couples desired a "nuclear" family experience: "his-mine-and-ours." Others felt that a baby would cement or legitimatize the new family, as if the marriage would not be taken seriously until the new couple had produced a child of their own.

The Need to Be Called "Mommy"

Some stepmothers simply felt the pull of biology, despite their previous negative feelings about child-bearing. It's hard to compre-hend the extent that day-to-day child-care plays in such a decision. Stepmothers who have been mothers approach motherhood in a sort of backwards fashion: Expected to assume responsibility for nurturing and rearing their stepchildren, they often begin to operate competently but with a marked feeling of "Is this all there is?" Those who enthusiastically jump into child-rearing find that they handled the responsibility well but yearn for the reciprocal love and affection that is missing from their relationships with their stepchildren. Often, this yearning leads to the desire to bear a child. Stepmothers who feel satisfied and fulfilled in their relationship with their stepchildren wanted a baby of their own, too: They are eager to undertake child-rearing from the beginning, with an infant. Then, of course, there are many childless stepmothers who simply want a baby because they've never had one. For these women, the decision to marry often was made with the strong intention of having a baby. Such stepmothers tend to see any existent stepchildren as "incidental" and are actually at great risk for feeling put-upon and resentful when the reality of *living* with children, rather than "entertaining them until the baby arrives" sets in.

HUSBANDS—SOMETIMES NOT SO SURE

Some husbands seem absolutely delighted to begin the fathering experience again. Many find that they are more financially secure than when their older children were born and that they have more leisure time to spend with their babies. Other fathers are less enthusiastic about the prospect of parenting. These men look forward to a romantic marriage that will grow in intimacy as their older children leave home, or are reluctant to experience the stresses of fathering again due to problems in their previous marriage or a fear of creating stress for their existing children.

The simple, commonsense approach for any woman contemplating marriage is to discuss the possibility of children before marriage. If having babies is important to her, she should clarify this issue before she walks down the aisle. It is not feasible to assume that a man with children will want to have more children. If, on the other hand, a woman does not want to have children, she may be foolish to assume that a man who already has children has ended his urge to be a father; he may be eager to have a baby with *her*. The prospect of adding children to a family is too important to be left unexplored.

A CHILD OF "OUR OWN"

For a stepmother who has been married previously and has borne children, a new and happy marriage may suggest a different brand of parenting. Involved in a committed relationship, she may feel a need to create a child that will belong only to her and her new husband. Couples with children from former marriages must share their children with others—the noncustodial parents. A new baby offers another chance—a chance to nurture a child within the confines of the couple relationship only, without the complexities of visitation and extended family relationships that have been severed by divorce. A husband is nearly as likely to feel this pull toward parenthood as is a wife.

A BABY "CEMENTS" A FAMILY

Some stepmothers spoke of the need for a child as if the new baby would "cement" and unify the family mixture. A baby would create a biological tie between stepchildren, stepparents, and stepsiblings, thereby creating a real connection among the family members. Many stepmothers also spoke of giving the family a feeling of legitimacy. Virtually all stepmothers who had had a new baby reported that a baby DID, indeed, give the family a feeling of togetherness and cohesiveness that had been lacking. More important was the stepmother's fulfillment of the need to love openly. After a period of perhaps strained or conflicted feelings toward stepchildren, these women welcomed the luxury of being able to love unconditionally.

Stepmothers frequently mentioned the need to have a baby all of their own, the need to be called "Mommy," the need, perhaps, to be accepted by a tiny, nonjudgmental human being who did not have to be shared with any other mother figure.

At twenty-eight, Judy married for the first time and became a stepmother to her husband's two preteen children. Within two years she and her husband decided to add a baby to their family. Judy seemed to speak for many stepmothers when she said, "I needed so badly to love *freely*. I was a wounded and rejected stepmother and I felt the new baby would pull us all together as a real family. I think that has happened to some extent."

Connie had raised her stepdaughter for six years before she had a powerful desire to become a "real" mother. Connie stated that "I think now I wanted to be "legal." She was surprised to discover that her feelings for her infant son did not surpass the intense feeling she had for her eight-year-old stepdaughter. Connie said that she "often

felt guilty that I didn't love him more than I loved my stepdaughter."
Connie was surprised that her feelings for her infant son were not
immediate; she needed to get to know him first.

Anticipating the Response

FROM YOUR STEPCHILDREN

"When the baby came home from the hospital, Timmy wanted to
pick her up right away to soothe her. I felt very good about that.
Later, he'd get mad when he was asked to feed her when I was busy.
I was disappointed."

"John loves having a baby brother, although sometimes he cries
too much. I explain that babies need to cry. The most negative
reaction was John being upset that he couldn't do more with the
baby. We helped John find more ways he could help."

"Jenny spends time with the baby and loves her very much. Her
teacher told me that Jenny acted as if the baby were hers. Jenny calls
him 'my' baby."

FROM YOUR HUSBAND

The big news is really no surprise: Fathers who were generally uninvolved with their first set of children continued to be uninvolved
with the new baby. This was a source of great disappointment for
women who felt that their husbands would be very different with a
child from the new marriage—a child of their "own." These stepmothers seemed to have forgotten that their stepchildren *are* their
husband's "own" children. Although there were several cases where
fathers became much more involved with later additions than with
their older children, this was the exception rather than the rule. Very
few leopards seemed to change their spots.

FROM YOURSELF

Stepmothers found that they were more relaxed with their stepchildren after the arrival of the new baby. This probably has far less
to do with anything mystical or psychological than with the simple

fact that there is less time for "harping," as one stepmother put it. "Comfortable, relaxed, less strict, easy, casual." These words were often repeated when stepmothers relayed what had changed in their families after the arrival of the new baby. There seemed to be a general release in tension, perhaps because the birth of a baby signaled the end of the period of trying so hard to prove they were "mothers." Now, they *really* were.

INCREASED CONFIDENCE

Stepmothers also looked forward to and realized a sense of closeness with their babies that had been missing from their relationships with their stepchildren. Miranda, a stepmother with a new baby girl, expressed this sense of confidence. Even though her baby was just an infant, Miranda felt truly comfortable with her. Miranda verbalized a hidden suspicion of many stepmothers: She would feel more comfortable with her own child because, as she put it, "She has no choice but to stay with me."

INCREASED SENSE OF POWER

Many stepmothers seemed to relax with the feeling that they would be accorded unconditional rights to raise their new babies in the manner in which they saw fit. So many stepmothers mentioned the word "rights" when referring to their new babies that this need to raise a child without outside intrusion seems to be more than speculative.

LESS CONTROLLING

The advent of a baby encouraged the other children in the family to assume a more independent role. As Hillary stated, "When the new baby came I was so busy that I didn't have time to constantly remind my teenaged stepson to "take a jacket" or to "take out the garbage." Because the baby demanded so much of her time, the other children were expected to do more for themselves. This expectation seemed actually to lead to increased independence.

BONDING AS A FAMILY

Many, many stepmothers decided to have a baby with the idea that the baby would make everybody "feel like a family." And did that happen? The answer is YES! Stepmothers reported feeling "more secure," "more normal," even, as one stepmother stated, "more real."

Julie strongly felt that baby Iris had created a "blood tie" among members of the family that had not existed before her birth. "It's made the kids feel more a part of each other by sharing a blood tie in Iris. They can feel a little bit of each other in her. They are *all* brothers and sisters when Iris is discussed."

Women desired to have their "own" babies in an effort to meet strong emotional, psychological, and biological drives. These new babies at first seemed to carry a heavy load, to function as "glue" bonding together pieces of a family that didn't always fit. At first glance this may seem too tall an order for a baby, but these new-family babies seemed to meet this demand: Their arrival often relaxed household tensions and supplied a focus that everyone could share and enjoy.

CHAPTER 12

Special Occasions

Holidays, birthdays, anniversaries, and other special occasions are times when people share happiness in a traditionally accepted manner. For many people the thought of such special days may prompt visions of happy family faces smiling from the pages of photograph albums or flickering on a movie screen or a home videocassette. We are a culture of occasion celebrators. Brightly wrapped gifts and crinkly paper, flowers and candy on Mother's and Valentine's days. Holidays, birthdays, anniversaries, and personal events permit all of us to give in to our penchant for celebration. The dream of the happy family celebrating together is perhaps one of the most closely guarded "national treasures."

Stepmothers share this dream, too. Stepmothers revel in the Mother's Day bouquet, the lacy Valentine, the happy family around the laden holiday table. But alas, many stepmothers are disappointed and unhappy around holiday times, finding that what should be happy occasions are instead tests of their personal worthiness and collective validity as families. They find that traditions are largely defined by families and that differences in the "way things are done" can cause unnecessary complications. Special days, including stepmothers' birthdays, anniversaries, holidays, and that special nemesis for stepmothers, "Mother's Day," can be joyful events for stepmothers. But it takes some doing.

The handling of birthdays, anniversaries, achievement celebrations, and holidays is simply a matter of limit setting and taking charge. Stepmothers have to be sure of themselves and their right to happiness; stepchildren need to be made aware of expectations and should be protected from impossible decision making. Unacceptable behavior must not be tolerated. A hostile, sullen stepchild can ruin a celebration or a vacation. Set the limits, work as a team with your husband, and stick to your guns.

The stepmother who creates traditions will orchestrate the mood of those celebrations. She must always set the "tone" of the day. Stepmothers who define limits, avoid competition, and create their own traditions will avoid senseless wrangling and unnecessary tension and unhappiness.

What is a family if not a group of people with shared traditions? Traditions and celebrations weave together through time to create a unique family pattern. Stepmothers who accept the importance of traditions not only feel more in control of their lives but happier for this sharing of life's special events.

Getting Started

PLAN AHEAD

The easiest way to avoid disappointment is by setting up expectations before the event. Stepchildren have no psychic powers. If, for example, a stepmother would enjoy a "day off" on her birthday, it would be more helpful for her to announce, "Today is my birthday and I'm taking a day off" than to grumble through a day of chores. Many stepchildren may need reminding of birthdays and other special days. If your husband is not particularly diligent about reminding the children of special days, make a calendar with everyone's birthday or put a note on the refrigerator or bulletin board a few days before the event. It will save everyone a lot of unnecessary grief.

BY THE SAME RULES

In order for the stepmother and her stepchildren to form a "family" relationship they have to be playing by the same rules. Stepchildren need to know what is expected in order to feel safe and cooperative. The stepmother must always remember that she is the adult in this relationship, and adults are straightforward about what they want; they don't play games or expect miracles, as Lisa did. She kept silent about her birthday and "just hoped," letting an entire weekend pass without saying a word. Her husband and stepchildren went about their business, oblivious to her pain. As a result, Lisa lost the opportunity to celebrate her first birthday with her new family. She never mentioned her birthday to her stepchildren, and they had no way of knowing that this was her day. Her husband simply forgot. How much better for everyone if Lisa had announced, at some earlier point in the week, that she was having a birthday and wanted to celebrate it!

CREATING NEW TRADITIONS

In order to avoid disappointment and to keep holiday occasions happy, make them special. Stepmothers need to create their own family and personal traditions that are different from those celebrated by their stepchildren in the past. Creating new traditions that do not conflict with old ones serves three important purposes:

- The stepmother assumes control of the occasion;
- The stepchild will not feel that loyalties are being tested;
- The stepfamily begins to establish an exclusivity of its own rather than competing with the former family's rituals.

ACCOMMODATING THE NONCUSTODIAL MOTHER

When the children's mother is living nearby and visiting regularly, holidays may be particularly stressful. For her own happiness and the success of her relationship, the stepmother should try to avoid placing the children in a position of deciding between families. Any stepmother who has ever tried to decide between celebrating with the in-laws or with her own family will empathize with this dilemma—a dilemma that is intensified for children. Try to avoid shifting the child around from holiday to holiday. This will only give everyone the feeling of celebrating on alternate years. You and your new family can celebrate each holiday without tearing the child apart. Having a Thanksgiving feast on Friday instead of Thursday does not diminish the importance of the holiday. Some stepmothers suggested specific techniques. If the stepchild has other commitments for Thanksgiving dinner, the stepmother might choose to establish her own Thanksgiving dinner at an earlier or later day—and perhaps serve a goose instead of a turkey.

Celebrating Traditional and Other Holidays

BIRTHDAYS

Birthdays seem to be a particularly sensitive issue for stepmothers. For a stepmother who may feel shaky in her relationship with her stepchildren, a forgotten or disappointing birthday may rock self-confidence and be perceived as an outright attack. If you've always enjoyed birthday celebrations, these traditions must be explained to your stepchildren—and to your new husband. You should also think about starting *new* traditions with your stepchildren. Special dinners, treats, trips, presents, or rituals are fun for children of all ages. Any new way of celebrating can be introduced as just that: something new. Children may feel uncomfortable, at first, about a new way of celebrating, so take care that no one feels that the old way is being devalued.

THE ANNIVERSARY

The stepmother and father's anniversary is another area that may be particularly sensitive. She may perceive her stepchildren's response to the wedding anniversary as a statement of their feelings about the marriage and the family. The wedding anniversary in stepfamilies does indeed assume a different connotation than it does in biological families. The anniversary commonly marks the family beginning rather than honoring the couple's own relationship. Again, in order to avoid disappointment, set up expectations early—and keep plans simple. Remember that this is your wedding anniversary; there is really little need for the children to join in the celebration. The anniversary can be a good opportunity for a couple to reaffirm their feelings for each other—to do something alone. The anniversary does not have to be a family event. For stepparents who have fallen into the pattern of doing everything as a family, this is the one day that they may guiltlessly celebrate as a couple.

MOTHER'S DAY

Mother's Day is a real bugaboo for most stepmothers. It is perceived as the day on which they receive—or do *not* receive—recognition for "mothering" their stepchildren. Even the most level-headed stepmother may find herself swept away when a grade-schooler hands her a lopsided handmade Mother's Day card. A bouquet of flowers from a teenage stepson will melt the coolest stepmother's heart. Consciously or not, many stepmothers set up Mother's Day as the big test. Mother's Day becomes the day they receive their "grade" for the job they have been doing.

When stepchildren have a living mother, the holiday becomes more complicated: Mother's Day often serves to highlight the duality of a stepmother's role. Many stepmothers resent a role that involves acting as a mother all year, perhaps even being called "Mother" or "Mom" only to relinquish their stepchildren to a woman whose relationship is defined in biological or legal rather than emotional or practical terms. The more distanced the relationship between stepchildren and biological mothers, the greater the resentment felt by stepmothers in sharing or relinquishing the holiday.

A stepmother of two little girls, Sandra positively glows when she describes the "cards, kisses, hugs, and handmade gifts" she receives from her stepdaughters. However, her face quickly falls when she adds, "But when they have to—as part of the visitation agreement—go off with their mom, it hurts so much."

Of course it hurts. For a woman who has played "Mother" for 364 days of the year, it simply doesn't seem fair to release children on the day set aside to celebrate such dedication. And yet in some bizarre form of "fair play" the stepmothers themselves are often most reluctant to challenge the Mother's Day rights of the biological mother. They bend over backwards, almost literally stepping into the background so that the stepchildren can have their day with Mother. One solution to the pain of this day is shifting the celebration either to before or after the actual holiday. Your own Mother's Day celebration can be established as a tradition and celebrated every year.

Stepmothers must also find the strength to overrule unreasonable dictates of the biological mother that affect her relationship with her stepchildren. Mary's nine-year-old stepdaughter is afraid to commemorate Mother's Day with her stepmother because she claims "her mother would kill her." The mother in this case abandoned her child at eighteen months—the girl's mother had stayed out of contact until the child was seven. At that time the mother began phoning infrequently and had visited with the child two or three times.

This mother is clearly placing her child in an unfair position by her demands that she refrain from celebrating Mother's Day with her stepmother—yet despite the inherent unfairness the child is still painfully torn. What can a stepmother do to help the child deal with such unhealthy "guilt trips" without adding further guilt and confusion? You can remove yourself from the role of coconspirator by refusing to honor demands that result in discomfort for both you and your stepchild and by helping your stepchild understand that the responsibility for facilitating a relationship lies with the people *involved* in the relationship. A smart stepmother will respond to fears that "my mother will kill me if . . ." by suggesting that the mother communicate directly with the child's father. Children need to be taken out of the middle of such unpleasant demands. Mary could tell her stepdaughter, "I'm sorry your mother is upset that you will celebrate Mother's Day with us. Maybe she'll call me some time and talk to me about this." After a response such as this, the planning and enjoyment of the holiday can continue.

PRESERVING THE HOLIDAY SPIRIT

Whereas birthdays and Mother's Day highlight the individual stepmother, and anniversaries are special to the couple, other holidays seem to pinpoint feelings of family loyalty. In this respect, they are harbingers of tremendous discomfort. In a more perfect world everyone would be able to compromise. Unfortunately, holidays circumstances often force stepchildren and the adults in their lives to make choices.

Disappointment, hurt, anguish, anger—these are just some of the feelings stepmothers experience on days that are supposed to be happy occasions. Let's not kid ourselves: Stepchildren harbor a great deal of anger, and special occasions are ideal times to ventilate their negative feelings in front of an audience. Many stepchildren and their parents feel pulled in all directions around holidays and special occasions—occasions when their feelings of divided loyalty are most severely tested. If the children's biological mother is living, "where" the holiday is celebrated may be an issue, as well as "how." If the biological mother is no longer alive, memories of past holidays may cloud present attempts at celebration. Past traditions tend to assume a sacred quality, and the stepmother's efforts to add her own style may be rejected out of hand. Discussing your stepchildren's fears may relax them enough to accept a different way of celebrating. Assuring children that new traditions do not erase past memories may be a big help.

Many stepmothers spoke of the heartache of Christmas. Several stated that they had simply instituted different gift-giving traditions. For example, if stepchildren will be visiting their mother on Christmas Day, then the big stepfamily gift-giving ceremony could take place on Christmas Eve. For stepmothers who are fed up with bickering, tears, and resentment around Christmas time, Three Kings' Day, Boxing Day, or other gift-giving occasions may be borrowed from other countries and adopted as the traditional day of gift-giving.

Stepmothers who chose to delay their gift-exchanging until Three Kings' Day were pleased with their solution to this unwieldy problem. The Feast of Epiphany commemorates the first manifestation of Christ to the Gentiles, through the coming of the Magi. In the middle of the fourth century, when the Eastern Church began to adopt December 25 for Christ's nativity, the Western Church introduced the Feast of the Epiphany on January 6, giving primary importance to the visit of the Magi. Later Epiphany became popularly known as the Feast of the Three Holy Kings, especially in Catholic Europe.

Celebrating Three Kings' Day offers several advantages. Because it falls nearly a week after New Year's, the stepmother and her family will be able to enjoy an exclusivity of their holiday celebration. The stepchildren will most likely welcome the prospect of extending their Christmas celebration.

Other stepmothers celebrate Chanukah by selecting one day as their special day for gift-exchanging and a festive dinner and candle-lighting in the evening. Because this Feast of Lights spans an eight-day period, stepmothers can usually find one day that can be reserved for their family's special celebration.

The Feast of Passover, commemorating the Jewish exodus from Egypt and the journey through the desert to the "Promised Land," typically involves two large holiday dinners at the beginning and end of a period that encompasses eight days. Although the first seder (dinner) is accorded primacy over the second, it is again more beneficial for the stepmother and her family to modify a tradition than to haggle over winning the children for the first seder.

In addition to the "big-name" holidays, here are many, many additional ones of religious, national, and personal significance that can be elevated in importance within the stepfamily and celebrated in unique and consistent ways—Valentine's Day, Memorial Day, Halloween, "Moving-In Day," even Labor Day can be occasions for special family celebrations.

GRADUATIONS—CONFIRMATIONS—WEDDINGS— SPECIAL DAYS

Most stepmothers can come up with a list of very rational reasons why their stepchildren's mothers or maternal relatives don't "deserve" to attend various special events in their stepchildren's lives. However, such reasons are simply irrelevant. The stepmother need ask herself only one question when confronted with such occasions: Who is the *center* of the special event? If the answer is herself or her husband, then obviously the children's mother can be excluded. If the answer is the stepchild, then the best interests of the child must be primary. Who is graduating? Who is getting married, or receiving the honor, or rushing to the finish line, or making the speech? The stepchild is the focus of his own special event. Neither stepmother, nor biological mother, nor father, grandmother, grandfather, aunt, uncle, or little cousin is the focus of that person's special day. The committed stepmother is sensitive to her stepchild's wishes and puts aside petty competitiveness and jealousies. She is able to see how this event fits into the larger picture of her stepchild's life. Such a stepmother does not fall into the trap of perceiving such events as public validations of her role in her stepchild's life.

Stepmothers should not be excluded from events, but they should be gracious and loving enough to think about expanding traditional roles to include *all* desired participants. Two sets of parents may walk down the aisle before and after the bride; two women may respond to the "mother's" prayer at a boy's Bar Mitzvah ceremony. Stepmothers are instrumental in shining the limelight where it belongs—on the celebrating child.

Vacations

Vacation periods are often difficult to negotiate because these time periods are not always under the control of stepmothers and fathers. Vacation plans usually revolve around the adult's work schedules and the school and extracurricular schedules of the children involved. Given the fact that many different schedules are often involved, such plans can be difficult to arrange. In addition to the real problems posed by schedules that overlap or conflict, some adults may choose vacations as the time to "power trip," making planning seem almost impossible. Stepmothers and fathers may find, to their unpleasant surprise, that their vacation plans are continually undermined by the children's mother. This does not have to happen. Planning a vacation involving three or more adults and children is not simple, but it *is* possible. The safest rule is to *plan well in advance*. Because of the number of individuals involved and unforeseen problems that may crop up—such as illness or injury— *make contingency plans* as well. Imagine your worst-case scenario and plan how to have a happy vacation despite it!

Many stepmothers spoke of having their *own* vacation plans sabotaged by mothers who changed plans at the last moment, leaving the children stranded. Don't let a vacation be totally dependent on your stepchildren's mother. Make an alternate plan in case she backs out: Willing grandparents, camp, or live-in baby-sitters can be arranged long in advance.

Other stepmothers found enthusiasm for family vacations dampened when their stepchildren were pressured by their mothers to change their plans and vacation with *her*. Help stepchildren avoid guilty feelings by taking adult responsiblity for vacation plans. Communicate directly or by mail with the noncustodial mother confirming travel plans—and go!

CHAPTER 13

Legal and Financial Considerations

Although a full-time stepmother functions as the primary parent in her stepchildren's lives, she has in effect no legal relationship with her stepchildren. Stepmothers may clean up after the child at home, may administer the alcohol rubs and take temperatures at 4:00 A.M., but their caretaking does not legally empower them even to sign a consent form for a school outing. Stepmothers, despite their day-to-day involvement and the intensity of their relationship with their stepchildren, find themselves in a state of legal oblivion. As far as the law is concerned, stepmothers are nonpersons with neither rights nor responsibilities for their stepchildren.

In addition to the lack of a legal relationship to her stepchildren, stepmothers may unhappily discover that they are involved in protracted court battles—litigation that has either begun before or after their marriages. The extreme discomfort many stepmothers suffer as a direct result of protracted and often ugly court battles is an important contributing factor to the failure of many stepmothers' marriages. The very definition of a full-time stepmother implies that stepchildren are living with their father on a full-time basis; however, the legal custody of children is always subject to review and modification either by the father or the mother. Because custody and visitation are subject to changing circumstances, stepmothers often find that a good portion of the time they spend with their stepchildren has an undercurrent of ongoing litigation.

Custody

Most statistics put the recorded number of children living with fathers at about ten to eleven percent. (This figure may indeed be much higher, as many children live with their fathers without benefit of legal custody awards.) It is still much more common for children to live with their biological mothers in the event of divorce than with their fathers. Fathers seeking custody are frequently told that unless the biological mother is psychiatrically or physically incapacitated—confined to an institution or hospital—they would do better to save their time and money and forget a custody battle. In fact, one stepmother reported that her husband was given this advice despite the fact that the children's biological mother did *not* want custody!

BUT THINGS ARE CHANGING

As women enter the work force as the norm rather than the exception, and as divorce becomes increasingly more socially acceptable, the roles of motherhood and fatherhood are being redefined. The courts are beginning to reflect this phenomenon: In cases where fathers dispute the mother's right to custody, they are now winning a resounding 63 percent of the time. These changing custody decisions imply more full-time stepmothers on the horizon.

STEPMOTHER'S ROLE IN CUSTODY BATTLES

Many stepmothers describe custody battles as excruciatingly uncomfortable. Persistent legal action causes them to suffer the sensation of participating in their husband's ongoing and seemingly never-ending divorce action. The emotional devastation of divorce is a commonly acknowledged phenomenon; such devastation often escalates into a full-scale conflagration upon the introduction of a stepmother.

Stepmothers suffer from these courtroom battles on many levels. Their marriages suffer as the language and strategies of the courtroom seem to dominate their lives. Often stepmothers feel that their own lives are being put on hold until custody decisions are finally resolved. Stepmothers may resent the lack of attention given to the children they bear with their husbands, and may grow increasingly upset living with constant tension, feeling that their actions and relationships are monitored by the adversary attorneys. Indeed, stepmothers involved with their husband's custody battles may feel dominated by legal actions from which they are *excluded*— stepmothers are *not* part of custody battles which are treated as modifications of, and therefore tied to the original divorce action. Many stepmothers describe a blend of shame and frustration surrounding court-related issues.

Even if they have been living with and raising their stepchildren for *years*, stepmothers are often excluded from the courtroom proper—prevented even from witnessing events that will directly affect their own lives. Although they are often expected to make themselves available for various interviews and examinations related to the custody procedure, they will probably never be permitted to witness the presentation of these reports in court. Stepmothers may be excluded on the request of the biological mother from attendance within the court unless they are specifically named in the custody action. Since custody is usually tied to the original divorce action, the stepmother's name will not appear on the action. If custody *is* awarded, it will be awarded to the father only—not to the stepmother and father, together.

The very language of the courtroom may be hurtful to the average stepmother. Most custody issues are treated as modifications of previous separation and/or divorce agreements; the language of such custody actions is the language of divorce. Despite the passage of time and changing circumstances of the parties, the stepmother eerily discovers that her husband has been returned, for the purposes of the court, to the children's biological mother, who has now resumed the title of wife. A stepmother in court quickly feels invisible, troubled by the sensation that she is functioning in a time warp, living in a period that predates—and negates—her very existence as a wife and stepmother.

The stepmother exists on the edge of a sharply honed two-edged blade. If she attempts to support her husband and is committed to her stepchildren, she will necessarily find herself included in "living in her husband and stepchildren's past" in a way that is often humiliating.

WHAT TO EXPECT: COMMON CUSTODY PROCEDURES

Despite the statistics, stepmothers speak again and again about the tremendous amount of pain and emotional toll exacted by custody battles, battles that usually end with *everyone losing*! The courts have become fond of repeating the expression "best interests of the child" in attempting to arrive at custody decisions. However, the best interests of the child are terribly subjective. Who determines the criteria? The father? The biological mother? The new father/step-mother couple? The children? The court? In an attempt to decide, the court often attempts to garner as much "expert" opinion as possible. A custody battle may involve court-appointed forensic examination of all involved parties. These are individual interviews with a court-approved psychiatrist, usually at a state-regulated agency. In addition, the homes of both parties will usually be visited by a worker from the city or county social service agency: The children will be interviewed and reinterviewed and asked to state and restate their preference and reasons for such preference. A case can be made for interviewing anyone involved in the present or proposed life of the children, including teachers, friends, extended family members, friends of the children and *all* the parents, and religious and community leaders. These reports are submitted to a judge by the attorneys representing the biological mother and the father. Sometimes the children involved in this battle will be given a court-appointed attorney of their own who is supposed to represent their interests in court.

Unfortunately, many fathers, stepmothers, and biological moth-ers become embroiled in a battle that is in everyone's *worst* interest. The custody battle assumes a life of its own. Stepmothers speak of years of nonstop conversation about custody, legal ploys and maneuvers, and changing of attorneys. Often the months turn into years. As one veteran attorney at a New York family court confided, "The family court has two speeds: SLOW and STOP." However, while the reports are garnered, while the interviews continue, while the court appearances drag on, while the attorneys' fees mount (and good custody attorneys *are* expensive), children have a way of continuing to grow. And such battles take their toll on the way children grow. Custody battles become a way of life for these children. The stepmother and the father may find that they are helplessly "trapped in the past," never developing a life of their own. In this sad way, the present is sacrificed to the past.

For these reasons it is best to avoid the courts if at all possible. Too many fathers, stepmothers, and biological mothers enter the courts for the wrong reasons, seeking validation and confirmation of personal worth rather than any real legal recourse. Unless the father has a clear legal reason to enter litigation, try to keep him away from the court.

ARBITRATION

Arbitration is a much more expedient and satisfying route than the courtroom. The hiring of a professional mediator can resolve emotional issues in a way that is both more satisfying and more practically applicable. In addition, arbitration really gets to the core of the issues that are being fought and is less expensive in terms of time, money, and emotions.

Although arbitration and mediation may be a less painful route for resolving custody and visitation issues, this decision is often not in the stepmother's control. What can a stepmother do to protect her marriage, her stepchildren, and her self-esteem if she does find herself involved in a custody or visitation battle?

WHAT TO DO

Many stepmothers, finding themselves involved in a process that excludes them, seek to take over the role of "attorney" or husband's advocate. These women become quasi-attorneys, reading legal journals, conferring with attorneys, keeping court papers, driving to court appearances. The more control these stepmothers seek to assert, the harder they suffer when they are excluded from the court procedure. A short personal letter to the presiding judge defining your relationship to the stepchildren and your interest in the proceedings may prompt the judge's permission for your attendance in the court as more than an "interested party." Then again, it may not.

Support Your Husband but Remember It Is His Fight

Stepmothers need to step back and away from issues where they have no real control. Jill almost destroyed the happy life she shared with her husband, Joel, and her two stepdaughters. Jill now finds that she must live with the effects of the can of worms she opened by exerting pressure on her husband to bring action against the children's biological mother who had left the country five years before. Jill prodded her husband to terminate the biological mother's rights and clear the way for her to adopt her adolescent stepdaughters. Litigation was begun and Jill became immersed in the procedure of the court. However, what Jill assumed would be a simple issue became incredibly entangled when the girls' mother returned to the country and decided to countersue for full custody. Further complicating the issue was Jill's exclusion from all courtroom procedures. That left her husband, who was not as well-versed nor as *vested* in the sole-custody issue, fighting a battle he had not begun!

Don't Look for Bargains—Hire the Most Competent Attorney

Custody battles are, sadly, often nothing more than business as usual for the courts. Although there is frequent reference to "best interests," the legalese of the court applies to custody decisions as well as to corporate takeovers. "Old boy" networks operate in all courts, and a well-meaning but unknown attorney who gives satisfaction outside the courtroom may be disastrously ineffective inside it. Seek out the services of the best-known and most influential custody attorney. The more competent and experienced attorney can move a case more quickly through the courts. Although such expertise is expensive, it is well worth the money it costs in terms of personal satisfaction and what really is at stake.

Once you've hired such an attorney, turn the case over to him and step back! There is no need to become embroiled with the issues of the court. Find the attorney you trust, check out his or her track record, then listen to the professional advice. Too often stepmothers and their husbands become embroiled in tortuous custody/visitation battles simply because they fail to realize that family law is a "game" of sorts. Failing to perceive this "game," they persist in viewing all the "players" from an emotional vantage point. Compounding this misconception, the stepmother and father often refuse to listen to the very advice they have sought and further extend and complicate proceedings. Remember, it doesn't matter if you have a royal flush if you don't know how to play poker. Leave the game to the professionals.

Continue with Your Life

Discussions revolving around court actions must be confined to a particular time and place. If possible, all such discussions should occur outside the home, preferably within an attorney's office. Stepmothers often realize, before anyone else does, that "custody" exists only on paper and in the imagination of those who desire it. Although a legal "win" in the court is satisfying, custody decisions are ultimately secured in the home rather than in the courtroom. Indeed, the very term "custody" is at best a misnomer, suggesting either ownership or coercive confinement. Outside of children of divorced parents, WHO do the terms "custody" and "visitation" apply to but criminals and social deviants? Such terms are the language of jails and institutions; children are not chattels, subject to ownership by anyone. A stepmother's relationship to her stepchildren is defined neither by legality nor by biology. Her relationship depends upon interaction, shared experience, and commitment. Stepmothers understand a secret truth that seems to elude the participants of custody battles: "Custody" lies within the heart. Respect, loyalty, affection, and love cannot be required or demanded; they must be earned. A child's feelings are not subject to court mandate or legislation. No one understands this secret better than a stepmother.

Remembering this may save your marriage, your relationship to your stepchildren, and your sanity.

CASE CLOSED AT EIGHTEEN

There *is* an end to custody cases. At the very least, stepmothers can look forward to the future by remembering that there is an eventual finiteness to debates over custody. Sometimes, in the heat of battle, everyone seems to lose sight of the very real fact that even the best attorney cannot prevent a child from growing up. When children reach eighteen, cases are marked "Closed." However, stepmothers realize that a child's *life*, barring unforeseen tragedy, does *not* close

at eighteen, and with that thought in mind a stepmother will continue to attempt to live in the present—to raise her stepchildren.

As one eighteen-year-old wrote to his stepmother after years and
years of a protracted and ultimately unsettled court battle, "Thank
you for being the only one who seemed to remember that *I* was
having a *life* while they were having a *battle*."

Other Legal Matters: Estates, Adoption, Guardianship, Stepmother-Custody, Financial Responsibility

Although stepmothers do not have a legal relationship with their
stepchildren, many seek to protect the interests of the children they
raise by including them as primary recipients of their estate. Stepchildren will *not* automatically be entitled to any inheritance from
their stepmother's estate unless they are specifically named in her
will.

Most stepmothers who had a will, or carried life insurance, stated
that their stepchildren were beneficiaries, to share in equal amounts
with any biological children.

ADOPTION

Only a tiny percentage of the stepmothers surveyed reported that
they had adopted their stepchildren. In the cases where the mother
was not living, they didn't feel it was necessary: Their stepchildren
were "their children." In cases where the biological mother was
living, they usually didn't feel that she would permit this. This is
interesting in view of the fact that many stepfathers (whose stepchildren have living fathers) *do* adopt. It is also interesting in view of
the fact that the overwhelming number of stepmothers viewed
themselves as the primary maternal figure in their stepchildren's
lives. One can only speculate on the stress caused by living under
such contradictory circumstances.

LEGAL CUSTODY FOR THE WIDOWED STEPMOTHER

Although stepmothers time and time again protested that they
functioned as mothers in every way, their statements about what

would happen in the event of the death of their husbands belied their protestations. It was astounding to learn that a majority of stepmothers felt that if their husbands were to die, their step-children would return to their biological mothers. Stepmothers voiced this opinion despite the quality of the mother's relationship with the children or the suitability of the mother's living situation and/or personal circumstances. A small but adamant percentage of stepmothers were determined to keep their stepchildren with them in the event of their husband's death. Some of these stepmothers described financial arrangements they had made—trust accounts and financial guardians—to rule out the possibility of financial gain providing the biological mother with a motive for custody.

Mary was the exception to the rule—a widowed stepmother who secured legal custody. Mary's husband died after they'd been mar-ried for only a short time, leaving Mary with two young stepsons and an infant daughter. Mary fought for, and won, custody of her young stepsons, and has raised them to adulthood as a single parent.

Many stepmothers voiced passiveness, not their wishes, when they predicted that their stepchildren would be returned to their mothers in the event of their husbands' death. Their responses seem to reflect what they felt *would* happen rather than what they would *want* to happen. When asked to describe the type of legal relation-ship they felt a stepmother *should* have with her stepchildren, they presented a very different picture.

Anne married Joe when she was in her mid-twenties. It was her first marriage and his second. Anne had no children; the mother of Joe's two sons had left when the boys were little more than infants. At the time of marriage, her stepsons were eighteen months and three years old. Anne and Joe had been married for nine years when Anne became pregnant and gave birth to another son. However, before the new baby was a year old, Joe filed for divorce. Anne's stepsons, who were ten and twelve, were sent cross-country to live with their paternal grandparents. Neither mother nor father assumed or wanted custody of the boys. Because there are no legal provisions for divorced stepmothers, Anne was awarded no visita-tion. Although she has tried repeatedly to locate the boys, she has not been able to. She still hopes that at some time in the future, when they reach their majority, they will locate their stepmother and their younger half-brother.

FINANCIAL RESPONSIBILITY

Many stepmothers did not realize, at the time of their marriages, that they might be financially responsible for their stepchildren. Although there is no standard legal obligation for a stepmother to support her stepchildren, many women discovered that they were expected to contribute to the support of the children, and did so willingly. In cases where the mother was living, most stepmothers were surprised to learn that those mothers had no financial responsibility for the support of their children. Although most states support the notion that biological parents should be financially responsible for their children, the term "parents" seems to translate to "fathers only."

Stepmothers also found that their personal financial background weighed heavily when their stepchildren reached college age. Many colleges in the nation determine financial eligibility based on computations that include the stepmother's financial status. The stepmother's salary and other assets become a factor in determining eligibility for financing and loans.

LEGAL GUARDIANSHIP

Most stepmothers were unaware that they could be appointed guardians of their stepchildren. Check with an attorney for procedures; they differ from state to state.

HOPE FOR CHANGE

As more children begin to live in stepmother-headed households, more changes will occur. It may be that *all* parents—step and biological—could come together to renegotiate a legal agreement that delineates responsibilities when the father and stepmother marry and/or assume full-time responsibility for the children. A new agreement, thus negotiated and arbitrated, would give all the adults in a child's life a sense of power and control over the new situation and perhaps desensitize the feelings of jealousy, insecurity, and low self-esteem that underly many court actions. Such an agreement would serve to modify previously existing custody and visitation agreements and would take into consideration the new circumstances of the newly created family in the best interests of *all* parties. Biological mothers would feel that they had some say in what was going to happen with their children in their new family situation.

Legal responsibilities and privileges accorded to stepmothers will certainly make them feel more definite about their role as primary caretakers and less like "mothers in name only," constantly engaged in competition with an idealized biological mother.

Such negotiations and arbitrations would serve to bring the new family into the present. Any future modifications would involve *all* parties: stepmothers, fathers, biological mothers, and stepfathers!

Life experiences are not subject to legislation. Life does have a way of "intruding" on the best-laid plans of stepmothers. Major life events and crises have an impact upon stepmothers and their families and must be handled sensitively. Stepmothers may find that their day-to-day lives are played out against a background of complicated crisis issues.

PART III

Changes, Challenges, Crises

CHAPTER 14

What Do I Do Now?

Life goes on—even for a stepmother. Her stepchildren's mother dies, or moves away or out of their lives. Custody is changed; stepchildren move in or out, or away from home. Husbands die or divorce. Stepchildren grow up and move away.

Coping with Change

THE DEATH OF THE CHILDREN'S BIOLOGICAL MOTHER

In situations where unresolved conflicts have remained for step-children, their grieving may be particularly intense and burdened by guilt.

Stepchildren often feel unduly responsible for the unhappiness or death of their mothers despite the disappointing quality of their relationship with her during life. The death of a mother represents the death of a dream—a dream of reconciliation between mother and child, or between mother and father. The death of a mother, despite her lack of involvement or even her complete absence from a stepchild's life, will be a bitterly painful event.

Stepchildren, in their pain, often lash out at their stepmother, implying either directly or through their attitudes or actions that they hold her responsible for their mother's death. What to do? As with any inappropriate behavior, calm response, support for the child's pain, and a limit to inappropriate acting out is the order of the day.

LOSS OF CONTACT WITH THE BIOLOGICAL MOTHER

A mother who just fades away can send even the most well-adjusted child into an emotional tailspin. The stepmother's role here is cautious support. Typically, children will question their own role and that of their stepmother and father in the disappearance of their mother from their lives. Rejection, or perceived rejection, by a parent is always painful. Children need to be helped to deal with the reality of the loss and to avoid feelings of guilt—either unrealistic guilt over their part in "driving off" their parent or the feeling that they "should" feel guilty or sad, but really don't, about losing a relationship that was either minimal or unsatisfactory. A stepmother can help by reassuring the children that she has no intention of changing her own relationship with them because of the disappearance of their mother. It is comforting for children to know that some things do not change and there is still someone they can count on.

CUSTODY CHANGES

Stepchildren often face changes in custody, due to the decisions of the court, because of a parent's decision, or because of their own preference. However the change of custody comes about, it will affect the child's life and the stepmother's. If the change of custody is from the stepmother's home to the biological mother's, the stepmother will have to deal with the deep emotional effects of loss of control and status as a full-time parent as well as with the real sadness at losing day-to-day contact with the child.

If the change is welcomed by the stepmother, there may be a relaxation of stress; the stepmother and stepchild may get along better when freed of the daily tension of trying to live together. If the change was against the wishes of the stepmother and her husband (and perhaps of the stepchild) the stepmother will have to deal with her personal feelings of loss as well as with those of her husband and stepchild. Although the stepmother may grieve or decide to continue to "fight," either in or outside the courts, her time spent with her stepchild should be kept as free as possible from feelings of grief and powerlessness. Children need to perceive parents as strong and in control. An out-of-control and vulnerable stepmother is *not helpful* for a child who may already feel coerced and unhappy in a new living situation. A stepmother can help her stepchild through an unsettling custody change by maintaining her own calm, efficient, and loving household as a safe haven for the stepchild to come home to.

Some children seem to bounce from parent to parent, depending upon whim or upon who is offering the best situation at the best time. Bouncing is not good either for parents or for children. Changes in custody should be serious decisions, not subject to the whims of children or their parents. Any change in custody should, ideally, be on a trial basis, with the child "visiting" in the new home for a protracted stay before any formal change in custody is effected.

DEATH OR DIVORCE OF FATHER

If the stepmother should become widowed or divorced while her stepchildren are still legally minors, she will be faced with painful custody decisions. If the stepmother and her husband divorce, the stepmother will often lose all rights to her stepchildren, including visitation; some stepmothers of long duration are beginning to test this lack of visitation rights in the courts, but at present most stepmothers who divorce lose all contact with their stepchildren unless the children themselves elect to maintain contact with her.

If her husband dies, the stepmother will be faced with similar difficulties, despite any provisions in her husband's will or the choice of the children she has raised. Some stepmothers have successfully challenged custodial decisions in the courts, but at the present time the chances for a stepmother to retain custody of her minor children following her husband's death remains remote. If stepchildren are no longer minors when death or divorce occurs, stepmothers may be forced to confront the realities of their personal relationship with their stepchildren. If the relationship has been tied primarily to the stepmother's marriage to the children's father it will founder, but if the stepmother has developed a real connection with her adult stepchildren, that relationship will, in all likelihood, continue.

Family Crises

Many stepfamilies are formed as an indirect result of a crisis situation. A mother dies or becomes mentally or physically unable to care for children; a stepchild gets into trouble at school or cannot break the yoke of substance addiction; sometimes a child and his mother, and perhaps a new stepfather, simply can't get along. Other crisis situations spring from complications inherent in the unique character of the stepfamily—a family without biological ties or accepted cultural taboos. Stepmothers often have to become familiar with a wide range of crisis situations in order to deal effectively with their new families.

WHAT TO EXPECT

Many stepchildren harbor secrets they have been unable to share with anyone. The move into a stable and secure environment may prompt a stepchild to entrust these secrets to a stepmother, who is perceived as caring and committed. Often the kinds of secrets that stepchildren choose to confide involve neglect, abuse of one kind or another, or family behavior that is unacceptable by anyone's standards.

The abuse may be of a physical, sexual, or emotional nature. Dealing with a child who confides in you about such problems requires a cool, clear head. You must decide when—and how—you should get involved, and you'll also have to deal with your husband, who may respond by "shooting the messenger."

Past Abuse

Sometimes stepchildren remember incidents of abuse that occurred long before the stepmother appeared on the scene.

Andrea, a twenty-eight-year-old physical therapist, was married for five years before her stepdaughter came to live with her. Caroline had been abused by her mother's husband for a period of two years. When Caroline began to trust her stepmother, she felt secure enough to share her long-hidden secret. Such delayed "telling" is common between stepmother and stepchild. It may take years for a child who has been abused to trust and feel self-confident enough to share such "secrets." Stepmothers who are so entrusted must view the confidence as an indication of the stability and security that the stepchild perceives in the new relationship, and must *not* over-react or rush to share the news with the child's father. It is usually best to get professional help and advice for the child, even though the abuse occurred in the past.

Current Abuse

When the stepchild confides abuse that has occurred in the past, the stepmother can achieve some sort of distance and delay immediate action. Sometimes, however, stepchildren confide abuse that is going on in the present—the stepchild may be abused or neglected during current visitation periods. It is very difficult to terminate a mother's right to visitation through the courts. However, a child who is being treated badly during visitation deserves protection, and every effort should be made to shield the child from any further danger. Again, great delicacy will be required in sharing the bad news with the child's father—and dealing with the consequences of his reaction.

WHAT TO DO

The typical stepmother is not a psychologist and most stepmothers don't have experts in residence. When a child shares a confidence, a stepmother must react immediately, wisely, and calmly. It helps to take the process step by step:

Listen

Let the child talk. Ask questions. Try to get the facts as clearly as possible without getting into too many details. If you are unsure about anything, don't be afraid to ask.

React

Don't be afraid to react to your stepchild's confidences. Stepchildren need honest reactions to their trust. Such confidences are made in the hope that something will be done!

Commit to Action

It is not enough just to listen or to respond sympathetically. The most important contribution a stepmother can make is to act in the child's interest. A stepmother, like the fairy in "Sleeping Beauty," cannot undo the past, but she can and should try to lessen the impact and improve the prospects for the future. A stepmother may not know what can or should be done, but a stepchild needs to hear that her stepmother will help—or will *get* help.

Discuss with Your Husband

Stepmothers will need to discuss their stepchildren's confidences with their husbands. Fathers may be shocked, appalled, unbelieving, or plagued with guilt. If the abuse occurred in the past and was unknown to the father, he may suffer guilt over his lack of knowledge and protectiveness. If the problem is ongoing, the father may be enraged. The stepmother is caught in the middle.

Find a Solution

The decision to prosecute or not is a very personal one. The possibility of gaining a conviction will depend upon a variety of factors including the child's willingness to testify and the presence of physical or other evidence of abuse. Family court systems are notoriously slow, and investigations involve long, complicated procedures.

Many families seek to change or modify legal custody or visitation based on their commitment to their child's veracity. Family court is not the province for retributive justice. Many stepmothers find that family court is prejudiced in favor of keeping family relationships *together* and restructuring fractured family relationships. Because of the family court's predisposition to maintaining or reconciling family relationships, stepchildren are often subjected to long, complicated processes that end with no change in custody or with *renewed* visitation. The most important thing to remember before deciding upon court action is that once the issue is before the courts, you lose a great deal of control over your family's life. If a child is in real danger or distress during present visitations then the reporting of such abuse belongs in *criminal court*—not family court.

Many stepmothers spoke discouragingly of the court system in relation to situations involving the abuse or distress of their step-children. The court has shown itself to be generally sympathetic to the claims of biological mothers in areas of custody and visitation; courts are still loath to accept the realities of incest and maternal abuse. When abuse or neglect occurs between mother and child, the court seems to have difficulty accepting this distortion of the "sanc-tity of the mother-child relationship."

A Cautionary Tale

Aimee's stepson began having academic, social, and personal prob-lems during his junior year in high school. A characteristically timid boy, Kevin suddenly began to be plagued by skin rashes and insom-nia, and his grades plummeted. When Aimee questioned the boy, he confided that he had just recently "remembered" that he had been sexually abused by his mother beginning when he was about seven years old. Because the mother lived in another town and had had no contact either with Kevin or with his thirteen-year-old sister for the past two years, Aimee and her husband arranged for private therapy for the boy and continued with their lives. After several sessions with the therapist, the boy recalled a more recent episode of sexual abuse occurring during his last overnight visit with his mother. Shortly after this new disclosure, Aimee's stepdaughter slid a letter under her stepmother's bedroom door.

> Don't want to ruin your day but you always say to write if I have a problem. Here goes. I don't want you to be upset but Kevin is not the only one who was "abused." I was too. I guess I was a different kind of kid but I just told her after the first couple of times to cut it out. Now, you know why I don't care if I don't see her. Now you know why it's kind of hard for me sometimes to talk about personal stuff. I know noth-ing can be done about this stuff but I just didn't want Kevin to think he was the only one and that I got away free.
>
> Luv, Me

Aimee decided to act. She called a state hotline for child abuse and reported the mother. Child Protective Services responded quickly. Within twenty-four hours a caseworker had been sent to the house and spoke with both children. Aimee assured the kids that they would be able to "close" this issue. By the time the report was made, Kevin was seventeen and his sister, Kimberly, was fifteen. Both children were eager to speak about the abuse and seemed relieved that something would be done at long last. The caseworker for the Department of Social Services suggested that the case be remanded to the family court so that visitation (which was still a legal "right" for the mother, although not exercised) could be terminated. The family agreed. Neither Aimee nor her husband sought an attorney, feeling that the case was straightforward. The mother adjourned the case twice and by the time it came up the third time, Kevin was away at college. Aimee and her husband decided to drop his name from the petition, as he would soon be eighteen anyway. When the judge ordered forensic examinations (for all parties), Aimee, her husband, and her stepdaughter attended eagerly, convinced that such an examination would validate Kimberly's allegations as well as determine the mother's mental incompetence. The court-appointed psychiatrist was a warm and concerned professional who related well to all three members of the family: She felt that Kimberly was a well-adjusted child and did not require any additional therapy.

Aimee and her husband returned to court. Aimee asked for, and was granted, permission by the judge to be present in the courtroom. At this procedure, the judge stated that he had *no* reports of abuse and that the children had denied all the charges. Aimee, who held copies of all the investigative reports in her lap, desperately tried to get the judge's attention. The judge took notice of her waving hand and interjections and cautioned her to remain silent. When he continued to chastise her husband for repeating "unfounded" allegations, Aimee ignored the judge's warning and spoke aloud. She didn't get much further than a beginning, "What . . ." before she was ejected from the courtroom. This might have been for the best—Aimee's exclusion allowed her to miss the judge's order that visitation between Kimberly and her "natural" mother begin immediately in a private therapist's office, with all such expenses paid for by the petitioner—Aimee's husband. When

Kimberly informed her law guardian that she had no intention of seeing her biological mother unless it was in court, she was informed that she had no choice and that if she refused she and her father could be held in contempt of court: Jail for Dad and a foster home for Kimberly could be the punishment if she did not abide by the court's decision.

Aimee secured the services of an attorney well-known for her advocacy of women's issues such as rape and battering. The attorney met with Kimberly and suggested that Kimberly did have the right to refuse visitation—which she did. Kimberly's failure to comply with the judge's recommendations caused him to become enraged; when the court convened again, he ordered weekly visitation supervised by a social worker at the Department of Social Services. Aimee's husband was ordered to drive Kimberly to these meetings and threatened with imprisonment and Kimberly's removal to a foster home for failure to do so. Kimberly was forced to comply. She placed a headset on her ears, turned up her music, and read a magazine each time she was forced to visit with her mother.

Kimberly is now seventeen years old and currently defying court orders by refusing to "visit" with her mother. Neither child has any contact, nor any desire for contact, with the biological mother—and the case continues.

If a child is in present danger, obviously the abuse will need to be reported, but if the problem occurred in the past and is but a recollection, private therapy is probably the least intrusive and most effective recourse. Remember, if you open up a can of worms you will have to live with the consequences.

SEXUAL ISSUES WITHIN THE NEW STEPFAMILY

Stepfamilies are not, by definition, related by biology, and therefore sexual attraction may not seem subject to the same taboos that apply in biological families. However, many stepfamilies "function" as biological families and would like to see stepsiblings regard each other as *siblings*, rather than as possible mates.

Incest taboos are not biologically programmed; they are *created* by society. Incest taboos are "taught" in biological families and need to be taught in stepfamilies as well. What is and what is not acceptable must be stated simply and with great clarity.

Set Limits

Stepmothers can set clear limits about what is or is not considered acceptable behavior within the family. The way stepsiblings dress around one another, the way in which she and her husband dress and behave in front of the children, and the way in which the stepmother will demonstrate and receive affection from her step-children must be consistently reinforced by both statement and action. Initially, stepmothers may find that a good deal of testing of boundaries goes on, especially when older children and adolescents begin living together and especially in situations where the stepmother and her stepchildren are close in age.

Obviously, it will be difficult for individuals who are initially strangers to develop a family feeling when faced with a parade of sexuality. Bonnie came to her marriage with two teenaged daughters; her husband brought one son aged fifteen to the marriage. Bonnie's new stepson had a good deal of trouble beginning to think about his new "sisters" as sisters when they continued to march between their rooms in various stages of undress. The air of sexual tension became intolerably charged for Bonnie's adolescent stepson. He chose to deal with his normal sexual attraction for his new stepsisters by acting out and becoming uncharacteristically aggressive—prompting his mother and stepfather to "get on his case" and encourage him to be "nicer and more loving to his sisters."

Kathy's seventeen-year-old stepson, faced with a similar situation, chose a different route. After two months of living in the next room and sharing a bathroom with his new sister, his father and stepmother were pleasantly surprised at how quickly the "children" learned to get along. Both parents thought it was sweet when Kathy's fifteen-year-old daughter would kiss her "big brother" good night. Both parents thought it was also sweet that the boy blushed when his "sister" would compliment him on his good looks or ask him to apply suntan lotion to her back. And when the girl began to walk around the house in her bikini underwear they thought it was a sign that the kids really considered themselves brother and sister, a notion that was quickly dispelled by a scream one summer night. After a day in the sun and an evening snuggling in the T.V. room with a sister dressed only in sheer shorty pajamas, the boy entered his "sister's" bedroom and made sexual advances to her.

The family was shocked and the boy was sent to finish out his senior year with his grandparents in another town. This situation could have been avoided by clearer expectations and a limit to provocative behavior.

Basic Rules for Teenage Stepsiblings

Limits that are placed on behavior can prevent or at least curb inappropriate stepsibling behavior.

- Opposite-sex stepsiblings should have their own sleeping quarters.
- Bathroom doors should be closed during use.
- Robes and cover-ups are proper attire for all members of the household.
- Discussion of individual sexual behavior is inappropriate.
- Parents' sexuality remains a private issue.

Sexual Issues for Stepmothers and Stepsons

Sometimes women become stepmothers to adolescent and older "boys" who are unable to think about their fathers' wives in a "maternal" or nurturing sense. Stepmothers can do much by their action and behavior to set the tone for the kind of behavior they find acceptable. The stepmother who lounges about in a sheer negligé, having intimate talks with her teenage son while waiting for "Daddy" to come home, is sending out mixed messages and asking for trouble. When stepmothers are much younger than their husbands they may find themselves confronting stepsons who are their own age-mates. The fact that these "boys" are often younger versions of their own husbands may prompt unsettling feelings in a young stepmother. Watch out!

Becoming Aware

Stepmothers needn't be scared off by images of sex-crazed adolescents invading their homes—or by their "own" children suddenly changing into monsters. Most of the problems reported by stepmothers resulted from a denial of the sexuality of adolescents—a sexuality that needs to be redefined within the context of the new family.

Children who have grown up in single sex, single parent homes often have difficulty knowing just what is, and what is not, appropriate "family" behavior. A balance must be struck somewhere between overemphasizing sexuality (by hovering and unfounded suspicion) and oblivion—such as thinking it's cute when teenagers flaunt their sexuality.

Girls who grow up in all-female homes will tend to be freer about their manner of dress. They may need help understanding the changing mores of the new home that now includes male family members—including your husband, who may be as uncomfortable with inappropriate dress or flirtatious behavior as his sons are.

Women who have raised sons may be accustomed to expressing physical affection in a manner that is misinterpreted with stepsons who have no history with the stepmother as a caretaker.

Boys who have been raised in all-male homes will, like their stepsisters, need to be reeducated about their manner of dress or undress in the house. Boys who have been raised in an all-male household may have grown accustomed to a "locker-room" mentality when at home and may at first resent or misunderstand the need for covering up.

Girls who have been raised by their fathers may resent even the implication that their former casual behavior with their fathers was at all provocative.

Time Helps

With time, living-together taboos seem to emerge, just as they do in college dormitories where young men and women share facilities. As many adult couples have found, living together is sometimes the best remedy for inappropriate romances. The act of sharing living quarters and all manner of personal items, from toothpaste to the telephone, coupled with day-to-day proximity, adds an insider's view of another person's private life. Curlers, pimple cream, sulks, screaming matches with parents, tears, and giggles may do a lot to extinguish the inappropriate flame of sexual attraction. If familiarity does *not* dull the edge, the family must confront the problem and either deal with it themselves or seek professional help.

Children with Special Problems and Needs

Many children come to live with their fathers because of problems that their mothers are unable or unwilling to handle on a full-time basis. Such children may have difficulties with substance abuse— either drugs, alcohol, or both—or a history of antisocial behavior involving truancy, running away, or acting out in an aggressive or sexually promiscuous manner. Other stepchildren are plagued by emotional problems—eating disorders, depression, even suicidal tendencies. Others have physical disabilities or conditions that make their care difficult. Stepmothers in such circumstances require a great deal of personal and family support and the assistance of qualified professional resources.

You will need to become as knowledgeable as possible about your stepchild's particular problem in order to deal with it. You will need to learn, and face, all facts about the child's difficulty and how it will affect the daily lives of everyone in the family. A child with special needs must be treated as normally as possible, whether the handicap is a physical disease, a learning disability, a disfiguring birthmark, or just simply a difficult or unlovable disposition.

As Dr. Spock tells us, a handicapped child's happiness and effectiveness depends on that child's own attitude toward the difficulty, and the attitude of other family members as well. The important factors that make a person (with or without defects) grow up happy and outgoing are parents who thoroughly enjoy and approve and who do little worrying, urging, fussing, or criticizing. The handicapped child who grows up learning to give and take with other children from an early age is the child who grows up happily. It is those parents who are unhappy or ashamed about their child's appearance, always wishing he were different, who will tend to produce an unhappy child. In growing dissatisfied with him or herself, Dr. Spock feels that the child becomes exactly what the parents feared: a burden. "If they take his disfiguring birthmark, or the deformed ear, as of no great importance; act as it they consider him a normal child; let him go places like anyone else; don't worry about stares and whispered remarks—then the child gets the idea he is a regular guy and thinks little of his peculiarity. As for the stares and whispers, the child with a noticeable defect has to get used to them, and the younger the easier." Dr. Spock feels strongly that children are much better off without pity. "Pity is like a drug."

Stepmothers can be more helpful to a disabled child than the actual parent, who may be burdened by a sense of guilty responsibility for their genetic contribution to the disease or deformity. Because of their lack of a biological relationship and their more objective demeanor, stepmothers can help their stepchildren reach their full potential. "Naturally a child with a defect needs understanding, and he often needs special handling," cautions Dr. Spock. "The slow child should not be expected to do a job that is proven to be beyond his mental development, and one with stiff hands shouldn't be criticized for poor penmanship. On the other hand, don't sell your child short by assuming that he can't do something, or be taught to do something. It is the confidence of parents and teachers that keeps a child moving forward. But the child with a defect can be reasonably polite, take turns, do his share of the chores. Everyone is happier and more pleasant when he knows he's expected to be considerate. The child with a handicap wants to be treated the same, held to the same rules as other children."*

Dr. Spock and other child-care experts agree that in order to grow happily and to contribute to families and the larger community, children need to be loved and accepted for who they are. A child's disability may be profound or may be only a matter of the adults' perception. Treating a child with overconcern and refusing to accept the child as he or she is can result in lowered self-esteem. Dr. Spock relates the example of a ten-year-old boy who is short for his age. Although the parents have been assured that he has no disease, they view his small stature as a deformity and continue to show their concern by urging the boy to eat larger portions so that he will grow faster. Being compared favorably for other qualities—telling a child that his looks don't matter because he is so smart, or so witty—only emphasizes the idea of competition and rivalry. There are times when a short child, or a homely one, or a nearsighted one, wants to be told how unimportant the handicap is. Confident reassurance is then a great help. But if the parents are uneasy, always bringing up the subject, the child becomes convinced that he is an inferior person.

* Spock, Benjamin, *Baby and Child Care*, pp. 666-667.

SET THE TONE FOR ACCEPTANCE

Brothers and sisters take their attitude from the parents: If the parents accept the handicapped child wholeheartedly and matter-of-factly, the other children in the family are likely to do so, too. They become indifferent to the remarks of other children.

Stepmothers may find that they are inundated by friends and family with unsolicited advice about experts and treatment programs concerning their stepchild's disability. In order to feel comfortable with the particular handicap, stepmothers will need to confer with the child's physician and any specialists with whom the child is interacting. Sometimes stepmothers find it helpful to attend or organize a support group for children with similar special needs.

DON'T HESITATE TO SEEK HELP

Caring for a child with a handicap or a "difficult" child usually means extra effort and extra strain. To make the best plans for that child requires real wisdom, which is hard to come by, especially when you have little experience. All this adds up to the fact that you as the parents of troubled or handicapped children need guidance. Find an opportunity to discuss whether or not it is feasible to manage the care of the child at home and, if so, what practical strategies are involved in this care. Educate yourself to cope with the impact of the child's disability on other family members, the advantages and disadvantages of various educational programs both local and residential, and a host of other issues. Clarifying such matters may take months, even years of researching and discussing findings and questions with qualified professionals and other parents. There are usually social workers in state bureaus for the blind, deaf, crippled, and retarded and also on the staffs of the schools and clinics that care for such children. In rural districts there might be a county welfare worker, and in cities there are social workers in family and children's social agencies.

If you are not sure where to get help, write to the Department of Welfare in your state capital. If you live in a city, call the United Way or United Good Neighbors. They can tell you the right agency to contact. Parents of children with various handicaps and conditions have organized themselves into local chapters and national associations that share their special problems and solutions. They hear talks by professionals in the field and exert their influence to get better facilities for their children. They raise funds for research and treatment. You can get information about special schooling from your state Department of Education, and about professional resources from your state Department of Health.

Once the stepmother feels that she has a good working knowledge of the child's disability, current limitations, and prognosis, she can usually treat her stepchild as a person rather than as a disability. Some well-meaning parents and friends become so involved with the child's disability that they lose sight of the child. A stepmother, unshackled from the debilitating burden of guilt that many biological parents carry, can provide the love and confidence her stepchild needs.

Crisis situations affect families deeply. Stepmothers have to be careful not to become overcontrolling and obsessive about protecting and redressing previous or current wrongs, or to grow resentful about the impact of such weighty problems upon their daily lives. Husbands may either turn away from problems that began in, as one husband called it "another lifetime," or may turn inward with guilt. Other husbands are unable or unwilling to take responsibility for their children's current symptoms. Although crises can and often do bring families together, a crisis that originated outside the present family can often serve to divide it.

Don't hesitate to seek professional advice. If you are unsure about how to find a therapist, ask a doctor you trust for a referral, contact a local hospital or mental health association, or ask a rabbi, minister, priest, or any other person you trust and respect for assistance. Try to get several names and shop around until you find a person with whom you feel comfortable. Many stepmothers don't realize that initial consultations with therapists are often free of charge.

WHEN YOU CAN'T GET HELP

Obviously, the best solution is to find a family counselor and haul the whole bunch into family therapy. Realistically, this doesn't always work. Often, husbands and/or stepchildren are unwilling to enter therapy, or feel that they can't afford it. If you are in a situation where counseling is not a real option, *read, read,* and *read some more!* Become knowledgeable about your stepchildren's particular problem. Share what you have learned with the family. Present age-appropriate options for the child to consider and help him make choices in working through, and ultimately moving away from, his problems. Encourage your stepchildren to talk through their concerns.

Living with problem situations is extraordinarily stressful for a stepmother. In order to avoid feeling overloaded, resentful, and overwhelmed, it is important to have a place where you can unload your feelings safely. When you are stressed out, or angry, you need an outlet. Whether or not the family is in counseling, stepmothers may benefit from individual therapy or the warmth of a good stepmother group.

Stepmothers who are bewildered or frustrated about their roles often lack self-confidence; frequently they find that struggling to cope with difficult and pressing family concerns sends stress levels soaring to unmanagable heights. You can learn to manage your stress and become calmer and happier in the process.

CHAPTER 15

Stress Management: First Aid for Stepmothers

Stepmothers suffer from an incredible amount of stress. Attempts to juggle demands of career, a new marriage, and the added demands of building a new family, often from resistant members in a climate of nonsupport or outright hostility, create increasing buildups of stress.

Stress results when a person's best attempts seem thwarted. Many stepmothers begin to feel that they have no "homes"—no place where they can unwind and recharge. Indeed, when there are conflicts with stepchildren and/or husbands, home may feel like territory dotted with dangerous land mines, rather than the calm, safe haven you would like it to be. A home filled with tension can actually be perceived as a *cause* of stress.

What to Expect: Five Common Areas of Stress

LACK OF RECOGNITION

It has long been recognized by mental health experts that a one-sided relationship is both stressful and doomed to failure. When a person perceives that she is doing "all the giving," she is bound to feel resentful. Many stepmothers willingly assume the bulk of child-care responsibilities only to discover that their efforts are unrecognized by their husbands. Compounding the buildup of stress is the stepmother's feeling that she is somehow unable to ventilate her feelings; she feels that speaking out is either inappropriate or impractical.

Jackie is one such stepmother. At twenty-nine she feels that "most disappointing is when, after all the consideration, after all the doing and caring as if they were your own, there is not an ounce of gratitude, thanks, or appreciation." Most disappointing is an attitude from your husband that "you're expected to do all that, that you have no right to feel tired, hurt, or angry about any part of the situation."

Other stepmothers feel cheated: They feel that they are always on the "short" end of the stick—that they have been assigned all the responsibility for their stepchildren, without any of the fun times, celebrations, and recognition. Jane, a thirty-three-year-old stepmother of three, often feels as though she's "paying the penalty for other people's irresponsibility." Jane states that "I feel I'm always expected to clean up, or correct other people's messes or mistakes. It makes me angry when my own family or my own son must pay consequences for actions and deeds they didn't have any part of. I'm angry at the injustice of the situation, the blindness and injustice of people, and the pomposity of a court system and appointed representatives that treat me like I don't exist."

This question of "invisibility" crops up again and again among stepmothers; they feel that they are "just not there." In some cases, this perception is anything but illusory, as stepchildren seek to reconcile loyalty conflicts by ignoring their stepmothers. Sally can't stand it when the kids "act as if I'm a stranger" when she picks them up from a weekend with their mother. Sally feels betrayed and incredibly angry, even though she knows they're coping with a difficult situation that involves loyalty conflicts.

Rebecca reports that her very existence is ignored by their stepchildren. Even two years after her marriage, her stepdaughter is still having problems adjusting to "having a stepmother"—she just "forgets to tell people" that she has one. Rebecca is hurt and upset when she meets teachers, camp counselors, parents of the child's friends, and others who don't even know the girl has a stepmother. Rebecca claims that she feels eerily "dead."

Other stepmothers have their existence recognized, but fail to receive any approval for their role in child-rearing. Harriet is still dismayed over her need to hear some support from her in-laws. Even though Harriet has raised her sixteen-year-old stepson for the past nine years, her in-laws persist in ignoring Harriet, "crediting only their son, or grandson, luck, or even themselves for any achievements or accomplishments." Harriet realizes that she shouldn't care so much about approval or recognition from others, but she, like many stepmothers, continues to seek approval and recognition from their in-laws, husbands, and stepchildren long after it becomes obvious that this recognition will not be forthcoming.

"Sometimes it's just little things that get to me, like the time I helped our boy with a big school project on dogs. We worked for days, gathering the materials, going to the library, and making the actual project. When it was all finished I took him out for pizza and bowling. Weeks later, I found a report that he had written where he praised his 'mother' for taking him to a dog show. I never told him I saw that report but it still hurts to think about it!"

LACK OF AFFECTION

While some stepmothers are upset about their lack of recognition, others feel most stress about the lack of affection between themselves and their stepchildren.

Dorothy, a stepmother with grown children, remembers this lack of affection as a prominent cause of the stress that gradually eroded her relationship with her stepchildren. Dorothy missed any feeling of warmth or affection from them. A biological mother of four and a stepmother to three, Dorothy had expected that her hugs and kisses would eventually be returned. However, after some initial tries, she was hurt and backed off when her stepchildren struggled from her embraces. From time to time Dorothy would reach out again, only to be rebuffed. The years passed and Dorothy grew used to living without any demonstrations of affection by her stepchildren. Now that they're almost adults, she no longer even tries to be affectionate. The coolness during the past eleven years has affected her feelings for her stepchildren—feelings that she and others like her perceive to be stunted by a lack of demonstrativeness.

Irene invited all her nine-year-old stepdaughter's classmates and friends for a huge surprise birthday party. Irene even went so far as to dress up in a clown costume and bake the birthday cake herself. Much to her disappointment, her stepdaughter refused to be in any pictures with her. When Irene tried to sneak into one picture, the girl ran from the room and screamed in front of all her friends that she hated her. Irene was crushed.

LACK OF ACCEPTANCE

Many stepmothers are rattled by the lack of stability, acceptance, and respect for their role in their stepchildren's lives. Stepmothers may, with all good intentions, create important roles for themselves in their new families. They may continue executing these roles, only to find themselves occasionally thrown off balance either by the chilling devaluation of their role by insensitive remarks or by "surprise" appearances by the children's mother. Remarks from those outside the stepfamily can be especially stressful for a stepmother who has chosen to be primarily responsible for her stepchildren. A teacher's "But where is her real mother?" may ring in the ears of a stepmother who has raised this child for six of her ten years of life.

Tanya, stepmother to two boys aged nine and seven, says, "It's the inconsistency that really gets to you; not knowing what I'm expected to do. Like taking my stepsons to their Little League dinner after attending every game all season and finding 'her' in my seat, or going to the school open-house and finding 'her' sitting in the boys' seats. There's no rhyme or reason to it. She disappears from their lives for months at a time and then resurfaces at these public times, just as if she'd never been gone. Of course, to the world she looks like a great mother, and I look like the wicked jerk if I say anything at all." Such inconsistency builds stress; being unable to prepare for the future and feeling unbalanced, attacked, and incapable of receiving support is stressful.

LACK OF CONTROL

The *most* stressful issue for stepmothers is their perceived lack of control. Stepmothers usually function as primary parents for their stepchildren and as such begin to feel possessive and responsible for their day-to-day lives and instrumental in affecting their future. When these parental efforts are frustrated or blocked, many stepmothers feel a tremendous amount of stress.

Diane finds that she is faced with unrelenting stress every other weekend when she is forced by court order to send her eight-year-old stepson, against his wishes, to his mother's home. Diane "can't stand being unable to protect my stepson from the negative, abusive aspects of his life." The boy's mother is an alcoholic and frequently abusive, both physically and emotionally: Although Diane and her husband have repeatedly sought a termination of such visits in the court, they have been unsuccessful, and they just don't have the money to continue fighting. Diane has sought to counterbalance the instability of her stepson's life by providing a positive example and a "dry" household. Diane well knows the effects of being the child of an alcoholic; her own father was one. Diane has been prevented by the child's mother from permitting the boy to attend Al-Anon meetings; the biological mother still retains joint custody, which gives her the legal power to consent or decline consent for any and all of the boy's extracurricular activities. Since the biological mother denies her own alcoholism, she denies her permission for him to attend the A.A.-sponsored meetings. "Sometimes I feel so frustrated I could cry and I often do. It kills me to have to encourage him to go on these visits—if this wasn't his mother, I wouldn't even let him spend one minute there."

Other stepmothers find that they are not permitted to assume parental roles for their stepchildren either by their husbands or through the resistance of their stepchildren. Such stepmothers are often confused about exactly what they are supposed to be "doing." Ultimately, their very sense of identity begins to suffer.

Marie finds that not being a primary central figure in this house really bothers her. Like all too many stepmothers, Marie has found an uncomfortable dichotomy between her professional and personal life: Professionally, she is a middle manager who functions in a leadership position. At home, she seems to have no control—"I go from respected executive to nonperson as soon as I walk through my front door." Marie finds that it is very stressful to be expected to switch gears so abruptly.

Other stepmothers are frustrated by trying to influence their stepchildren's lives in ways that just don't seem to work. Renée discovered, after five years of marriage, that she was not going to raise stepchildren who would "turn out just like her" after all. It was very difficult for Renée to accept the fact that patterns of behavior, and personality traits, are often so firmly entrenched that a stepmother has little chance, if any, of influencing *who* stepchildren "really" are.

Another primary cause of stress for stepmothers is feeling unjustly blamed for events and issues over which they have little actual control. Too often, stepmothers feel that they are the family "dump" into which everyone's garbage is spilled. Merryl, a new stepmother of two teenagers, feels blamed for issues over which she has no power at all. Last year her husband blamed her for her stepchildren's bad grades. After all, says he, Merryl had been "told over and over again to check the girls' homework each evening." Yet, her husband is aware of the girls' uncooperativeness. Merryl had tried to check the girls' homework and had been told to "get out of our room and off our case"; her husband told her to back off, stop nagging, and to respect the girls' privacy. Although Merryl knows that she is not at fault, she feels powerless and constricted by these contradictions.

Other stepmothers *really* have no sense of control: Their control is totally tied to their husband's physical presence in the home. When the husband leaves, so does any hope of control. Carol is one such stepmother. Her husband often travels on business and when he leaves, her two preteen stepchildren seem to become "totally different children." They refuse to "mind" Carol, telling her to her face that if she tells their father they will just deny everything they've done. At these times Carol feels like a hostage in her own home. The stress builds as Carol struggles with deciding between capitulation and "tattling" to her husband, or trying to handle this out-of-control situation on her own.

NO TIME OFF

Many stepmothers are "stressed out" when they discover that, contrary to previous expectations, they have no time "off" from child-rearing. Often stepchildren, even those with living mothers, do not visit with her because of unsatisfactory situations or relationships.

Stepmothers often feel uncomfortable requesting that in-laws, their own relatives (or even their husbands'!), act as "baby-sitters," fearing that others will question their commitment to their stepchildren. Because of this unwillingness to ask for help and the very real problem in finding people who are willing to "baby-sit" for one, two, three, four or more children at one time and in one place, stepmothers often find that they have committed themselves to unrelenting child-care.

Marlene didn't expect that she'd *never* have a vacation. When she and Neal married, she thought her three stepchildren would be spending their vacations with their mother, as they always had. That arrangement changed when Marlene came on the scene. Now the kids stay home for vacations, which leaves no vacations or weekends alone for Marlene and her husband.

What to Do

Stepmothers do not have to wait for recognition, appreciation, and control of their lives; they can take charge by themselves. Stress can be minimized by changing one's perspective—*you* cause your own stress and *you* can reduce it.

Stepmothers need to be kind to themselves. They are after all, stepping into a difficult situation. Stress levels will be greatly reduced by a simple retuning of perception. You do *not* need to wait for anyone's approval and validation. *You* must validate, confirm, and accept the importance of your role in your stepchildren's and husband's lives.

In order to reduce stress immediately and substantially, try to view yourself as you would wish yourself to be—gracious and calm and able to tolerate stress competently and with dignity.

REFUSE TO BE STRESSED

Stress is a killer. In the same way that a stepmother watches her diet, her alcohol intake, and other unhealthy factors, she must refuse to participate in the creation of her own stress. Managing stress is really not very complicated. We manufacture our own stress, and as such we can overcome it by changing the way in which we perceive a stressful position. Most stepmother stress, and indeed most of all stress, is caused by a feeling that one has lost the ability to manage a situation or to prevent an unpleasant event from occurring.

Try these simple steps:

Ask for What You Need

"I need a hug. I need to be left alone. I need to be told you love me . . ." Say the words. There is no crime or shame in asking for what you need. More often than you would imagine, husbands, stepchildren, in-laws, your own relatives, and friends will be happy to comply. You don't come with an instruction manual—people won't know what works for you unless you tell them. Waiting around for people to figure out what you need is unfair to them and to you.

Give Yourself What You Want

If it's a hug, take it. If it's to be left alone, remove yourself from the room. If it's a candlelight dinner, orchestrate it! People who are not "needy" are more attractive to others because they're more fun to be around. You may find that once you give to yourself, others are more willing to give to you, too. Or you may find that you just don't *need* so much coddling anymore.

There is never any reason for a human being to feel invisible. No one can make us feel unworthy but ourselves. It is very true that respect is accorded only to those who respect themselves.

Focus on the Practical

Sometimes, in response to the tremendous emotional issues that seem to bombard them, stepmothers get totally mired in the undercurrents of life. Bright, highly educated women begin to lose sight of both the forest *and* the trees in their overly analytical approach to life. These women tend to pick apart and analyze each statement uttered, to look for hidden meanings in the most casual behavior. Such overanalysis produces a tremendous amount of stress in *everyone*. Whenever possible, try to focus on the practical and do-able, leaving the heavy analysis and introspection for only the most critical issues.

Let Go of the Things That Are Not in Your Control

The most stress-producing feature of a stepmother's life was her perceived lack of control. The best way to obliterate this type of stress is: LET GO! Stepmothers need to acknowledge that *there are certain aspects of their stepchildren's lives that are outside their control.* The stepmother who can separate herself successfully from those things that she truly cannot control will find that she is living a life relatively free from stress.

Accept Responsibility Only for Your Own Actions

A primary stress producer is accepting blame and responsibility for others' actions. Stress builds up when a stepmother seeks to rewrite history, to redress past wrongs, or to live someone else's consequences. The simple way out of such nonproductive stress is to opt out of this game. Psychologists call this "not buying in." Don't buy in to accepting anyone else's responsibility. The stepmother who accepts responsibility only for her *own* actions will lead a much more serene life. Stepchildren can be helped toward this goal as well by not being permitted to blame their stepmothers for events that she did not cause or share and by being required to focus their complaints on the here-and-now instead of on the past. Stepchildren then learn to become more responsible for their own actions and thereby lessen their stepmother's stress.

Find Support Systems

Stepmothers often feel that they have no one to talk to about their concerns. They are often correct in this perception. Friends, family, and even some professionals may be unaware of the concerns that are typical for most full-time stepmothers. Indeed some stepmothers have spoken about reaching out to people who were inappropriate sources, only to find that their ignorance and lack of sensitivity *added* stress to the situation rather than reduced it. Stepmothers *do* need support systems.

Individual therapy provides an arena where women can talk about themselves in a noncritical, nonjudgmental setting. It's a welcomed luxury that boosts self-esteem and speeds the ability to handle the challenges of stepmothering.

"People need people." Most full-time stepmothers don't know

any *other* full-time stepmothers. This isolation is in great part responsible for the stress many stepmothers feel. Breaking this isolation isn't always easy, but it *is* always helpful. If there is a stepfamily group in your area, seek out other full-time stepmothers. If there is not a "group," create your own. Groups may be formed by advertising in the local newspaper in the Personals column.

If it is impossible to get into therapy or to find or create a stepmother group, or even to locate another stepmother to talk to, get out a pen. Stepmothers who are isolated will find that "spilling" their feelings into a journal or diary is very helpful. In addition to getting those feelings "out" and onto paper, you can also chronicle your progress through the various stages of stepmothering.

Date Your Husband

Stepmothers often shelve their role as *women*. Good couple-time—and a vacation from superparenting—are refreshing. Try to remember what you loved about your husband when you were dating and *why* you thought you'd be able to handle all this! Recapture that feeling and you will find your stress melting away.

Work Outside the Home If Possible

Many women leave their jobs when they marry and become stepmothers. Sometimes they enjoy being able to give up their work, only to find that they were unprepared for the negative side effects they suffered. Stepmothers who had not worked outside the home tended to identify themselves through their families; they expected to work harder at making everyone happy. Such stepmothers, unfortunately, tended also to expect too much too soon; more often than not, everyone was unhappier than might have been expected.

Whether working within or outside the home, stepmothers need to define themselves through some other means than their families. Since a new family takes years to build, a woman who insists on defining herself through the family tends to magnify each success and failure and to react to family matters much too personally. Stepmothers who have some other means of fulfilling themselves will find that they are less stressed and, ironically, that they are more, rather than less, successful in their family relationships.

Keep hobbies, activities, and personal interests alive, too. You'll be less stressed and more interesting to your family, and, most important, to yourself.

HOW TO DEFUSE A STRESSFUL SITUATION

Despite careful planning and self-preserving tactics, most stepmothers will occasionally bump into a situation that is especially stress-producing. In order to minimize personal stress and retain a measure of dignity and self respect:

- Remember how you would like to "be" and act as though you "are."
- Take deep breaths.
- Speak in low tones.
- Speak slowly.
- Avoid responding if you're feeling overly emotional.

Sometimes stepmothers are faced with stress in the form of direct "attacks" by their stepchildren. Such statements more often than not cause stepmothers deep pain—pain and stress that can be easily sidestepped by being prepared and by recognizing that such hurtful statements are little more than window dressing for some deeply felt emotions.

There is a certain repetition to the type of remarks that children most frequently level at their stepmothers. Those are the remarks that hit way "below the belt" and snatch the breath away from the most composed stepmother. It is possible to take the sting out of these commonly launched barbs; it is possible to desensitize stepmothers and thereby lessen the possibility of stress.

Try to respond to the *feelings* underlying the following statements (and others like them) rather than responding to the statement itself. Each statement has been followed by a suggested retort—a response which attempts to exemplify the technique of desensitizing the remark and lowering the level of stress for both stepchild and stepmother.

> **"You're not my mother!"**
> "Of course not. I'm your stepmother."

"I hate you!"
"I'm sorry you're angry."

"I wish my father never married you!"
"I know, but *I'm* glad he *did*."

"You ruin everything!"
"I'm sorry you're disappointed."

"My brother [sister, grandmother, mother, teacher] says that . . .
"That's interesting, but how do *you* feel?"

"Don't kiss me! [touch me, tickle me, etc.]"
"Okay—for now."

"This is not your house! [boat, car, dog, etc.]"
"You're right. It's not mine, it's ours."

The way to avoid stress is simply to avoid "playing the game." Children are not proper adversaries for arguments. Children, step or otherwise, are really not to be "argued" with. A child's statements, even if they are hurtful, can be used to forge a deeper and more understanding relationship. A stepmother need not be saccharine or phony, but need only *refuse to argue* with children—to refrain from responding to statements that are really nothing more than bait for arguments.

STRESSFUL REMARKS FROM OTHERS

Stressful remarks do not come only from children: Teachers, neighbors, family, and friends often inadvertently or even intentionally make statements that cause stress levels to soar. Heading the "Hit Parade" for tension is that classic statement "Are you so-and-so's mother?" Most stepmothers think it sounds "cold" to respond, "No, I'm his [or her] stepmother." On the other hand, just saying "Yes" may make the stepmother feel a little uncomfortable, especially if the person continues, as many do, "I mean so-and-so's *real* mother." Probably the best response is something like "Yes—everything but the giving birth. I'm so-and-so's stepmother." A response like this reduces your stress, identifies exactly who you are and how important you consider your role. The general rule of thumb is to avoid getting emotional and either to provide the information you want the person to have or to turn the question back to the questioner, as you've learned to do with your stepchildren.

SAVE TIME ALONE

Stepmothers need time alone, away from the concerns of family life, whether this time consists of a bubble bath for one or a dinner out once a month with a group of college chums. Whether you do something as rigorous as attending an aerobics class or as introspective as practicing the piano or taking an evening walk, you need individual time that is apart and separate from your role as a stepmother. Because so much of a stepmother's energy is directed outward, this individual time is necessary for restoring balance. It helps release and reduce stress.

RECOGNIZE YOUR POWER

Although many stepmothers feel powerless and become stressed in their attempts at recognition and validation, they are often perceived as anything *but* vulnerable by those they seek to impress. Stepmothers are much more powerful than they imagine. In fact, much of the stress they bump up against is in direct reaction to their perceived strength. The resistance from stepchildren, the bad-mouthing from biological mothers, the devaluing by in-laws—all are often nothing more than reactions to the stepmother's perceived *power*.

Stepmothers spend too much time trying to justify their existence; such attempts lead to unending stress. There is no need for a stepmother either to define or to justify her existence. Stepmothers, like mothers, brothers, sisters, grandmothers, and grandfathers, uncles, and aunts, just *are*. They are as different and as alike as members of any other family group. When stepmothers stop trying to defend themselves and to justify their actions, they will feel a tremendous decrease in their level of stress.

A stepmother's relationship with her stepchildren can prove to be one of life's most challenging tasks; it can also provide deep personal satisfaction. Many people have asked, "Why would anyone want to become a stepmother?" The answer lies in a stepmother's heart. Stepmothering can and does "work," and when it does, a family is forged. That adds immeasurably to a woman's personal fulfillment.

The primacy and critical nature of a stepmother's relationship with her stepchildren is obvious; stepmothers live with and care for their stepchildren on a daily and ongoing basis. "That is all she wrote," and stepmothers need say no more.

EPILOGUE

It Can Work: Success Stories

As I researched this book, stepmothers asked time and time again for ways in which to contact one another. Many stepmothers were frustrated by their isolation. Yet, despite the challenges, despite the intrusions and stress, most stepmothers had developed close and rewarding relationships with their stepchildren. Most stepmothers felt that their experience had deepened them and taught them lessons about life and love that would never had been learned without their stepchildren.

> **Stella**, stepmother to one boy nine years old, felt that she had been a "total" mom to her stepson, doing everything from buying a puppy together to making him pick up the mess.

> **Sylvia** felt that her life had been enriched immeasurably by her nightly heart-to-heart talks with her stepdaughter.

> **Pamela's** three girls, now adults, brighten her
> life each time they telephone "just to say they
> love me."

Other stepmothers are proud of their contribution to their stepchildren's accomplishments. **Cynthia** remembers that day when
"our boy's teachers unanimously told *me* that they saw a marked
improvement in his grades and attitude since we got custody of
him."

> **Georgia** felt her heart swell with love when she
> realized just how much she really meant to her
> stepchildren following a hospital stay.
>
> **Janet's** two stepdaughters, now in their twen-
> ties, gave her the greatest gift of all; the ability to
> LOVE. Janet's own family background provided
> very little experience with loving feelings. She
> found a love and commitment in caring for her
> stepdaughters since toddlerhood.
>
> **Carla,** stepmother to two girls and one boy,
> stated that being a stepmother required a big
> effort. That effort enabled her to relate to the
> sensitivities of others in a more understanding
> way. In fact, Carla went so far as to say that
> being a stepmother made her a more forgiving,
> more loving person.

The experience of stepmotherhood is deeply and personally
rewarding for many women, requiring the testing of feelings about
family relationships and the personal endurance that leave many
women feeling stronger and more self-assured.

Being a stepmother "definitely keeps you on your toes," states
Kim. Her experience has brought her closer to her husband. "Having a child in the house to take care of together brought us new
experiences."

> **Chrisann** felt that being a stepmother brought
> an understanding of herself and the knowledge
> that she could "survive in one piece."

> **Jennifer** learned that "nothing is forever. Children do grow up." Jennifer's stepdaughters gave her years of their childhood and their lives. She feels strongly that she "has a past filled with everything that "antistepmotherists" could never believe I could possess and a future of that past locked in love forever."

Many stepmothers felt that they had become more tolerant people. **Wanda** "became much less controlling of other people" and felt a patience, tolerance, and wisdom grow within her that she had never realized she was capable of feeling.

Most of all, stepmothers learned that they are not fairy-tale creatures, not wicked, not evil, not owners of talking mirrors. Just women who are willing, as one stepmother put it, "to pick up the pieces that other people had left." Women who learned that

> There is more to being a mother than giving birth . . .
> This is a stepmother's secret: a secret knowledge we all share . . .

Where to Get Help

There are many types of help available to stepmothers who need information, assistance and/or support in meeting the challenges of raising their stepchildren. Child guidance centers, mental health clinics, family service agencies, and groups organized around specific areas of concern may be helpful. In order to locate such groups in your area contact your local and/or state Mental Health Association, Department of Health or Department of Social Services.

Referrals for counseling services in your area may be obtained from:

Family Service America
11700 West Lake Park Drive
Milwaukee, WI 53224
414-359-2111

Additional agencies, groups and organizations:

For a Stepfamily Association chapter in your area, write:
Stepfamily Association of America, Inc.
National Headquarters
602 E. Joppa RD.
Baltimore, MD 21204
301-823-7570

Step Family Foundation
National Headquarters
333 West End Avenue
New York, NY 10023
212-877-3244

*The Stepfamily Association of America and the Step Family Foundation are nonaffiliated.

Incest Survivors Resource Network International
P.O. Box 911
Hicksville, NY
516-935-3031

Child Abuse and Maltreatment
1-800-342-3720

Drug Abuse Information Hotline
1-800-522-5353

Missing Children (KIDWATCH)
1-800-543-9282

For additional telephone numbers of groups, organizations, and agencies in your area consult your telephone directory. Most have crisis hotline numbers and government agencies under separate headings that are located either in the front or back pages of your directory. In addition to professional organizations and groups, religious leaders, teachers, school counselors, friends, magazine articles, and your children's pediatrician may be appropriate sources to turn to for guidance.

Some stepmothers just yearn for someone else to share with. If this is your situation, try beginning your own stepmother group: seek out interested stepmothers in your area. Place ads in your local newspaper, hang up notices in your local market, workplace, beauty shop, coffee-shop, etc. Be creative.

BIBLIOGRAPHY

Beard, M. Ruth. *An Outline of Piaget's Developmental Psychology.* New York: Mentor, 1969.

Berman, Claire. *Making It as a Stepparent: New Roles, New Rules.* New York: Doubleday, 1980.

Bettelheim, Bruno. *The Uses of Enchantment.* New York: Knopf, 1976.

Clingempeel, Glenn W. and Eulalee Brand and Richard Ievoli. "Stepparent-Stepchild Relationships in Stepmother and Stepfather Families: A Multimethod Study." *Family Relations,* July 1984.

Coleman, Marilyn and Lawrence H. Ganong. "Effect of Family Structure on Family Attitudes and Expectations." *Family Relations,* July 1984.

Despert, J. Louise. *Children of Divorce.* New York: Doubleday, 1953.

Einstein, Elizabeth. *The Stepfamily: Living, Loving and Learning.* Boston: Shambala Publications, 1985.

Esses Lillian M. and Richard Campbell. "Challenges in Researching the Remarried." *Family Relations,* July 1984.

Fischer, Judith L. "Mothers Living Apart from Their Children." *Family Relations,* July 1983.

Francke, Linda Bird. *Growing Up Divorced.* New York: Fawcett-Crest, 1983.

Ganong, Lawrence H. and Marilyn Coleman. "Stepparent: A Pejorative Term?" *Psychological Reports,* 1983.

247

Ganong, Lawrence H. and Marilyn Coleman. "The Effects of Remarriage on Children: A Review of the Empirical Literature." *Family Relations,* July 1984.

Ganong, Lawrence H. and Marilyn Coleman and Jane Henry. "What Teachers Should Know About Stepfamilies." *Childhood Education,* May/June, 1984.

Ginott, G. Haim. *Between Parent and Child.* New York: Avon, 1969.

Giles-Sims, Jean and David Finkelhor. "Child Abuse in Stepfamilies." *Family Relations,* July, 1984.

Lutz, Patricia. "The Stepfamily: An Adolescent Perspective." *Family Relations,* July 1983.

Maddox, Brenda. *The Half-Parent: Living with Other People's Children.* New York: M. Evans, 1975.

Mills, David M. "A Model for Stepfamily Development." *Family Relations,* July, 1984.

Noble, June and William Noble. *How to Live with Other People's Children.* New York: Hawthorne, 1979.

Papernow, Patricia L. "The Stepfamily Cycle: An Experiential Model of Stepfamily Development." *Family Relations,* July 1984.

Paskowicz, Patricia. *Absentee Mothers.* New York: Allanheld/Universe, 1982.

Piaget, Jean. *The Grasp of Consciousness.* Boston: Harvard Press, 1976.

Robinson, Bryan E. "The Contemporary American Stepfather." *Family Relations,* July 1984.

Roosevelt, Ruth, and Jeannette Lofas. *Living in Step.* New York: McGraw-Hill, 1977.

Rosenbaum, Jean and Veryl Rosenbaum. *Stepparenting.* California: Chandler and Sharp, 1977.

Skeen, Patsy, and Bryan E. Robinson, and Carol Flake-Hobson. "Blended Families—Overcoming the Cinderella Myth." *Young Children,* January, 1984.

Stone, L. Joseph and Joseph Church. *Childhood and Adolescence.* New York: Random House, 1966.

Turnbull, Sharon K. and James M. Turnbull. "To Dream the Impossible Dream: An Agenda for Discussion with Stepparents." *Family Relations,* July 1984.

Visher, Emily B., and John S. Visher. *Stepfamilies: A Guide to Working with Stepparents and Stepchildren.* New York: Brunner-Mazel, 1979.

Visher, Emily B., and John S. Visher. *Stepfamilies, Myths and Realities.* New Jersey: Citadel, 1979.

Visher, Emily B., and John S. Visher. *How to Win as a Stepfamily.* December, 1982.

Walker, Glynnis. *Second Wife, Second Best.* New York: Doubleday, 1984.

INDEX